BOOKS AND READING
IN THE LIVES OF
NOTABLE AMERICANS

BOOKS AND READING
IN THE LIVES OF
NOTABLE AMERICANS

A Biographical Sourcebook

JOHN A. McCROSSAN

Gerard B. McCabe, Advisory Editor

GREENWOOD PRESS
Westport, Connecticut • London

Library of Congress Cataloging-in-Publication Data

McCrossan, John Anthony, 1930–
  Books and reading in the lives of notable Americans : a biographical sourcebook /
John A. McCrossan.
    p. cm.
  Includes bibliographical references and index.
  ISBN 0–313–30376–2 (alk. paper)
  1. Celebrities—Books and reading—United States. I. Title.
Z1039.C45M34   2000
028'.9—dc21   99–045598

British Library Cataloguing in Publication Data is available.

Library of Congress Catalog Card Number: 99–045598
ISBN: 0–313–30376–2

First published in 2000

Greenwood Press, 88 Post Road West, Westport, CT 06881
An imprint of Greenwood Publishing Group, Inc.
www.greenwood.com

Printed in the United States of America

The paper used in this book complies with the
Permanent Paper Standard issued by the National
Information Standards Organization (Z39.48–1984).

10 9 8 7 6 5 4 3 2 1

For all of my students and for those of all ages who love books and reading.

CONTENTS

ACKNOWLEDGMENTS

I want to express my appreciation to the many librarians, school library media specialists, and classroom teachers who gave me so many valuable suggestions on ways to make this a useful book for students of all ages. I am also especially grateful to Gerard B. McCabe and my editors at Greenwood Press—George Butler, Emma Moore, and Alex Petri. Without their constant help and suggestions, I would never have been able to complete writing this volume.

INTRODUCTION

The purpose of this book is to provide a reference source for teachers, students, parents, librarians, media specialists, and the general public on the role books and reading have played in the lives of a number of notable Americans from early to modern times. The book will also be useful in general library collections for those interested in learning more about this aspect of the noted people included.

All of those profiled have found reading important in their lives. Most loved reading and read many books and other materials for education, information, and inspiration. A few of those included read little but were strongly influenced by just a few works. Most also loved libraries, a number considering a library a "second home," and they encouraged others to read and to use libraries.

Major questions considered are: What types of reading were especially enjoyed by the biographees? Which books or other reading materials had major impacts on their personal or professional lives? Did parents, teachers, or other adults influence their reading as children? To what extent did those profiled use libraries and promote the use of books and libraries by others?

Educators and government and business leaders place increasing emphasis on the importance of good reading skills for students and adults. Such slogans as "readers are leaders," "leaders are readers," and "read to succeed" clearly highlight the importance of books and reading in one's personal life and in success in school and in the workplace.

The book contains discussions of the reading interests of unique people from different walks of life: scientists, entertainers, writers, social activists, athletes, government officials, and business and labor leaders. Also profiled are people from different racial and ethnic backgrounds in our increasingly multi-cultural society. Including a variety of individuals from various professions, as well as those of different racial and ethnic backgrounds, should stimulate identification with the biographees by students and adults reading the text.

Most notables covered in this book are studied by students in middle school, high school, and college classes, and are featured prominently in textbooks. Works by and about them are also held by school library media centers and college and public libraries. The few which may not be included in texts are popular with students and adults, and books by or about them are found on most library shelves.

The importance of promoting children's reading is stressed throughout the book. Oprah Winfrey became a lifelong book lover after being encouraged to read by her grandmother, then taken to the library by her stepmother and quizzed on the books she had read. Young Ronald Reagan and his brother sat in rapt attention while their mother read stories to them. Jimmy Baldwin was a frail, unattractive, lonely child. His reading and writing skills were recognized and encouraged by caring public school teachers. Noted Latina author Sandra Cisneros, brought up in poverty in Chicago, was taken to the library where she found a whole new world in books. Helen Keller, both deaf and blind, learned to love books and reading, and learned about the world she could neither see nor hear because her faithful teacher Anne Sullivan took time to teach her.

The importance of reading in the development of the biographees' careers and philosophy of life is also highlighted. According to his biographers, extensive reading as a child helped John F. Kennedy prepare for his great leadership role as president of the United States. As a college student, Kareem Abdul-Jabbar read *The Autobiography of Malcolm X*, which taught him that a central philosophy of life was needed in order to lead a meaningful life, and reading about Malcolm X led him to read many more books. Jane Addams, founder of Hull House, was strongly influenced by Tolstoy. She accepted his philosophy that in order to effectively serve the poor one had to live among them, not just bring them help and then go back to an upper class existence, such as the one from which she came.

A number of those profiled, upon realizing the value of reading in their own lives, have made major efforts to make books and libraries more accessible to the public. Andrew Carnegie, Eleanor Roosevelt, Bill Gates, and Shirley Chisholm are just a few who have contributed time, money, and/or their personal prestige and celebrity to increase the dissemination of books and other reading materials for readers of all ages.

In summary, a major aim of the book is to provide education and inspiration to those reading about the notable Americans profiled—to point out how reading improved their personal and professional lives. Those who are already dedicated readers should have their love of and appreciation of books and libraries strengthened. It is hoped that those who are not presently readers will discover how important books and reading have been to notable people and incorporate a reading program into their own lives.

BOOKS AND READING
IN THE LIVES OF
NOTABLE AMERICANS

KAREEM ABDUL-JABBAR (1947–)

Kareem Abdul-Jabbar, known as Lew Alcindor until he converted to Islam and changed his name, has been hailed as one of history's greatest professional basketball players. A book lover, an intellectual, and an excellent example of the scholar-athlete, Kareem has read a great deal, has recommended reading to others, and has written a number of books and articles.

Lewis Ferdinand Alcindor was born in New York City on April 17, 1947. His fame as a basketball player began while he was in high school. At a height of 7 feet 2 inches he towered over the other players. His great record of achievement continued in college and on professional teams. He broke numerous records in professional basketball, and in 1984 became the National Basketball Association's (NBA) all-time leading scorer.

With his parents' encouragement, Alcindor learned to read when he was very young. When he was enrolled in Catholic grade school, where almost all the students were white, Lew Alcindor excelled.

I was always a good reader, generally faster than most of my class, and in the time we were supposed to be plowing through one story I could absorb three. At school I would read the assignment and then flip through the book until I came to a story that never failed to please me. (Abdul-Jabbar and Knobler, 15)

It was the story of the ugly, black duckling, tormented by the other ducklings because he was so ungainly. Eventually, however, he grew to be a beautiful black swan. "Other, lighter children may have seen only the duckling as black, not the swan. I saw otherwise" (Abdul-Jabbar and Knobler, 15).

Ever since he learned to read, Lew read the sports pages and marveled about the exploits of sports heroes. By the time he was fifteen, he had begun to read about himself in those pages. Glowing reports of his phenomenal talent appeared in the newspapers.

When the first article about him appeared in the *Journal-American*, Lew's father got so excited he bought fifteen copies and distributed them to friends and relatives "all over the place" (Abdul-Jabbar and Knobler, 43).

One summer Lew made a momentous discovery. He walked into the New York Public Library's Schomburg Center for Research in Black Culture to find information for an article he was writing. He had seen the building a few times but did not know anything about it.

Once he discovered the Schomburg library, he "became a fixture" there. It was there that he learned so much about Harlem and black history, things that had never been taught or even mentioned to him before. He was introduced to black heroes, including Marcus Garvey and W.E.B. Du Bois.

He was fascinated by black writers. He read the novels of Richard Wright and the works of the great black poets—Langston Hughes, Countee Cullen, and Paul Lawrence Dunbar. "The Schomburg," he wrote, "was an entire building filled with facts each one of which I wanted to put under my skin" (Abdul-Jabbar and Knobler, 71).

When he started college, Lew experimented with drugs. After a few tries, however, he learned that he did not need them. He had found something else that would become very important to him. "More significant than any mind-altering drug was the overwhelming change in perspective I found when I read *The Autobiography of Malcolm X*" (Abdul-Jabbar and Knobler, 139). Lew had known very little about Malcolm X. He remembered that he would call the black radio station in New York and declare that all white people were devils. He also knew that Malcolm had broken with the Black Muslims and had been assassinated.

He couldn't put the book down. He read it during every spare moment. It touched him "very personally." Malcolm left him a legacy. He had discovered himself through religion, moving from a white-hating radical to a true believer in Islam who no longer thought all whites were evil. The great basketball star himself came to believe that there is no room for racial hatred, and that all men, black and white, are brothers. He learned that a central philosophy is necessary in order to live a meaningful life. He was so impressed with Malcolm's autobiography that he recommended it to friends. In a magazine article he encouraged people, especially young blacks and whites, to read it.

Lew undertook an intensive study of Islam and other religions. He cherished the Koran and read it whenever he had the chance. He accepted Islam, and became a "genuine" Muslim, rejecting the ideas of the Nation of Islam, which taught that blacks are a superior race. Kareem could not accept that idea. He believed that "the genuine Muslim bears witness that there is one God, that his name is Allah, and that all men—black and white—are brothers" (Thacher, 23).

This religious belief became very significant for Kareem.

The teachings of Mohammed suddenly put things into place for him. Islam teaches that life on earth is a period of testing for the life to come. Kareem was being tested very hard, but he could now see beyond the present. (Thacher, 23)

Another work that influenced Kareem was *A Book of Five Rings* written by the renowned Japanese samurai warrior Miyamoto Musashi who had been inspired by the teachings of Zen. Musashi changed the military arts into a high form of spiritual study. He taught that "to win in battle, you must prepare yourself for everything, but without attachment to outcome. . . . His few thousand words from the seventeenth century became *A Book of Five Rings*. I read from it constantly" (Abdul-Jabbar with McCarthy, 52).

Pramahansa Yogananda's *Autobiography of a Yoga* also inspired the basketball star. The book made him realize the benefits of yoga and enabled him "to adapt those lessons to conditioning my body" (Abdul-Jabbar with McCarthy, 204). At one point he claimed that without yoga he would never have been able to last in the NBA as long as he did.

In 1996 Abdul-Jabbar published his landmark book, *Black Profiles in Courage*. In it he described the great contributions made by blacks to American culture. In the book he refers to the importance of reading to the progress made by African Americans. One example cited is that of Frederick Douglass, who began life in the nineteenth century as a slave. Douglass realized that to progress he would have to learn to read, which he did. By applying himself he became one of the great leaders in the emancipation of blacks and also played a leading role in the suffrage movement to give women the vote.

Black Profiles also contains a discussion of a pamphlet about the life of Nat Turner, the famous black leader of a slave uprising, written from Turner's point of view and widely circulated. It got out the message about oppression of slaves, a message many whites previously had not heard or had ignored.

One person who followed the great basketball player's advice to read Malcolm X's autobiography was the noted scholar Henry Louis Gates, Jr., who was at the time a high school student. Years later in a foreword to *Black Profiles*, Gates described the effect the book had had on him.

I sat up all night reading that book. . . . I went on to read other books by black authors. . . . Slowly, gradually, inevitably, I became engulfed in reading books about the Black Experience. (Abdul-Jabbar and Steinberg, xi)

A tragic fire took place in Kareem's home in January, 1983. While he was on tour in Boston, he got word of the fire. When he returned home, he found that everything was destroyed, including the sizable collections of books and recordings he had built up through the years. His possessions had been reduced basically to only those things he had with him on the road. The story had a happy ending, however.

As word got out about the fire, albums and books began finding their way into my hands from every part of the country. Friends and strangers, fans, people I never knew were there before, tried to help replace my collections and my loss. (Abdul-Jabbar with McCarthy, 55–56)

It reminded him of the classic film *It's a Wonderful Life*. The James Stewart character in that movie was in deep financial trouble. Then all kinds of townspeople showed up and brought him things, much more than he needed. "I felt something like that," he wrote (Abdul-Jabbar with McCarthy, 56).

Kareem Abdul-Jabbar is a great role model for all young people, especially African-American youth, a role model not only in athletics but also in the development of one's mind. Referring to the publication of *Black Profiles*, Henry Louis Gates, Jr., wrote:

By his example, Kareem Abdul-Jabbar . . . has performed a service for our youth far greater even than the remarkable triumph he achieved on the court . . . mind triumphs forever—as long as one can read and write. (Abdul-Jabbar and Steinberg, xiii)

IMPORTANT DATES IN KAREEM ABDUL-JABBAR'S LIFE

1947	Born in New York City.
1967, 1968, 1969	Member of National Collegiate Athletic Association (NCAA) championship teams.
1970	Named National Basketball Association (NBA) Rookie of the Year.
1971, 1972, 1974, 1976, 1977, 1980	Won Most Valuable Player titles, more than any other player in pro basketball history.
1983	Published *Giant Steps*.
1984	Became the NBA's all-time leading scorer.
1990	Published *Kareem*.
1996	Published *Black Profiles in Courage*.

SOURCES

Abdul-Jabbar, Kareem, and Peter Knobler. *Giant Steps*. New York: Bantam, 1983.
Abdul-Jabbar, Kareem, with Mignon McCarthy. *Kareem*. New York: Random House, 1990.

Abdul-Jabbar, Kareem, and Alan Steinberg. *Black Profiles in Courage: A Legacy of African American Achievement.* New York: William Morrow and Co., 1996.

Porter, David L., ed. *African-American Sports Greats: A Biographical Dictionary.* Westport, Conn.: Greenwood Press, 1995.

Porter, David L. *Biographical Dictionary of American Sports: Basketball and Other Indoor Sports.* Westport, Conn.: Greenwood Press, 1989.

Thacher, Alida. *In the Center: Kareem Abdul-Jabbar.* Milwaukee, Wis.: Raintree Editions, 1976.

JANE ADDAMS
(1860-1935)

Jane Addams, the renowned social reformer, with the help of a friend, Ellen Starr, founded a settlement house named Hull House in the slums of Chicago in 1889.* A settlement house is a community center set up to help the needy. Hull House provided many educational and recreational opportunities for a poor, ethnically mixed population, mostly immigrants from a number of foreign countries. It became a model for other settlement houses and for a variety of other social programs. Addams became one of the most influential voices on behalf of a variety of social reforms and world peace.

Addams became so successful in her work that she was called the greatest American woman of her time, the greatest woman in the world. She was compared with Saint Francis of Assisi, Joan of Arc, and Abraham Lincoln.

Jane Addams was born in the small village of Cedarville, Illinois, on September 6, 1860, the daughter of John Huy Addams, a well-to-do businessman and politician who represented his district in the Illinois Senate from 1854 to 1870. Her mother, Sarah, died when Jane was only two.

By the time she was six, Jane had seen the grinding poverty and dilapidated small houses in which so many people lived. Even those who worked long, hard hours were destined to live in poverty. She determined that she would do something to improve the lives of such people when she grew up.

Years later Addams established Hull House. Hull House was somewhat similar to—but also very different from—previous religious missions and philanthropic attempts to work with the poor in the cities. Addams' approach was quite radical for the time. Addams and the other staff lived

---

*In older works Hull House is hyphenated (Hull-House). In most modern works it is not. This writer has not used a hyphen.

among their poor immigrant neighbors. They did not simply visit and then go home every evening. Moreover, unlike previous attempts that relied on well educated, prosperous do-gooders to develop programs for the poor, at Hull House everyone, including the slum dwellers themselves, worked together to develop its programs. In addition Hull House was totally nonsectarian, and no attempt was made to convert people to a particular religion.

Within a few years, Hull House had grown from one house to many houses. Its programs included reading clubs, play productions, and a day nursery. It also had athletic programs and a labor museum where residents demonstrated different types of work.

Before attending school, Jane learned a great deal from the many books which abounded in her home—classics, geographies, histories, biographies, as well as magazines. In addition to the family's books she had access to books in the local subscription library, which was housed in the Addams' home.

Every morning Jane's father would arise before dawn to read. Jane, determined to be like him, whom she considered the greatest man in the world, also got up early and embarked on an ambitious reading program. She read the Iliad, Virgil, histories, and studied the biographies of many great people. "Reading and absorbing quickly, she made book reports to her father who encouraged her liking for history" (Wise, 52).

Jane's formal education began in the town school. Then she entered Rockford Female Seminary where she pursued courses in Literature, Latin, Greek, Ancient History, Philosophy, and French. English composition was a favorite subject, and she was especially fond of the English writers Coleridge and De Quincey. She wrote a number of papers on various literary topics, including Shakespeare's *Macbeth* and Goethe's poetry. Some of her papers were published in the *Rockford Seminary Magazine*.

Jane started to work on the college magazine when she was a freshman. The next year she became "Home Editor." By her senior year she was editor-in-chief and could boast that for the first time in its history the magazine had money in the bank.

Before Jane became editor, the magazine's articles and stories had been very moralistic, preaching about the evils of drink, the rewards of missionary work, and other such topics. Under Jane's leadership, the magazine became much more philosophical and critical with poetry, articles about famous writers, and even one article by Jane's classmate and lifelong friend Ellen Starr on the beauty of Roman Catholicism, not a very popular concept at an evangelical protestant college.

Jane read Darwin's *Origin of Species* and *The Descent of Man* while at Rockford. She accepted Darwin's theory of evolution, the survival of the fittest, as related to the physical development of species. She questioned, however, that the survival of the fittest ideas should be applied to moral and social questions, especially when used to defend a corrupt system against change.

She was a great admirer of Tolstoy. She had first read his small book, *My Religion,* when she was twenty-one and continued to read it for many years afterward. She also read any other works of his which she could "lay her hands on" (Linn, 288).

She was especially impressed with his efforts to put himself into right relations with the humblest people. She decided, as Tolstoy had, that one could not really serve the poor simply by giving alms from a distance. One had to live among them. She agreed with "his inevitable conviction that only he who literally shares his own shelter and food with the needy, can claim to have served them" (Addams, *Twenty Years,* 260).

In addition to Tolstoy, Addams read and carefully studied the works of many of the great writers who emphasized one's duty to help the less fortunate. They included Thomas Carlyle, Matthew Arnold, and John Ruskin. Ruskin, for example, had undoubtedly shocked many upper class Englishmen when he told his students at Oxford:

I have not yet abandoned all expectation of a better world than this. . . . I know there are many who think the atmosphere of rebellion and misery which wraps the lower order of Europe every day is as natural as a hot summer. But God forbid! (Linn, 89)

Although Addams was inspired by such writers, she did not agree with them in all respects. In particular she disagreed with the idea that reform should be brought about by an aristocratic, elite leadership. Along with Tolstoy, she always believed in the importance of community cooperation in the development of programs. She maintained that she learned as much from her immigrant neighbors as they ever learned from her.

Jane Addams and Ellen Starr were not reformers. They did not begin or go on with the insistence either of reformers or providers. They wished to make a place, if they could, in and around which a fuller life might grow, for others and for themselves, a happier life, a life richer in interest. (Linn, 111)

Books and reading were always an important activity at Hull House. Addams believed that literature could lift people above their monotonous, care-filled lives. Most of those who came to Hull House had very little money and worked for long hours for low pay in local businesses.

One of the first literary activities was a series of Hawthorne readings done by a woman who came to Hull House because she wanted to be in a place where "idealism ran high."

Our "first resident" as she gayly designated herself, was a charming old lady who gave five consecutive readings from Hawthorne to a most appreciative audience, interspersing the magic tales most delightfully with recollections of the elusive and fascinating author. (Addams, *Twenty Years,* 61)

"Reading parties," in which books were read aloud, often featured books of special interest to particular groups of foreign born who came to the settlement house, including Russian Jews, Greeks, and Italians.

Romola by George Eliot was selected for the first reading party partly because the story takes place in Italy and had special interest to Italian immigrants. Also, the fact that both Addams and Starr were fluent in Italian undoubtedly impressed the participants that the two women appreciated Italian culture.

Another reason for selecting *Romola* was its theme. There were many similarities between events in the novel and the work at Hull House. The character, Romola, is inspired to work with the poor for purely humanitarian reasons. Certainly the lesson was not lost on the participants at Hull House.

Romola points up the moral of the novel: "It is only a poor sort of happiness that could ever come by caring very much about our own narrow pleasures. We can only have the highest happiness . . . by having wide thoughts, and much feeling for the rest of the world as well as ourselves." (Farrell, 61)

Although many other activities took place at Hull House, literacy, books, and reading always remained an important part of the effort. The smallest children came to listen to simple stories, older boys to heroic tales of medieval knights. Adults read and discussed such great writers as Shakespeare, Plato, and William James.

Every day a newsboy would bring "a broad selection" of newspapers to the door. The reading room was available for use by everyone. Some of the books in it were contributed by the immigrant neighbors and local organizations. English instruction was given for the many neighbors who had little understanding of the language.

Writing and performing both traditional and original plays became a staple at Hull House. The plays ranged from simple productions given by children to sophisticated plays performed with great pride by members of different ethnic groups.

Plays performed by especially talented neighbors included those by Sophocles, Ibsen, Shaw, and Galsworthy. Each ethnic group put on plays about life in the old country. One Italian, for example, wrote a play about conflict between generations, "and his neighbors saw that their own family conflicts were not unique" (Levine, 62).

Many distinguished figures, including writers, politicians, and union leaders visited Hull House, participated in discussions, and answered questions. How proud the poor immigrants must have felt to host meetings with such luminaries as John Dewey, Clarence Darrow, John P. Altgelt, young Harold Ickes, and Vice-President Theodore Roosevelt. "Hull House very quickly became one of Chicago's well-known 'sights' as well as one of the centers of the city's intellectual life" (Levine, 55).

Addams spread her ideas by lecturing and writing. According to Linn she made her reputation during the first ten years of Hull House by lecturing. She spoke before numerous women's groups, businessmen's associations, labor unions and legislatures. She always drew examples from her own experience with the people with whom she worked at Hull House. She told their true stories, sometimes tragic, usually inspiring and often lightened with appropriate humor.

In time she began to write these talks for articles which were published in many different magazines. Then she started putting these articles together into a book.

She eventually published several books: *Democracy and Social Ethics, Newer Ideals of Peace, The Spirit of Youth and the City Streets, Twenty Years at Hull-House,* and *The Second Twenty Years at Hull-House.*

Her books were neither sensational nor academic. They were written in a readable, popular style which appealed to many. Her books were called masterly and revolutionary, and some called her the greatest psychologist of democracy in the world.

During her final years, Jane Addams received numerous honors from throughout the world. In 1931 her efforts on behalf of peace were recognized with the most prestigious peace prize in the world. She shared the Nobel Peace Prize with Nicholas Murray Butler.

IMPORTANT DATES IN JANE ADDAMS' LIFE

1860   Born in Cedarville, Illinois.

1881   Graduated from Rockford Female Seminary.

1889   Opened Hull House in Chicago.

1910   Published her autobiographical masterpiece, *Twenty Years at Hull-House.*

1919   Presided at a congress in Zurich which established the Women's International League for Peace and Freedom.

1931   Shared the Nobel Peace Prize with Nicholas Murray Butler.

1935   Died in Chicago.

SOURCES

Jane Addams: A Centennial Reader. New York: Macmillan, 1960.

Addams, Jane. *The Second Twenty Years at Hull-House: September 1909 to September 1929, with a Record of a Growing World Consciousness.* New York: Macmillan, 1930.

Addams, Jane. *Twenty Years at Hull-House, with Autobiographical Notes.* Urbana: University of Illinois Press, 1990. (Originally published in 1910.)

Farrell, John C. *Beloved Lady: A History of Jane Addams: Ideas on Reform and Peace.* Baltimore: Johns Hopkins Press, 1967.

Hagedorn, Hermann. *Americans: A Book of Lives.* New York: John Day, 1946.

Levine, Daniel. *Jane Addams and the Liberal Tradition*. Madison: State Historical Society of Wisconsin, 1971.

Linn, James Webber. *Jane Addams: A Biography*. New York: D. Appleton-Century Co., 1935.

Wise, Winifred E. *Jane Addams of Hull-House*. New York: Harcourt, Brace, 1935.

ARTHUR ASHE, JR.
(1943–1993)

"I have always been an avid reader of books and also of newspapers and magazines of all types," Arthur Ashe, Jr. wrote in his best-selling autobiography *Days of Grace* (Ashe and Rampersad, 280). Ashe, one of America's greatest tennis stars, was also a bibliophile, a serious book collector, and a book lover who built up a significant library of his own.

He was also one of the most admired athletes in history, admired not only for his athletic skill but also for his good sportsmanship, humility, grace, and gentlemanliness.

Arthur Ashe, Jr., was born in rigidly segregated Richmond, Virginia, on July 10, 1943. He began playing tennis as an adolescent and soon won numerous national boys' tennis championships and later many men's tennis championships. He was often the first African American allowed to play in such events and to win them. Year after year Ashe was ranked among the top American men tennis players, usually first, second, or third.

Ashe had always deeply resented the way he and other blacks were treated. In Richmond, he had to attend segregated schools, live in the "colored" section of town, and play on a segregated playground. Segregation and racism had made him hate some aspects of the white South, but he did not become radicalized by his experiences.

He played an important role in the civil rights struggle, but he disagreed strongly with the more radical civil rights leaders, such as Stokely Carmichael, who preached black power. Ashe always believed, as did Dr. Martin Luther King, Jr., in the reconciliation of the races rather than separatism.

In addition to his athletic ability, Ashe was an accomplished scholar and writer. He wrote numerous articles for newspapers and magazines, and several books. These include his mammoth history of African-American athletes: *A Hard Road to Glory* and his autobiography, *Days of Grace*.

Ashe suffered major health problems beginning in 1979. He had three heart attacks, two heart bypass operations, and underwent brain surgery after his right arm became paralyzed. In 1988 he was diagnosed with AIDS, which he believed he had contracted from blood transfusions during his operations.

From then until his death in 1993, Ashe became a major spokesman for education about AIDS, founding the Arthur Ashe Foundation for the Defeat of AIDS. Even facing death he maintained his lifelong positive attitude and faith. "God's will alone matters," he wrote, "not my personal desires or needs" (Ashe and Rampersad, 290).

Brought up in a religious family, Arthur started reading the Bible when he was a child. He continued reading it throughout his life, and it always remained one of his favorite books.

In the Richmond schools, black children were allowed to read only "safe" books about blacks, including Harriet Beecher Stowe's *Uncle Tom's Cabin*. Despite being "safe," it became one of Ashe's favorite books. He commented:

It's a haunting story for a southerner. . . . The hero in *Uncle Tom's Cabin* had to eat a lot of crow and go through life hat in hand, but ultimately he survived, and succeeded. (Hurford, 88)

Nonetheless, he was sorry other writers were not taught. He commented as follows: "Marcus Garvey was not part of the curriculum, and I didn't even hear of W.E.B. Du Bois until I was well into high school" (Hurford, 88).

Ashe always craved information, and he read constantly to learn. He generally favored nonfiction over fiction. He read books on a variety of topics. He also read several newspapers a day and several magazines a week.

In his autobiography he discussed his love of and reasons for reading.

I like to know something about everything, from economics and geography to science and philosophy. I want information, not to enliven exchanges at dinner parties or in some other way to show off my collection of facts before less-informed people but because—as I tell myself—if I am proud to be a citizen of the world I must know as much as possible *about* the world. (Ashe and Rampersad, 280)

Ashe was a critical reader, forming his own opinions about what he read. For example, he noted that some Christians used the Bible to support slavery. In response to that notion, he argued that although a verse or two might support the concept of slavery, the whole history of Judeo-Christian morality did not.

He also criticized those who cited a verse of the Bible (Leviticus 18:22) to condemn homosexuals. Ashe argued that some Bible verses also condemned other activities, which today are considered quite ordinary kinds of behavior.

Ashe also opposed the censorship of *Heather Has Two Mommies*, the story of a girl being brought up by two lesbians. He was not sure he wanted his daughter to be taught about lesbian parents in the first grade, but he wanted her to have a tolerant and enlightened attitude towards homosexuals.

Ashe sometimes read the radical newspaper *Muhammad Speaks* "to find out what was going on or what the Muslims thought was going on" (Ashe and Rampersad, 154). Their "white devil" rhetoric, however, made little sense to him.

He also read *The Autobiography of Malcolm X*. He was fascinated by it. He admired Malcolm's courage, his efforts to educate himself, and his ability to grow. He did not, however, share the passion for Malcolm that many people had. He especially disagreed with Malcolm's preaching of black separatism. "Having lived under white-imposed segregation," Ashe wrote, "I was not about to deliver myself to the black-imposed segregation central to the Nation of Islam" (Ashe and Rampersad, 154).

Besides the Bible, books most important to Arthur Ashe were the two dozen or so volumes written by the mystic, philosopher, and theologian Dr. Howard Thurman. Those books gave special help to Ashe "both in my moments of crisis and in my extended struggle with disease" (Ashe and Rampersad, 288).

Thurman was co-founder of a large, integrated church, probably the first such congregation in America. Born black and poor, Thurman was to Ashe, a wonderful example of an African-American with an ability to achieve spiritual growth and maturity despite the problems of racism.

He admired Thurman's emphasis on the existence of a God who gives humans "sufficient strength" for all their needs.

He [Thurman] notes how virtually all the religions of the world affirm this point, no matter how each religion interprets or represents God. Divine power is sufficient to aid every human being, no matter what his or her trials and needs. This belief is true of all the major religions, including Judaism, Islam, Christianity, Taoism, and Buddhism (Ashe and Rampersad, 288).

Ashe quotes extensively from Thurman's work. One of Thurman's many prayer-poems quoted by Ashe describes the process of "centering down," which appealed so strongly to the athlete.

> How good it is to center down!
> To sit quietly and see one's self pass by!
> The streets of our minds seethe with endless traffic;
> Our spirits resound with clashings, with noisy silences,
> While something deep within hungers and thirsts for the still moment and
>   the resting lull.

With full intensity we seek, ere the quiet passes, a fresh sense of order in
   our living;
A direction, a strong sure purpose that will structure our confusion and
   bring meaning in our chaos . . .
(Ashe and Rampersad, 288)

For many years Ashe collected books. He described himself as one of
those who had to own books, unlike most readers who will pass a book
along after finishing it. In the 1960s he started to specialize in books written
by and about African Americans. He put a great deal of research into locating such books, looking them up in rare book catalogs and ordering them
from book dealers in New York, Boston, and Chicago, and he built up a very
impressive library.

In the early 1980s he decided to write a history of black athletes in America. He had begun looking for books on the topic and was very discouraged. "Ashe was startled to find only one pertinent work on the topic, *The
Negro in Sports*, written by Edwin B. Henderson in 1939 and updated in '49"
(Hurford, 88).

After several years of searching for information in all kinds of magazines, newspapers, and interviews, Ashe's dreams of publishing the history materialized. In 1988 *A Hard Road to Glory* was published in three
volumes and hailed by the critics as an essential work on the contribution of
African Americans to sports. The volumes cover the subject from 1619 to
the 1980s.

Some of the facts Ashe discovered were astounding. The accomplishments of many great black athletes were practically unknown to modern
Americans, even to Ashe himself. These included Josh Gibson, perhaps the
greatest longball hitter in baseball history; Marshall Taylor, the world
champion cyclist; and George Poage, the first American to win an Olympic
medal.

When the first Kentucky Derby was run, all the jockeys except one were
black. After that, the law required that jockeys be licensed, and black jockeys were replaced by whites. "Racism destroyed a tradition so effectively
that most people, black or white, probably assume that blacks had never
been a part of the Run for the Roses" (Ashe and Rampersad, 175).

Even knowing that he would die soon from AIDS complications, Ashe
maintained his optimistic attitude and wrote that he was "a fortunate,
blessed man." He stated that both his wife and daughter were in good
health, that he had "loving friends in abundance," and the support of
"skilled doctors and nurses." "So why should I complain? . . . I have God to
help me" (Ashe and Rampersad, 292).

He quoted a favorite prayer-poem from one of Dr. Thurman's books,
which maintains that there is a thread that connects one to God. It reads in
part: "One thread is a strange thread—it is my steadying thread . . . God's
hand holds the other end" (Ashe and Rampersad, 292).

IMPORTANT DATES IN ARTHUR ASHE, JR.'S LIFE

1943	Born in Richmond, Virginia.
1955	Won the American Tennis Association (ATA) National Boys Singles title. In succeeding years he won the title several more times.
1965	Won the National Collegiate Athletic Association Singles title and led his team, the University of California at Los Angeles Bruins, to the team championship.
1968	Ranked first in U.S. Men's Tennis and won ten tournaments.
1975	Ranked first in the United States and the world, winning nine tournaments.
1968–1985	First African American named to the Davis Cup team, he led the United States to five Davis Cup victories.
1981	Published *Off the Court*.
1985	Inducted into the International Tennis Hall of Fame.
1988	Published *A Hard Road to Glory*.
1988	Underwent brain surgery after his right arm became paralyzed. The surgery revealed a condition which led to the diagnosis of AIDS. Arthur believed he was infected by a blood transfusion.
1992	Created the Arthur Ashe Foundation for the Defeat of AIDS.
1993	Published his autobiography *Days of Grace*.
1993	Died in New York City.
1994	*Sports Illustrated* ranked Ashe among the top athletes of history.

SOURCES

Ashe, Arthur, Jr. et al. *A Hard Road to Glory: A History of the African-American Athlete, 1619–1918*. Vol. 1. New York: Warner Books, 1988.

Ashe, Arthur, Jr. et al. *A Hard Road to Glory: A History of the African-American Athlete, 1919–1945*. Vol. 2. New York: Warner Books, 1988.

Ashe, Arthur, Jr. et al. *A Hard Road to Glory: A History of the African-American Athlete since 1946*. Vol. 3. New York: Warner Books, 1988.

Ashe, Arthur, Jr., and Arnold Rampersad. *Days of Grace*. New York: Knopf, 1993.

Ashe, Arthur, Jr., with Neil Amdur. *Off the Court*. New York: New American Library, 1981.

`Hurford, Daphne. "A Man of Many Words," *Sports Illustrated*, November 4, 1991.

Robinson, Louie, Jr. *Arthur Ashe: Tennis Champion*. Garden City, N.Y.: Doubleday, 1967.

JAMES BALDWIN
(1924–1987)

James Baldwin was a brilliant author whose novels, dramas, and essays received numerous awards and honors. He also was hailed as "the most visible and respected literary figure in the civil rights movement" (Shuman, 127).

Born into poverty in Harlem, little Jimmy Baldwin became a great reader. According to his biographer, W. J. Weatherby, reading saved him. "It was an escape from his stepfather, his home life, the Harlem streets, the other boys, the cops. A book could take him far away, he soon learned" (Weatherby, 14–15). In addition to providing escape, his constant reading played an important role in his development as a writer and as a spokesperson for civil rights and other social causes. It assisted him on the road to fortune and fame.

James Baldwin was born in New York's Harlem on August 2, 1924, the illegitimate son of Emma Berdis Jones. After his mother married David Baldwin, not James' father, eight more children were born into the family. Baldwin's mother was a loving person. His stepfather, however, a laborer and preacher, was mentally unbalanced, often beat his children, and eventually died in a mental institution.

Jimmy attended New York public elementary and secondary schools. He was small and frail and not very attractive. He had large protruding eyes, which led other children to call him "Frog Eyes." They also made fun of him because he seemed effeminate to them. He was so thin that others felt sorry for him. When he first started school at age five, he looked so undernourished that a teacher fed him cod liver oil.

Despite many obstacles, Jimmy did well in school. Teachers recognized him to be a special child with a bright mind, and they encouraged his writing talent.

Baldwin's preacher stepfather wanted his stepson to be a minister too, and Jimmy began preaching as a young teenager. In his late teens, however, he suffered a crisis of faith and gave up preaching. For the next several years he worked at various menial jobs. He moved to Greenwich Village where he worked on his literary career, and he was fortunate enough to meet some famous American writers who counseled him and helped him get some pieces published.

Baldwin had often been the victim of racism in America. He was sometimes refused service in restaurants and not allowed to rent apartments because of his color. He also felt uncomfortable in the United States because he was openly homosexual, and at that time homosexuality was the object of discrimination and ridicule in his native land.

Growing disgusted with the attitudes of many Americans, he moved to France in the late 1940s. For the rest of his life he divided his time between France and the United States, to which he returned periodically to visit his family and many friends.

The oldest child, Jimmy Baldwin was often left taking care of his baby brothers and sisters. While babysitting he read constantly. Books taught the small, weak, far-from-handsome boy, "Frog Eyes," that his problems were not unique. "The hunchback of Notre Dame had been even uglier than Frog Eyes! The East End of London that Charles Dickens described was even worse than Harlem" (Weatherby, 15).

By the time he was thirteen, he had read avidly many, many books in the two Harlem libraries. Then he began to go downtown to the main New York Public Library on 42nd Street. The libraries became second homes to him.

His constant reading prompted him to try his own hand at writing. Encouraged by his teachers, he contributed a number of pieces to school publications, and then he served as editor of his school magazine.

Harriet Beech Stowe's *Uncle Tom's Cabin* was one of his favorite books. He read it so many times that his mother finally hid it from him, fearing he would damage his eyes. Although he vastly enjoyed the book in childhood, he became quite critical of it as an adult. He then judged the book to be "very bad," and that its portrayal of black people was "sentimental and dishonest" (Campbell, 63).

Among the other works he read as a youth were Robert Louis Stevenson's prose and poetry. He also enjoyed the rags-to-riches Horatio Alger stories.

After he read Dickens' *A Tale of Two Cities*, Baldwin began a lifelong fascination with the English author. He greatly admired Dickens who wrote so vividly about the poor in London as Baldwin himself would write about those ground down by poverty and racism in America. He read his works over and over. Years later Baldwin stated that Dickens' bravura writing style had a major influence on his own writing.

The Bible was also an important influence on Baldwin's writing. Although he was ambivalent about his stepfather, he was grateful that he had introduced him to the King James Bible, which he considered one of the greatest literary treasures in the English language.

Baldwin first discovered Richard Wright's work in high school. Wright's *Native Son* published in 1940, "was perhaps the first novel by a black American to be regarded in the literary world as a work of major significance" (Campbell, 21). Wright quickly became one of Baldwin's idols, the "greatest black writer in the world for him then" (Weatherby, 46).

For Baldwin, Wright was "real." The black middle class had produced a number of writers, but they did not interest Baldwin. They were as remote to him as well-off blacks who lived in affluent sections of Harlem. Wright's work, on the other hand, "touched his own life, the tenements, the rats, the street people, the churches" (Weatherby, 46). Baldwin wrote:

I found expressed, for the first time in my life, the sorrow, the rage and the murderous bitterness which was eating up my life and the lives of those around me. His work was an immense liberation and revelation for me. (Weatherby, 46)

Baldwin was personally introduced to Wright, and the latter offered to read some of his work. Wright was clearly impressed. He believed Baldwin had talent and helped secure a grant for him—a Eugene F. Saxton Fellowship. That grant was probably the first tangible recognition, outside the pages of the school magazine, of Baldwin's talent as a writer.

Baldwin's attitude towards other American writers was mixed. He had genuine respect for the achievements of such authors as Ernest Hemingway, F. Scott Fitzgerald, John dos Passos, and William Faulkner. He also criticized them, however, "for a failure to see the world from a cosmopolitan perspective." They exemplified "the American way of looking on the world, as a place to be corrected, and in which innocence is inexplicably lost" (Porter, 125).

In contrast Baldwin had unlimited admiration for Henry James. He called him "the greatest of our novelists." When Baldwin first read James' works he was "surprised to discover a kindred spirit and a new model" even though they wrote about quite different groups of people. James wrote about the wealthy and privileged, unlike Baldwin's concentration on the poor, oppressed, and dispossessed.

Baldwin thought, however, that Henry James was the only American writer "who seemed to have some sense of the American dilemma."

To Baldwin, Henry James in his fiction but above all in *The Ambassadors, The Portrait of a Lady*, and *The Princess Casamassima*, described a certain American inability to perceive the reality of others, just as many white Americans today failed to perceive the reality of blacks. (Weatherby, 178)

Baldwin argued that white Americans seem trapped inside their history, afraid to break out. One of his favorite quotations was a remark of Lambert Strether, a character in *The Ambassadors*, who advised a young American to defy convention and take a chance for happiness. " 'Live all you can; it's a mistake not to,' which he said he interpreted as meaning 'Trust life, and it will teach you, in joy and sorrow, all you need to know' " (Weatherby, 2). Baldwin said that James was his standard, a model. He even claimed he could never have finished *Go Tell It on the Mountain* without James.

Baldwin also read very widely in European literature. According to Mary McCarthy, writer and Baldwin's close friend, "Baldwin had read everything," not only the English and American classics, but also foreign literature, especially Russian and French. He read Dostoevsky's *Crime and Punishment* with great intensity. He knew Tolstoy's *Anna Karenina* so well he could quote passages from it.

Baldwin knew a great deal about France before he went there to live. The works he read by French writers, as well as American writers who lived in that country, were what drew him to France in the first place.

He had read Balzac, for example, who taught him a lesson about the place of French institutions, from the universality of bureaucracy to the role of the concierge; from Flaubert he learned about the play of morality and hypocrisy, and the importance of conventional behaviour; Hemingway advised him about food, drink and waiters; Henry Miller revealed the secrets of sex in districts which, once only places of legend, now became his haunts; Montmartre, Montparnasse, St-Germain-des-Pres. (Campbell, 51)

Baldwin's books were controversial. They were sometimes banned by those who did not approve of his progressive views about civil rights, interracial romantic liaisons, and homosexuality, because they defied conventional ideas of most Americans of that time.

Notes of a Native Son, published in 1955, although offensive to many conservatives, became one of the most influential books about racial equality during the civil rights movement of the 1960s. The book described the outrage that Baldwin, as a sensitive young black, felt because of the inequality that faced blacks and how it "destroys not only the objects of that hatred but also the people who are possessed by it" (Shuman, 124).

Even major publishers were sometimes afraid to publish some of Baldwin's controversial novels. Several turned down *Giovanni's Room* which included bisexuality and homosexuality, illegal in the United States. They feared legal action would be taken against them. Fortunately, the editors at Dial Press had more courage. When published, it became a best seller.

In his book of essays *Nobody Knows My Name: More Notes of a Native Son*, Baldwin emphasized the black search for love and acceptance by the larger society, a search often frustrated because of prejudice and hatred. It won critical praise and a large readership.

Baldwin's numerous magazine articles about the sad state of racial affairs in the United States, especially in the South where he traveled widely, reached a very wide audience and elicited support for his views among both blacks and whites. The articles appeared in both specialized and mass magazines, including *Harper's*, *Mademoiselle*, *Partisan Review*, and *Esquire*.

Reading was always important to Baldwin. Reading helped him become a great writer and civil rights leader. The dramatic stories in the Bible and the works of such writers as Dickens, Henry James, Richard Wright, and many others contributed to his phenomenal success. Perhaps even now in an economically deprived area of Harlem or elsewhere there is a boy or girl reading James Baldwin and dreaming that some day he or she will be as famous as he was and write books that will help change the world for the better, just as he did.

IMPORTANT DATES IN JAMES BALDWIN'S LIFE

1924　　　Born in New York City.

1938　　　Converted and preached in a Pentecostal church, which he later left after becoming disillusioned with that type of religion.

1940–1941　Contributed to and edited *The Magpie*, his high school magazine.

1944　　　Moved to Greenwich Village, met various authors, including Richard Wright.

1948　　　Published first essay and short story in *Commentary*. Received Rosenwald Fellowship. Moved to France.

1953　　　Made literary debut with *Go Tell It on the Mountain*.

1955　　　Published *Notes of a Native Son*.

1956　　　Published *Giovanni's Room*.

1960　　　Traveled in the South. Wrote articles on civil rights and participated in sit-ins.

1961–1979　Published a number of works, including *Another Country*, *The Fire Next Time*, and *The Amen Corner*.

1987　　　Died in St. Paul de Vence, France. Funeral service was held in the Cathedral of St. John the Divine in New York City and was attended by several thousand people.

SOURCES

Baldwin, James, "White Man's Guilt," in *The Price of the Ticket: Collected Non-Fiction, 1948–1985*. New York: St. Martin's Press, 1985.

Campbell, James. *Talking at the Gates: A Life of James Baldwin*. New York: Viking, 1991.

Leeming, David. *James Baldwin: A Biography*. New York: Knopf, 1994.

Porter, Horace A. *Stealing the Fire: The Art and Protest of James Baldwin*. Middletown, Conn.: Wesleyan University Press, 1989.

Pratt, Louis H. *James Baldwin*. New York: Twayne Publishers, 1978.

Shuman, R. Baird, "James Baldwin," in *Great Lives from History: American Series*, Vol. 1, Frank N. Magill, ed. Pasadena, Calif.: Salem Press, 1987.

Sylvander, Carolyn Wedin. *James Baldwin*. New York: Frederick Ungar Publishing Co., 1980.

Weatherby, W. J. *James Baldwin: Artist on Fire*. New York: Donald I. Fine, 1989.

CLARA BARTON
(1821–1912)

Clarissa Harlowe Barton (or Clara), was a shy person who suffered from ill health much of her life. Despite such problems, in founding the American Red Cross, she undoubtedly accomplished more for humanity than almost any other American of her time.

Barton always loved poetry and imaginative novels. The reading that had most influence on her, however, were works on phrenology, the theory that one could determine human characteristics by studying the shape of one's skull. Although later discredited, phrenology was very popular during Barton's lifetime. She claimed it helped her gain self-knowledge.

Jean Henri Dunant's influential work *Un Souvenir de Solferino* was also important to Barton. It detailed the horrors of war and the need for an organization to treat the wounded. It is considered the work containing the germ of the idea for the Red Cross.

Clara Barton was born on Christmas Day in 1821 near North Oxford, Massachusetts. She was the fifth child of Stephen Barton, a soldier and farmer, and Sarah Stone Barton, a determined social reformer whose opposition to slavery was well known.

As a child Barton was, although intelligent, very bashful and withdrawn. Intimidated by her elders, she only rarely asserted herself, frequently weeping. She said of her childhood, "I remember nothing but fear" (William E. Barton, vol. 1, 20).

Help came when the English phrenologist, L. N. Fowler, visited the Barton home, and introduced Clara to phrenology. Some feel it was not entirely quackery but a forerunner of modern theories in that it claimed that no two human beings are alike, and that each person must gain self-knowledge and find a role in life especially suitable for him or herself.

Upon analyzing Clara, Fowler argued that she would "never assert herself for herself—she will suffer wrong first—but for others she will be perfectly fearless" (Burton, 8). His analysis proved to be an unusually accurate estimate of Barton's life and work.

Although most noted for founding the American Red Cross, Barton had a significant career before she undertook that task. She taught school for about eighteen years. During the Civil War, she nursed the wounded on the battlefield. She collected clothing, soap, bedding, and other items which she gave the soldiers. She also read to them and wrote letters home informing their parents of how they were.

Ill and exhausted from her work, Barton traveled to Geneva, Switzerland, to recuperate in its invigorating mountain air. While there she was introduced to the need for a group such as the Red Cross.

After returning to the United States, she was appointed to lead the effort to establish an American branch of the society. After four years, President Chester Alan Arthur signed the Geneva Accords, and Barton became the first head of the American Red Cross.

During succeeding years she led Red Cross delegations assisting people in all types of disasters in the United States and abroad. These included wars, hurricanes, floods, fires, and other calamities.

Much of Clara's education was undertaken by her family members. With the help of brothers and sisters she learned to read by age three. Barton stated that she had no knowledge of any time when she could not read, "or of a time that I did not do my own story reading" (Clara Barton, 18).

Clara's father told her fascinating tales about his days fighting in the Indian Wars under Mad Anthony Wayne. He also taught her about government, politics, and the military. "Those were also strong political days—Andrew Jackson days—and very naturally my father became my instructor in military and political lore" (Clara Barton, 20–21).

Clara memorized many facts about government and military strategy and protocol. Her father listened proudly as she recited what she had learned. All that knowledge came in useful years later when Barton had to deal with politicians and military personnel.

Clara's older sister helped her overcome some of her extreme shyness and hermit-like tendencies. They enjoyed reading English and American literature together, especially Sir Walter Scott.

As usual, my blessed sister, Mrs. Vassall, came to the rescue. Taking advantage of an all-absorbing love of poetry (which I always had) she made a weapon of it by providing me with the poetical works of Walter Scott, which I had not read, and proposed that we read them together. (Clara Barton, 89)

They began with *The Lady of the Lake* and proceeded to read many other of his works. Clara was fascinated by the romantic, stirring tales. She was "immediately transported to the Highlands and the Bonny Braes, plucking the heather and broom and guiding the skiff across Loch Katrine . . . thrilling with, 'Saxon, I am Roderick Dhu,' and trudging along with the old minstrel and Ellen to Sterling tower and the Court of Fitz-James" (Clara Barton, 89–90)

After reading Scott, Clara and her sister proceeded to read much more poetry. They were inspired and entertained with "all the train of English poetry that a child could take in" (Clara Barton, 90).

Harriet Beecher Stowe's *Uncle Tom's Cabin* became a favorite book of Barton's. Its treatment of the horrors of slavery rallied many to the abolition movement and had great appeal to her. After she started teaching, she had her students read it. She wrote to a friend, "I suppose you have read *Uncle Tom's Cabin*—isn't it excellent. . . . My school boys, poor fellows, are reading and crying over it and wishing all sorts of good luck to Uncle Tom" (Dubowski, 34).

The great Quaker poet and reformer, John Greenleaf Whittier, was another favorite of Barton's. His strong faith in God, as expressed in the following lines, inspired her.

> I know not where His islands lift
>   Their fronded palms in air;
> I only know I cannot drift
>   Beyond His love and care.

While recuperating from illness in Switzerland, Barton came across Jean Henri Dunant's landmark book *Un Souvenir de Solferino*. While traveling on business in Italy, Dunant, a Swiss philanthropist came to the battlefield of Solferino where thousands of wounded and dead soldiers lay untended. He went to work bathing and dressing the wounds of the afflicted and recruited others to help. Barton was inspired by his book, which details his experience.

Clara now read it with the keenest interest and understanding. There was much about Florence Nightingale in its pages, and he wrote most movingly of the horrors of the battlefield. Dunant advocated an international principle to apply to the wounded of all belligerent countries. He proposed relief societies . . . who would aid the wounded in time of war. He urged a neutrality clause, to protect the work of these societies. (Ross, 109)

Clara then studied the progress made by those who had taken up Dunant's challenge to form what would become the International Red Cross. As noted above, she persuaded the United States government to establish the American Red Cross.

In her later years, Barton was asked which books had influenced her the most. She responded that a wide range of books had been of much interest to her but had not necessarily influenced her. She noted those she loved as follows:

"The Fables of Aesop," "Pilgrim's Progress," "Arabian Nights," "The Ballads of Scott," "The Benign Old Vicar," "The Citizens of the World," and mainly the mass of choice English classics. . . . In fancy I should have sat at the round table with Arthur's knights, searched for the Holy Grail with Sir Galahad, roamed Africa with Livingston and Stanley, breakfasted with the Autocrat, and dropped the gathering tear for the loved Quaker poet, so dear to us all. How grateful I am for all this; and to these writers immortal! How they have sweetened life! (William E. Barton, vol. 1, 48)

She noted she had been most influenced, however, by books and brochures on phrenology. She claimed that such works had enabled her to understand the mysteries about herself, to "know herself." It had changed her from an extremely timid, self-effacing person to one who had great strength.

"Know thyself" has taught me in any great crisis to put myself under my own feet; bury enmity, cast ambition to the winds, ignore complaint, despise retaliation, and stand erect in the consciousness of those higher qualities that made for the good of human kind even though we may not clearly see the way. (William E. Barton, vol. 1, 49)

Thus reading was a very important factor in Barton's happiness and growth. Although she remained shy and sensitive personally, she became aggressive and fearless when working to help other people.

IMPORTANT DATES IN CLARA BARTON'S LIFE

1821   Born on Christmas Day, North Oxford, Massachusetts.

1838   Began teaching career.

1852   Opened first free public school in New Jersey.

1861   Began work with soldiers in the Civil War. Collected provisions and comforted those on the battlefield.

1869   Traveled to Europe for an extended rest as ordered by her doctor. Learned about the Red Cross.

1870   Began tending the wounded in the Franco-Prussian War.

1882   President Arthur signed the Geneva Convention, thus establishing the American Red Cross. Barton became its first president, retaining that position until 1904.

1905–1912   Founded and headed the National First Aid Society.

1912   Died in Glen Echo, Maryland.

SOURCES

Barton, Clara. *The Story of My Childhood*. New York: Baker & Taylor, 1907.

Barton, William E. *The Life of Clara Barton: Founder of the American Red Cross*. 2 vols. New York: AMS Press, 1969. (Reprinted from the 1922 edition published in Boston.)

Burton, David H. *Clara Barton: In the Service of Humanity*. Westport, Conn.: Greenwood Press, 1995.

Dubowski, Cathy East. *Clara Barton: Healing the Wounds*. Englewood Cliffs, N.J.: Silver Burdett Press, 1991.

Pryor, Elizabeth Brown. *Clara Barton: Professional Angel*. Philadelphia: University of Pennsylvania Press, 1987.

Ross, Ishbel. *Angel of the Battlefield: The Life of Clara Barton*. New York: Harper & Brothers, 1956.

HUMPHREY BOGART
(1899–1957)

Humphrey Bogart, one of filmdom's greatest and most enduring movie stars, was a fast reader, and he read all kinds of materials. While reading, he was always on the lookout for roles he might play in the movies, and some of his most memorable performances were based on characters from novels and plays.

Entertainment Weekly rated the 100 best movie actors and proclaimed Humphrey Bogart the number-one movie star of all time. The article noted that Bogart was "the mythical Bogey" perceived as "the last honest man punching with surly nobility at whatever authority presented itself" (Burr, 40). According to critic Leonard Maltin, Bogart "remains arguably the most popular male star of Hollywood's Golden Age" (Maltin, 85).

Humphrey DeForest Bogart was born in New York City in 1899; the exact date of his birth is disputed. His father was a prominent surgeon and his mother was a successful illustrator specializing in pictures of children. He attended private schools and Phillips Academy in Andover, Massachusetts, from which he was expelled for neglect of his studies. He joined the navy six weeks after leaving school and served in it for the next two years.

During the 1920s Bogart appeared in many stage plays, usually drawing-room comedies. Finally, he got the opportunity to play the type of "tough guy" that would make him famous. He received critical acclaim for playing the sinister character, Duke Mantee in the stage play *The Petrified Forest*. He later played the same role in the film version of the play.

From that time on he was a major movie star. He portrayed many gangster roles as well as sympathetic, sometimes noble characters. He received his first Academy Award nomination for *Casablanca*, and he was awarded the Oscar for his performance in *The African Queen*.

Bogart married his fourth wife, Lauren Bacall, in 1945. They appeared in successful films together, including *To Have and Have Not* and *The Big Sleep.*

A politically active Democrat, Bogart publicly supported liberal candidates for public office and spoke out in favor of civil rights and other liberal causes. He received bags of hate mail in which some writers argued that actors had no right to speak out on public issues. In response, Bogart argued that all Americans, including actors, had a right and a duty to express their opinions on public issues and that he would continue to do so.

A number of Bogart's films are considered classics, are shown regularly on television, and are available in video shops and public libraries. He has become a beloved film icon for legions of fans, including many who were not even born before he died in 1957.

Many were surprised when they discovered that Bogart was an intellectual who read a great deal. One was Lauren Bacall. In an interview, she stated that when she first arrived in Hollywood, she was reluctant to appear with him in a movie. "You know, the 'dese' 'dem' and 'does' kind of guy who can't spell his own name. I was surprised he could speak the English language" (Goodman, 65).

She found, however, that he was a very intelligent, sensitive man. He got up every morning about 9 A.M., she noted, had breakfast and read the *Hollywood Reporter.* He also read *Time, Life, Newsweek,* historical books, and film scripts. He was "always reading," she said (Goodman, 68–69).

When working, according to Bacall, he usually went to bed by 9:30 and always took a book with him to read before going to sleep. He was a fast reader and, she noted, "could read a book a night" (Goodman, 68).

According to Meyers, Bogart read scripts, devoured newspapers, liked current best sellers and was addicted to murder mysteries. Also, while reading and talking with his literary friends, "he kept his eye open for good parts" (Meyers, 82). He had good literary taste, and that was "a crucial factor in his success as an actor" (Meyers, 230).

Books in Bogart's home reflected both his personal and professional interests: boats and the sea, films, writing, and politics. Some of the books in his collection were:

Assen Jordaneff's *Through the Overcast: The Art of Instrument Flying* (1938), which provided background for his aeronautical films: *The Middle Aged Man on the Flying Trapeze* (1940), a satire by James Thurber; *Great Sea Stories*, a nautical anthology that he read on the boat; *American Harvest: Twenty Years of Creative Writing in the United States* (1943), which provided ideas for future films; Bill Mauldin's popular *Up Front* (1945), with drawings and text about army life in World War II; and *Nothing to Fear: Selected Addresses of Franklin Delano Roosevelt, 1932–1945* (1946), published soon after the death of the president. (Meyers, 81)

Bogart loved socializing with prominent writers. He formed close friendships with some, frequently inviting them to the many parties which he and Bacall gave.

He sought screenplays from such writers as James Agee, Lillian Hellman, William Faulkner, and especially John Huston who wrote or co-wrote a number of Bogart movies.

He also chose to do films based on plays and novels written by such leading authors as Robert Sherwood, Sidney Kingsley, Dashiell Hammett, Raymond Chandler, Maxwell Anderson, and Ernest Hemingway.

Bogart read all of Hemingway's books and identified with some of the characters. According to Meyers, there was an uncanny similarity between Bogart and Hemingway. Both were born into upper-class families. Both loved their fathers, but not their domineering mothers. Both disliked their rather sissy first names, Humphrey and Ernest.

Both became heavy drinkers who mistrusted those who did not drink. Both married four times to people in their own professions. Bogart married movie actors and Hemingway, journalists. Both were active Democrats.

More importantly, Bogart played the type of tough guys Hemingway created in his novels. Hemingway, "actually created the natty dress, menacing wisecracks and unrestrained violence of the movie racketeers" (Meyers, 3).

One Hemingway book Bogart especially liked was *The Old Man and the Sea*, which he read when it appeared in *Life* magazine. He identified closely with the story, and wanted to make the picture. He gave the magazine to Bacall.

"Read that," he said. "That's how I feel." Hemingway had written that the old man "knew that no man was ever alone on the sea," and that the sea was the only place where a man could be really free. (Benchley, 178)

Bogart, thin, gaunt, and an excellent sailor was very well suited to play the Cuban fisherman. He was unsuccessful in his effort to get the part, however, and Spencer Tracy, although plump and otherwise miscast, starred in the picture the year after Bogart died.

Richard Brooks, who later directed *The Blackboard Jungle* and *Elmer Gantry*, was another writer who became a close friend of Bogart's. Brooks, just out of the marines, had written *The Brick Foxhole*, a popular book about the military. Bogart was impressed with the story, was introduced to Brooks, and liked his angry young writer personality. Brooks later collaborated with John Huston in writing Bogart's film *Key Largo*, and he later wrote the script for and directed him in *Deadline—U.S.A.* and *Battle Circus*.

On at least one occasion, Bogart's reading led to another star's playing in a film. He had read Henry Bellamann's novel *King's Row*. He recommended to Ann Sheridan that she play the female lead, which she did. She was very successful in the role.

Humphrey Bogart, movie tough guy, was more of an intellectual than most film stars. Some of his phenomenal success can be attributed to his reading of novels, plays, and movie scripts that contained characters he could portray successfully.

IMPORTANT DATES IN HUMPHREY BOGART'S LIFE

1899   Born in New York City.

1935   Played his first very successful stage role as Duke Mantee in *The Petrified Forest*. Repeated the role in the film version two years later.

1941   Furthered his screen career by appearing in two memorable roles that George Raft had turned down: *The Maltese Falcon* and *High Sierra*.

1942   Won his first Academy Award nomination for his role as Rick in *Casablanca*.

1944   Appeared in *To Have and Have Not*, the first of his movies with Lauren Bacall.

1951   Won the Academy Award for his performance in *The African Queen*.

1957   Died in Los Angeles.

Late 1960s   Bogart achieved cult status when his films were rediscovered by younger viewers.

SOURCES

Bacall, Lauren. *Lauren Bacall: By Myself*. New York: Knopf, 1980.

Benchley, Nathaniel. *Humphrey Bogart*. Boston: Little, Brown, 1975.

Burr, Ty. "Humphrey Bogart," *Special Collector's Issue: The 100 Greatest Movie Stars of All Time* in *Entertainment Weekly*, Fall, 1996.

Goodman, Ezra. *Bogey: The Good-Bad Guy*. New York: Lyle Stuart, 1965.

Maltin, Leonard. *Leonard Maltin's Movie Encyclopedia*. New York: Dutton, 1994.

Meyers, Jeffrey. *Bogart: A Life in Hollywood*. Boston: Houghton Mifflin, 1997.

Sperber, A. M., and Eric Lax. *Bogart*. New York: William Morrow, 1997.

ANDREW CARNEGIE
(1815–1919)

The railroad and iron and steel baron Andrew Carnegie was the greatest individual benefactor of free public libraries in history. He was often called the "Patron Saint of Libraries." He provided vast amounts of money for public libraries, which made books and other reading materials available to countless numbers of middle-class and poor people who otherwise would not have had access to such resources.

Despite having little education, Carnegie had enormous respect for knowledge and loved books and reading. He believed strongly in the importance of reading not only for himself but for all people.

There was, however, a less benevolent side to Carnegie. A ruthless businessman, he made platitudinous statements about the dignity of labor while his own workers toiled for long hours for very low pay. At times they were even treated brutally, as during the Homestead Strike in which a number of those on strike were killed.

Andrew Carnegie was born in Dunfermline, Scotland, in 1835, the son of a weaver. In 1845 his family emigrated to the United States, settling in Allegheny, Pennsylvania. Andrew went to work in a cotton mill for $1.20 a week. As a young man he also worked as a messenger boy for a telegraph office and a railway clerk. He improved his skills by going to night school.

As a young man he began to invest his savings in stocks, and he was delighted when he made considerable money from those investments. After the Civil War he became actively involved in the iron and steel business where he made a huge fortune. By the time he retired in 1901, his company had become the largest steel company in the United States, and he was one of the richest men in the world. Carnegie devoted the rest of his life to philanthropy, and much of his fortune was distributed to libraries, museums, and schools.

Andrew Carnegie learned his letters and a little Latin in school, but his "real education" was derived from home and relatives. Andrew was a very close friend of his cousin George Lauder, and Lauder's father took both boys under his wing and introduced them to books and reading. Under his tutelage, Andrew memorized a number of the Psalms.

Uncle Lauder concentrated, however, on teaching the boys more secular literature, including *The Lady of the Lake* and Shakespeare's histories.

One story that touched young "Andra," as he was often called, was the poem describing the tragedy of Queen Mary. Everything went well until that part of the poem in which Mary "placed her head upon the block, and at this point Andra usually broke down and wept" (Hendrick, vol. 1, 26).

The most important writer in Carnegie's early training, however, was the Scottish poet Robert Burns. "It is impossible to exaggerate the influence of the national poet on this particular worshipper. Carnegie had the rare experience of knowing most of Burns's important poems before he had learned to read" (Hendrick, vol. 1, 26). He continued to love Burns throughout his life.

Although Carnegie had little schooling, one teacher in particular, Robert Martin, had an important influence on the boy. Martin was a real taskmaster, not reluctant to whipping the boys if they neglected their lessons. But Carnegie was a model student and learned a great deal from him. In fact the other boys nicknamed him "Martin's pet." In later life he took pride in it. In letters to those who had been school friends, he humorously signed himself, "Martin's pet."

Carnegie was always grateful that Martin introduced the children to Chambers' *Miscellany*. It was a real storehouse of information and entertainment on all kinds of topics that aroused the interest of the boys. Andrew earned his first penny from anyone outside his home from Martin. He recited the Burns' poem *Man Was Made to Mourn* flawlessly, and Martin rewarded him with the coin.

After some years in Pennsylvania, Carnegie was invited to join the Webster Literary Club. The group met weekly to discuss literary masterpieces, especially the works of Shakespeare. It was generally forbidden to discuss partisan politics or sectarian religion.

About the same time Carnegie heard about Darwin and Herbert Spencer. He bought a copy of *First Principles* by Spencer, the British philosopher who coined the phrase "survival of the fittest." The book strengthened Carnegie's belief that one must struggle in order to succeed. "He then made the acquaintance of a mind that became the most important intellectual influence in his life" (Hendrick, vol. 1, 101).

Leading railroad people in Pennsylvania recognized that Carnegie had potential. One was Colonel Niles Stokes, general counsel of the Pennsylvania Railroad. He invited Carnegie to his impressive home for weekends. Andrew was especially impressed by Stokes' library. It was the most extensive private library he had ever seen. He was especially impressed by the representation of a book carved on the mantlepiece which bore the following lines:

> He that cannot reason is a fool,
> He that will not is a bigot,
> He that dare not is a slave.
> (Wall, 124)

Carnegie determined that some day he would be rich and have an equally impressive library. Eventually, he had two fine libraries, one at his home in New York City and another at his Skibo Castle estate in Scotland.

His friends and acquaintances noted that Carnegie could recite much of Shakespeare and other literature from memory. Dr. W. J. Holland of Pittsburgh recalled an incident on a lake.

Something reminded Carnegie of *The Tempest*, and he recited scene after scene verbatim. He could repeat the play . . . as well as *Hamlet*, from beginning to end. Sir Henry Irving used to comment on this knowledge. "He knows his Shakespeare backward," he would say. (Hendrick, vol. 1, 160)

In the autobiography, Carnegie often discussed and quoted from Shakespeare, Burns, and other writers. This was done frequently to clarify a point. When discussing his desire to distribute wealth, for example, he quoted from Shakespeare's *King Lear*: "So distribution should undo excess, And each man have enough" (Carnegie, *Autobiography*, 245).

He argued that Burns was right about life when he implied that the most important critic is one's self in the line "Thine own reproach alone do fear" (Carnegie, *Autobiography*, 3).

Recommending that young men should seek the perfect lady as their mate, he quoted Shakespeare's *The Tempest*. Ferdinand, speaking to Miranda, noted that he had eyed "full many a lady," but found they all were wanting in some way except her.

> but you, O you,
> So perfect and so peerless are created
> Of every creature's best. (Carnegie, *Autobiography*, 206)

A voracious reader all his life, Carnegie also developed friendships with some of his favorite writers. These included Mark Twain, Matthew Arnold, Herbert Spencer, and John Morley. He just as easily conversed with them as he did with business associates. Undoubtedly, his knowledge of literature impressed such famous writers.

Carnegie frequently extolled the value of reading, books, and libraries, and he encouraged others to read. In many letters and articles he wrote statements such as the following:

Be sure to read promiscuously, and know a little about as many things as you have time to read about. (Carnegie, *A Carnegie Anthology*, 2)

It is no disparagement of free libraries that most of the works read are works of fiction. On the contrary, it is doubtful if any other form of literature would so well serve the important end of lifting hard working men out of the prosaic and routine duties of life. The works of Scott, Thackeray, Eliot, Dickens, Hawthorne, and other of the same class, are not to be rated below any other form of literature for working-men. (Carnegie, *A Carnegie Anthology*, 96)

It is from personal experience that I feel that there is no human arrangement so powerful for good . . . as that which places within the reach of all the treasures of the world which are stored up in books. (Carnegie, *A Carnegie Anthology*, 146)

Carnegie's ideas about philanthropy are outlined in his essay "The Gospel of Wealth" and other writings. He argued that rich men should spend their money in ways that advance society. The millionaire, he stated, is only a trustee of the funds he possesses, and should award money for public good.

He listed seven fields of philanthropy to which the millionaire should give money. They were universities, public libraries, hospitals, parks, halls suitable for meetings, swimming baths, and churches, but only church buildings, since, he believed, church activities should be supported by the congregation. The best gift that could be given to a community, he stated, was a free library, provided that the community maintained it.

Carnegie's idea to build libraries began when his father, William Carnegie, who, with other residents of Dunfermline, combined their few books and allowed their less fortunate neighbors to use them. "I had followed in his footsteps by giving my native town a library—its foundation stone laid by my mother—so that this public library was really my first gift" (Carnegie, *Autobiography*, 249).

Carnegie funds were used to build more than 2,500 libraries in the United States, Britain, and other English-speaking areas of the world. The largest number, a total of 1,679 public library buildings, were constructed in the United States with Carnegie monies. Grants totaled over $40,000,000, an enormous amount of money for the time.

Each community requesting a free public library had to specify that a site for the building was available. It also had to indicate how much money it was "willing and legally able to tax itself for annual support of the library" (Bobinski, 39).

Most towns answered these and related questions satisfactorily. There-fore very few were ever refused funds.

Carnegie endowed the Carnegie Corporation with money to continue making grants after his death. Such funds were to be used for public librar-ies, schools, and other cultural and educational purposes.

From humble beginnings, Andrew Carnegie became one of the richest men in the world. He also became one of history's most effective philan-thropists. The many libraries built with his money provided books and other reading materials to multitudes of people who would otherwise not have had such access. Also, he was an effective promoter of reading, fre-quently extolling the value of books and libraries in his publications.

IMPORTANT DATES IN ANDREW CARNEGIE'S LIFE

1835   Born in Dunfermline, Scotland.

1848   Emigrated to America. Employed in a variety of jobs, gradually work-ing himself up in business.

1853   Appointed secretary and personal telegrapher to Tom Scott, superin-tendent of the Pennsylvania Railroad's western division.

1865   Began his active involvement in the iron and steel business.

1892   Homestead steel workers strike: Management had insisted on a cut in wages. Strikebreakers were brought in. A battle ensued, and eight men were killed, many wounded.

1901–1919 Endowed many public libraries, schools, and museums.

1919   Died at his summer home near Lenox, Massachusetts.

SOURCES

Bobinski, George S. *Carnegie Libraries: Their History and Impact on American Public Library Development*. Chicago: American Library Association, 1969.

Carnegie, Andrew. *The Autobiography of Andrew Carnegie*. Boston: Houghton Mif-flin, 1920.

Carnegie, Andrew. *A Carnegie Anthology*, arranged by Margaret Barclay Wilson. New York: private printing, 1915.

Graybar, Lloyd J. "Andrew Carnegie," in *Great Lives from History: American Series*, Vol. 2, Frank N. Magill, ed. Pasadena, Calif.: Salem Press, 1987.

Hendrick, Burton J. *The Life of Andrew Carnegie*, 2 vols. Garden City, N.Y.: Double-day, Doran & Co., 1932.

Swetnam, George. *Andrew Carnegie*. Boston: Twayne Publishers, 1980.

Wall, Joseph Frazier. *Andrew Carnegie*. New York: Oxford University Press, 1970.

RACHEL CARSON
(1907–1964)

From early childhood Rachel Carson enjoyed reading about nature. When she grew up, she published a number of books that became best sellers and exerted great influence on the public. Her masterpiece *Silent Spring*, brilliantly described the calamitous use of certain pesticides that kill many life forms, even the most beneficial. Robert B. Downs in his landmark work *Books That Changed America*, compared the impact of *Silent Spring* on society to that of some of the most influential books ever published.

Comparable in its impact on public consciousness, and demand for instant action, to Tom Paine's *Common Sense*, Harriet Beecher Stowe's *Uncle Tom's Cabin*, and Upton Sinclair's *The Jungle* was Rachel Carson's *Silent Spring* (1962), describing the disastrous effects on the balance of nature caused by the irresponsible use of insecticides and other pest controls. (Downs, 260)

Carson was born on May 27, 1907, in Springdale, Pennsylvania. From earliest childhood she loved both nature and reading. She spent many hours in the woods observing the birds, flowers, and insects; and she also spent endless hours reading. Rachel attended local schools where she impressed her teachers as a very able, well read, and highly motivated student.

When she entered Pennsylvania College for Women, later named Chatham College, she was determined to be a writer. While taking a biology class, however, she was so impressed, that she changed her major to science, but she never lost her love of writing. After graduation she continued her studies at Johns Hopkins University.

From 1936 to 1949, Carson worked for the U.S. Fish and Wildlife Service. While there she wrote radio broadcasts about ocean life, and thus found a way to combine her love of writing with her love of science.

She published several science articles in national magazines, and in 1941 published *Under the Sea-Wind*, which received very enthusiastic reviews. Her later book, *The Sea Around Us*, became an immediate best seller. In 1962 she published her masterpiece *Silent Spring*.

"For the first time in history," she wrote, "every human being is now subjected to contact with dangerous chemicals from the moment of conception until death" (Carson, *Silent Spring*, 15).

The book was condemned by agricultural interests and even the U.S. Department of Agriculture. Within a few years, the public outcry became so great, however, that vast changes were made in environmental laws strictly regulating the use of pesticides and other dangerous chemicals.

Rachel Carson had a close relationship with her mother, Maria Carson. Maria was a schoolteacher, but when she married Robert Carson she was forced to quit teaching because most teachers in those days were required to be unmarried.

Maria loved books, and she read to Rachel as soon as the child could understand. Frequently in the evenings she would read aloud to the whole family all kinds of adventure stories, which Rachel loved.

Mother read beautifully and enjoyed doing so. The children listened with their minds as well as with their ears. . . . "Could you read just a little slower, Mother? . . . Would you mind reading that last part again?" (Sterling, 21)

Rachel also often used the public library. One day she discovered two books in the library which had a lasting effect on her. One was *Tarka the Otter* by Henry Williamson, and the other was Henry Beston's *The Outermost House*. In *Tarka the Otter*, the writer beautifully and dramatically described the life of otters.

The Beston book described the life of the author when he lived alone in a little house by the sea. Carson felt it had a "feeling for the great rhythms of nature." "I have read and re-read them more times than I can count; they are among the books that I have loved best and that have influenced me most" (Brooks, 6).

Young Rachel's favorite publication was the *St. Nicholas Magazine*, a periodical very popular with children that published some stories by children. Not long after the United States had declared war on Germany during World War I, the magazine asked its readers to write articles about the bravery of American fighter pilots. The best pieces would be published.

Ten-year old Rachel got an idea for an article from her older brother Robert who had enlisted in the U.S. Army Aviation Service. She wrote the article, entitled "A Battle in the Clouds." "Rachel mailed it and waited for something to happen. Issue after issue of *St. Nicholas* arrived. She read each one with enjoyment as though she felt no disappointment at not finding her own story in it" (Sterling, 25). Finally, her patience was rewarded. The September, 1918, issue included her article. A short time later she got a check from *St. Nicholas* for ten dollars. Rachel was thrilled. Now she was a paid writer.

At least three more of Rachel's stories appeared in *St. Nicholas* during the following year. One of them won the top prize, a gold badge.

Albert Schweitzer's life had a profound, lifelong effect on Carson, and she dedicated *Silent Spring* to him. The dedication reads: "To Albert Schweitzer who said 'Man has lost the capacity to foresee and to forestall. He will end by destroying the earth.' " Like Schweitzer, she believed in the value of all life—human, animal, and plant.

Joseph Conrad was another favorite writer. She admired his awareness of the sea. In his book *The Mirror of the Sea*, she thought "the converse of wind and water over the wide spaces of ocean have never been more magnificently described" (Brooks, 7).

U.S. government documents were another inspiration to Carson. Not at all dull, as many might believe, she found them highly practical yet "intrinsically romantic." She found that such publications gave helpful directions for traveling along little-known coasts. They provided a fine vehicle for arm-chair traveling and seemed to her "the most rewarding reading" (Brooks, 7).

Throughout her life, Carson read for pleasure, relaxation, inspiration, and ideas. Describing her habit of writing and reading until late at night, she wrote:

> There was usually a volume of Thoreau's Journal or of Richard Jefferies' nature essays beside my bed, and I would relax my mind by reading a few pages before turning out the light. As might be expected, such great sea books as Tomlinson's *The Sea and the Jungle* . . . Beston's *Outermost House*, and *Moby Dick* are all favorite volumes. (Brooks, 5)

Rachel Carson used her considerable knowledge of literature in her own writing. In her books she refers to and quotes many poets and novelists, especially those who had something to say about nature or the environment. The following, for example, are a few of the quotes used in introducing chapters of *The Sea Around Us*.

> There is, one knows not what sweet mystery about this sea, whose gently awful stirrings seem to speak of some hidden soul beneath.
> HERMAN MELVILLE

> Till the slow sea rise and the sheer cliff crumble, Till terrace and meadow the deep gulfs drink.
> SWINBURNE

And the earth was without form, and void; and darkness was upon the
face of the deep.

GENESIS

Thus with the year seasons return.

MILTON

Silent Spring also contains many apropos literary references. One of the
most compelling is an allusion to Robert Frost's poem *The Road Not Taken*.
Alluding to the possible destruction of our environment unless mankind
changes its ways, Carson wrote:

We stand now where two roads diverge. But unlike the roads in Robert Frost's familiar poem, they are not equally fair. The road we have long been traveling is de-
ceptively easy, a smooth superhighway on which we progress with great speed, but
at its end lies disaster. The other fork of the road—the one "less traveled by"—offers
our last, our only chance to reach a destination that assures the preservation of our
earth. (Carson, *Silent Spring*, 277)

Among other writers Carson quoted in *Silent Spring* are John Keats, E. B.
White, and Justice William O. Douglas.

Rachel Carson received many honors for her pioneering work which did
so much to improve the environment and ecology. She was awarded honorary degrees from academic institutions. She received a number of awards
from prestigious societies, including the Audubon Society, the American
Geographical Society, the American Association of University Women, the
National Wildlife Federation, and the Royal Society of Literature in England.

Probably one honor which she cherished the most was the Schweitzer
Medal of the Animal Welfare Institute, named in honor of Albert Schweitzer, the man whom she had for so long admired for his respect for life.

Carson's death from cancer at the relatively young age of fifty-six came
as a shock to the nation and the world. Senator Abraham Ribicoff, in a
front-page obituary in the *New York Times*, wrote: "This gentle lady, more
than any other person of her time, aroused people everywhere to be concerned with one of the most significant problems of mid-20th century
life—man's contamination of his environment" (Downs, 268).

In 1980 President Jimmy Carter posthumously awarded Rachel Carson
the Presidential Medal of Freedom, an honor given to very few Americans.
He lauded her for her pioneering work in awakening the public to the importance of protecting the environment, to creating a degree of environmental consciousness that has never ebbed.

IMPORTANT DATES IN RACHEL CARSON'S LIFE

1907   Born in Springdale, Pennsylvania.

1918   Published her first story in *St. Nicholas*.

1929   Graduated from Pennsylvania College for Women.

1932   Graduated from Johns Hopkins University with a master's degree in zoology.

1936   Became one of the first professional women to be permanently employed by the Federal Bureau of Fisheries.

1937   Her article "Undersea" was published in the *Atlantic Monthly*. It was praised so highly that she was encouraged to write a book on the topic later published as *Under the Sea-Wind*.

1951   *The Sea Around Us* published. It became an immediate best seller and won the National Book Award.

1955   *Edge of the Sea* published.

1962   *Silent Spring* published.

1964   Died in Silver Springs, Maryland.

SOURCES

Brooks, Paul. *The House of Life: Rachel Carson at Work*. Boston: Houghton Mifflin Co., 1972.

Carson, Rachel. *Silent Spring*. Boston: Houghton Mifflin Co., 1962.

Downs, Robert B. "Upsetting the Balance of Nature," in *Books that Changed America*. New York: Macmillan, 1970.

Gartner, Carol B. *Rachel Carson*. New York: Frederick Ungar Publishing, 1983.

Graham, Frank, Jr. *Since "Silent Spring."* Boston: Houghton Mifflin, 1970.

Sterling, Philip. *Sea and Earth: The Life of Rachel Carson*. New York: Thomas Y. Crowell Co., 1970.

WILLA CATHER
(1873–1947)

Willa Cather, one of America's most important writers, read a great variety of literature from an early age, and her reading had a considerable impact on her own writing. Cather's reputation has grown with time. Her works, published during the 1920s and through the 1940s, are studied in colleges, included in high school anthologies, and are the subject of many scholarly articles and books. Writing in the tradition of American naturalism, Cather is an original. Although her work shows the influence of other writers, "her spare, lean style and bold characterizations made her unlike any author before her or since" (Forman, 436).

At a time when such careers were rare and almost unheard of for women, Cather became a successful magazine editor, a noted literary and music critic, and a famous writer of novels, poetry, and short stories.

Willa Sibert Cather was born on December 7, 1873, in rural Virginia, the eldest of seven children. In 1883 the family moved to Nebraska where Willa grew up among immigrants, the type of people she often portrayed so vividly in her stories.

After graduating from college, Cather worked for a number of years as a journalist. In 1906 she was appointed to the very prestigious position as an editor of *McClure's,* one of the nation's most important magazines where she achieved phenomenal success as a crusading editor. In 1912 she resigned that position in order to devote full time to her writing.

Cather's first novel, *Alexander's Bridge,* was published in 1912. Other novels include *O Pioneers!, My Antonia, A Lost Lady, Death Comes for the Archbishop,* and *One of Ours.* She received the Pulitzer Prize for the latter work. Cather received many other awards and honors for her writing. These included the Gold Medal award of the American Academy of Arts and Letters for *Death Comes for the Archbishop*. She was a recipient of the Prix Femina Americain for her novel about Quebec, *Shadows on the Rock*. She also received honorary doctorates from Smith College and from several large universities.

Cather did not attend school until she was almost eleven, but she could never remember a time when books had not been important to her. When she was a small child, her grandmother read to her from the Bible, *Pilgrim's Progress*, and Peter Parley's *Universal History*.

As soon as she learned to read, she read all the time. When the busy Cather household became too noisy, Willa would retreat to a little attic room where she found privacy. According to Woodress, "Cather's reading during her adolescent years was more important to her than her formal education" (Woodress, 49). In addition to English classics and the Bible, she read indiscriminately, good books, trashy books, just about anything she could lay her hands on. *Pilgrim's Progress* became one of Willa's favorite books. One winter she read it through eight times. Bunyan's story made a deep impression on her. She stated years later that it had "scenes of the most satisfying kind; where little is said but much is felt and communicated" (Woodress, 23).

Willa was fortunate in that there were many books in her home. The Cather book collection contained standard English and American classics, including Dickens, Scott, Thackeray, Poe, Hawthorne, Ruskin, Emerson, Carlyle, Shakespeare, and Bunyan. It also included anthologies of poetry, translations of Latin and Greek classics, books about the Civil War, and bound volumes of popular magazines. Since Willa was a voracious reader, "one can assume that she read everything in the collection" (Woodress, 50).

In addition Willa could use the library of Mr. and Mrs. Charles Wiener, a European Jewish couple who lived just around the corner from the Cathers. The Wieners had an extensive collection of French and German literature. When they found out that Willa had a great appetite for literature, "they introduced her to French and German literature in translation and gave her the run of their large library" (Woodress, 49).

Cather was fourteen when she discovered Tolstoy. His *Anna Karenina* became one of her favorites. She also read *The Cossacks*, "The Death of Ivan Illych," and "The Kreutzer Sonata."

For three years, she said later with characteristic exaggeration, she read Tolstoy all the time. Backward and forward. What she wanted at that age was vitality. She wanted to read about life, about characters who were in the midst of struggle. (Woodress, 51)

At the University of Nebraska Cather became bored with much that the professors taught. She "was eager to explore authors who had special value for her personal life and for the practice of fiction and poetry" (Brown, 61).

As an undergraduate she developed a real passion for French culture. She read many French literary masterpieces. She read Maupassant, Merimee, Dumas, and Gustave Flaubert. She became a real devotee of Flaubert, and especially loved his *Madame Bovary*. She was often seen carrying a copy of the novel around with her. In her personal life, Cather shared many commonalities with the French writer. Like Flaubert, she was very dedicated to her art, did not trust science, was not interested in politics, desired privacy, and was very loyal to her friends.

Another French writer she greatly admired was Paul Verlaine. When he died in 1906, Cather had an opportunity to show "her devotion to French literature and defend the reputation of a favorite poet," as well as her broad mindedness regarding the weaknesses of others. She admitted that he was a dirty old man, a vagabond, and even a criminal. All that mattered to her, however, was that he was a great poet. She never cared about a writer's morals if she loved his writing.

Cather developed an "enduring pleasure" in Robert Louis Stevenson's works. She bought a complete set of his works—"the first large set she acquired"—paying for it at the rate of a dollar a month. When she died, the Stevenson set was located on a shelf in her living room, conveniently accessible. "Like the rest of the reading that was important to her as an undergraduate, it was important to the end"(Brown, 62).

Cather also read and admired Henry James from her college years. She thought his prose style was superb and that he was the most interesting writer of that time. He became one of her masters. When Stevenson died, Cather noted her admiration for the masterful style of James. With Stevenson dead, she remarked that James was the only English-speaking author who stuck to perfection, "that mighty master of language and keen student of human action and motives" (Woodress, 108).

Cather was generally skeptical of women writers, whom she considered too sentimental. Two she greatly admired, however, were Georges Sand and George Eliot.

The one woman writer who perhaps meant most to her, however, was New Englander Sarah Orne Jewett, a quarter century older than Cather. She met Jewett just a year before Jewett died. The two women became close friends. More importantly, Jewett wrote a long letter advising Cather on her writing, which had a lasting effect on her, "the most important letter, beyond a question, that Willa Cather ever received" (Brown, 140).

Jewett was concerned that Cather's writing was not maturing. She advised her to find a quiet place and focus on her work. She regretted that Cather was spending so much time on her magazine work "when she should be writing, pointing out to her that when one's first working power is spent, it cannot be regained" (Bennett, 195).

Cather paid high tribute to Jewett. She noted that the three American books that had the possibility of enduring for a long time were *The Scarlet Letter, Huckleberry Finn,* and Jewett's *The Country of the Pointed Firs.*

Cather's books are filled with literary allusions and quotations from the Bible, English and American classics, and many other types of literature. According to biographer James Woodress, she wrote "with an awareness of her literary predecessors from the Greeks to the major authors of the twentieth century. . . . The reverberations from the past abound in her work and give the experiences of her Nebraska farmer universality" (Woodress, 247).

Just a few examples can be given here. In *Sapphira and the Slave Girl,* Cather wrote that the miller in the story read *Pilgrim's Progress* while contemplating the moral implications of slavery. At the first meeting between Marie and Emil in *O Pioneers!,* Emil is singing the "Jewel" song from Gounod's *Faust.* The romances in both stories end in tragedy. Myth used in *My Antonia* gives the novel universality. According to Woodress, "Cather mytholigizes American experience in creating Antonia as an embodiment of the westward movement, the pioneer woman, the symbol of the frontier" (Woodress, 295–296). Cather's masterpiece, *Death Comes for the Archbishop,* contains allusions from various works, including *Pilgrim's Progress,* the Gospels, and *The Divine Comedy.*

The bishop has been lost in the desert without water for a day. He remembers Christ's cry on the cross, "J'ai soif!" (I thirst!). He prays, and an hour later he finds water, seemingly a miracle. The bishop has embarked on "a Christ-like ministry."

[As] Dante traveled through the Inferno to Purgatory and finally to Paradise, or as John Bunyan's Christian toiled with his load of sins through the Valley of the Shadow of Death towards his heavenly destination. (Woodress, 407)

Cather's book columns reveal how much she had read herself, how appreciative she was of a variety of literature, and with what verve she recommended books to others. Her columns contain recommendations of numerous English-speaking writers, including Thackeray, Shakespeare, and Dickens; and French writers, such as Hugo, Dumas, Anatole France, and Daudet. She frequently praised Hugo's *Les Miserables.* She read the book over and over. Every spring she would re-read it.

As a child and young woman, Willa Cather had never liked Walter Scott. When teaching school one time, she had to teach Scott's *Ivanhoe.* She thought it "one of the dullest and most artificial of books" (Lewis, 195).

During her last years, however, she fell in love with Scott's works. Her friend Edith Lewis explained that one summer while they were visiting in Maine, Willa found a copy of Scott's works in the hotel library. She began to read all of his novels, one after another "and found them a revelation of delight" (Lewis, 195).

She read *Guy Mannering, Rob Roy, The Bride of Lammermoor, Old Mortality, The Heart of Midlothian, The Antiquary, Waverley*, and *Redgauntlet*.

In the succeeding summers we spent at the Asticou Inn, she always re-read them; and in New York she bought herself copies of the ones she liked best . . . she planned to write an essay on Scott, which she would call *Apologies in Heaven*. But this was never written. (Lewis, 195)

Cather wrote just a few other things during her later years, including a beautiful story, *The Best Years*. It was about her childhood when she and her brothers slept in the attic of their old house. When she finished it, she planned to send a copy to her brother Roscoe. Sadly, before she mailed it, she got a telegram saying he had died in his sleep.

Throughout her life, Willa Cather had great pleasure in reading. In the last year of her life, she continued to find joy and comfort in literature. Her days were filled with "the glory of great poetry."

She turned almost entirely to Shakespeare and Chaucer that last winter; as if in their company she found her greatest content, best preferred to confront the future. (Lewis, 196)

IMPORTANT DATES IN WILLA CATHER'S LIFE

1873   Born in Back Creek, near Gore, Virginia.

1892   Published "Peter," her first short story.

1895   Graduated from the University of Nebraska.

1906   Moved to New York where she began a spectacularly successful career as editor of *McClure's* magazine.

1912   Left *McClure's* to devote full time to writing.

1913–1940s Published numerous novels and collections of short stories.

1923   Received the Pulitzer Prize for her novel *One of Ours*.

1937   Houghton Mifflin began publishing the definitive edition of Cather's works.

1947   Died in New York.

SOURCES

Bennett, Mildred R. *The World of Willa Cather*. Lincoln: University of Nebraska Press, 1961.

Brown, K. E. *Willa Cather: A Critical Biography*, completed by Leon Edel. New York: Knopf, 1953.

Forman, Robert J. "Willa Cather," in *Great Lives from History: American Series*, vol. 2, Frank N. Magill, ed. Pasadena, Calif.: Salem Press, 1987.

Lewis, Edith. *Willa Cather Living: A Personal Record*. New York: Knopf, 1953.

McFarland, Dorothy Tuck. *Willa Cather*. New York: Frederick Ungar Publishing, 1972.

O'Brien, Sharon. *Willa Cather: The Emerging Voice*. New York: Oxford, 1987.

Robinson, Phyllis C. *Willa: The Life of Willa Cather*. Garden City, N.Y.: Doubleday, 1983.

Woodress, James. *Willa Cather: A Literary Life*. Lincoln: University of Nebraska Press, 1987.

CESAR CHAVEZ
(1927–1993)

Books about St. Francis and Gandhi and encyclicals of the Pope provided Cesar Chavez with powerful incentives to organize the first successful union of farm workers.

Cesar Chavez, the grandchild of immigrants from Mexico, was born on a small family farm near Yuma, Arizona, on March 31, 1927. When he was ten, the family lost the farm because they fell behind in mortgage payments. They migrated to California, and traveled up and down the state seeking work as migrant farm laborers. Such work, when available, often paid far less than a living wage. The Chavez family frequently went hungry and were forced to live in tarpaper shacks or tents. Chavez once counted sixty-five different elementary schools he had attended as the family moved across the country looking for farm work.

Cesar, like other migrants, experienced discrimination first hand. Schools were often segregated. Stores and restaurants would not serve migrants, especially Hispanic migrants. Even theaters were segregated, and Chavez had to sit in the "Mexican section."

After returning from service in the United States Navy, Chavez worked as a farm laborer. He also worked as a volunteer for the Community Service Organization (CSO), a group trying to help Mexican Americans. The CSO was concerned with such issues as civil rights, voter registration, police brutality, and housing discrimination.

It was during his work with the CSO that Chavez became convinced that only unionization could make meaningful improvements in the lives of the migrants. Efforts to form an effective union had always been defeated by powerful interests, especially large agricultural businesses and their political allies. Police brutality against union organizers was common.

Nonetheless, Chavez was convinced that a new union movement could succeed, and he organized the Farm Workers Association, which later became the United Farm Workers. Within a decade the union brought large increases in the meager wages earned by the California migrants. "For the first time, migrant workers were eligible for medical insurance, employer-paid pensions, unemployment insurance and other benefits, and they had a mechanism to challenge employer abuses" (Lindsey, 554).

Chavez attained such success through nonviolent means, such as picketing, marching, singing, boycotts, and fasting. His idealism and even "saintliness" convinced many American political and social leaders and celebrities of the justness of the cause—"La Causa"—and he received support from them. Robert Kennedy was one of the most effective supporters. He defended the union in a senate subcommittee hearing relating to violence against strikers by the growers. Union marches also attracted thousands of ordinary people—college students, nuns, priests, and union supporters—from all over America.

Chavez, shy, frail, and only five feet six inches tall, had a peculiar charisma that appealed to the American people.

He was shy and not an outstanding public speaker. But he showed a humility that, with his shyness and small stature, piercing dark eyes and facial features that hinted at Indian ancestors, gave him an image as a David taking on the Goliaths of agriculture. (Lindsey, 554)

Cesar Chavez learned to read both Spanish and English at about the same time. His uncle Ramon Arias taught him Spanish. After school Cesar would go to Arias' home, and, in addition to teaching him the language, Arias would offer him fruit, candy, or a soda. He enjoyed learning Spanish, and found reading it "a lot easier than trying to learn English in school" (Levy, 25).

One reason learning in school was so difficult, in addition to attending so many different schools, was the discrimination against the migrant children. Although most of the children in class were Spanish speaking, they were forbidden to say a word in Spanish, even on the playground. If they spoke Spanish, the teachers or principal would hit them with a ruler or spank them with a paddle.

Chavez learned a great deal about the skills needed to form a union from experienced organizers Saul Alinski and Fred Ross. Much of his philosophy of labor, however, came from readings suggested by his priest and close friend, Father Donald McDonnell.

Father McDonnell had been sent to the area to work with the migrants. He wisely realized they needed improvements in their living and working conditions as well as spiritual solace.

Father McDonnell traveled around the district talking with people about their problems in their homes. "In due course, he knocked on Cesar

Chavez's door. It was perhaps the most important single meeting in the history of the farm labor movement" (London and Anderson, 143).

Father McDonnell explained to Chavez that the church approved of unions and introduced him to the papal encyclicals of Pope Leo XIII, which stated that workers had a right to organize and engage in collective bargaining. At the priest's suggestion, Chavez read not only the encyclicals but also books on labor history and legislation and works on the life of St. Francis of Assisi and Gandhi. The works of both of these great men impressed upon Chavez the superiority of a nonviolent approach to accomplishing desired goals. Chavez noted:

When I read the biography of St. Francis of Assisi, I was moved when he went before the Moslem prince and offered to walk through fire to end a bloody war. And I still remember how he talked and made friends with a wolf that had killed several men. St. Francis was a gentle and humble man. (Levy, 91)

Father McDonnell recommended that Cesar read Louis Fisher's *Life of Gandhi*. Fisher's biography made such an impact on him that he went on to read everything available about the great Indian spiritual and political leader. Gandhi's philosophy of self-sacrifice for the good of others and nonviolence became major tenets of Chavez and the Farm Workers Union.

The Mahatma's values struck a responsive chord that echoed in Chavez's experience. Gandhi spoke about the complete sacrifice of oneself for others, about the need for self-discipline and self-abnegation in order to achieve a higher good. These were values that Mexican farm workers could understand, not only in the life of Christ but in their own family experience. Especially important to Chavez's moral development were Gandhi's ideas on nonviolence: they echoed his mother's admonitions. (Griswold del Castillo and Garcia, 23)

Chavez was also influenced by the ideas of Martin Luther King, Jr. He never met him but saw him on television and read about his activities in the newspapers. King's civil rights work greatly impressed Chavez.

Boycotts against agricultural interests that would not negotiate with the union were effective methods used by the Farm Workers Union. Chavez said he got the ideas for such boycotts from those initiated by King during the civil rights movement. "Martin Luther King definitely influenced me, and much more after his death. The spirit doesn't die, the ideas remain. I read them, and they're alive" (Levy, 289).

Chavez's union leadership often reflected the influence of the great men he studied. He sometimes went on fasts and invited arrest in order to bring attention to the union struggle against the growers. He spoke of the need to sacrifice one's self for the good of others, to use nonviolence to achieve just ends. He was sometimes spoken of as "saintly," "monastic," or even "messianic."

Chavez died unexpectedly in his sleep on April 23, 1993, shocking his supporters throughout the world. The many condolences that poured in were "testimony to his importance."

[Chavez] was a leader who had touched the conscience of America. In addition to President Clinton's "authentic hero" proclamation, Art Torres, a state senator, for example, called him "our Gandhi" and "our Dr. Martin Luther King." Lane Kirkland, president of the AFL-CIO, said that "the improved lives of millions of farm workers and their families will endure as a testimonial to Cesar and his life's work." (Griswold del Castillo and Garcia, 173)

More than 35,000 people attended Chavez's funeral. Cardinal Roger Mahoney said the funeral mass and read a personal condolence from Pope John Paul II.

The program for the day included a Gandhi-like statement spoken by Chavez years before expressing his own philosophy, his hope for "a new humanity":

I am convinced the truest act of courage, the strongest act of humanity, is to sacrifice ourselves for others in a totally non-violent struggle for justice.... To be human is to suffer for others.... God help us to be human. (Griswold del Castillo and Garcia, 178)

IMPORTANT DATES IN CESAR CHAVEZ'S LIFE

1927   Born near Yuma, Arizona.

1938   After losing their farm due to nonpayment of a mortgage payment, family moved to California where they became farm workers.

1952   Joined the Community Service Organization.

1962   Founded a labor union, Farm Workers Association, later named United Farm Workers of America.

1965   Initiated successful national boycott of California table grapes because of very poor wages, working and living conditions of farm workers.

1970   Boycott ended when California growers signed a contract with Chavez's union.

1975   California legislature passed the nation's first collective bargaining act, outside Hawaii, for farm workers.

1993   Died in San Luiz, Arizona.

SOURCES

Chabran, Richard, and Rafael Chabran. *The Latino Encyclopedia*. New York: Marshall Cavendish, 1996.

Griswold del Castillo, Richard, and Richard A. Garcia. *Cesar Chavez: A Triumph of Spirit*. Norman: University of Oklahoma Press, 1995.

Levy, Jacques E. *Cesar Chavez: Autobiography of La Causa.* New York: W. W. Norton, 1975.

Lindsey, Robert. "Cesar Chavez, 66, Organizer of Union for Migrants, Dies," *New York Times Biographical Service.* April, 1993.

London, Joan, and Henry Anderson. *So Shall Ye Reap.* New York: Thomas Y. Crowell, 1970.

Pitrone, Jean Maddern. *Chavez: Man of the Migrants.* Staten Island, N.Y.: Alba House, 1971.

SHIRLEY CHISHOLM
(1924–)

Shirley Anita St. Hill Chisholm was the first black woman elected to the United States Congress. She was also the first black woman to seek the nomination of a major political party for president of the United States. Chisholm learned to read before she was four years old, and loved reading. In her professional and political positions, she used her considerable influence to promote the idea that children should be taught to read when they are very small, just as she had been taught.

Shirley Anita St. Hill was born on November 30, 1924, in Brooklyn. Her father, Charles Christopher St. Hill, was an emigrant from British Guyana who worked as an unskilled laborer in a burlap bag factory. Her mother Ruby (Seale) St. Hill, a seamstress, was born in Barbados. Because of financial problems, the St. Hills sent three-year-old Shirley and her sisters to Barbados to live on a farm with her grandmother. She received her early education there.

Returning to Brooklyn, Shirley attended local public schools. She graduated from Brooklyn College with honors, and later went to Columbia University where she earned a master's degree in elementary education. She met her future husband, Conrad Chisholm, at Columbia.

Before entering politics, Chisholm worked for a number of years with small children and became a recognized authority on early childhood education and welfare.

Significant political involvement began when Chisholm helped organize the Unity Democratic Club, which campaigned to elect candidates to the New York State Assembly. Chisholm ran and was elected to the Assembly. After serving in that body for several years, she decided to run for a seat in the United States House of Representatives. Although she had little money, Chisholm worked very hard and was elected to that office. She made her unsuccessful but history-making bid for the Democratic nomination for president in 1972.

Retiring from Congress, Chisholm was appointed Purington Professor at Mt. Holyoke College in Massachusetts, teaching politics and women's studies. She also helped found the National Political Congress of Black Women, which sent a delegation of more than one hundred women to the Democratic National Convention in 1988.

Chisholm continued to be a popular lecturer. She stirred audiences when she spoke on such topics as the needs of children, women's issues, and civil rights.

From an early age, Chisholm was a great reader. She read not only for information but also for fun and relaxation. In school in Barbados, Shirley was taught reading and other lessons in the strict British-style school system. Teachers insisted that their pupils pay attention in class and work hard. If they did not, they were punished. Teachers kept rulers in the classrooms and would use them if children misbehaved.

Chisholm appreciated such a strict education.

Years later I would know what an important gift my parents had given me by seeing to it that I had my early education in the strict, traditional, British-style schools of Barbados. (Mueller, 45)

On returning to Brooklyn, Shirley proved to be very good in reading and writing, but teachers were horrified that she knew so little about American history. Therefore, the school made a special effort to teach her about American history and geography.

Shirley undoubtedly got part of her love of reading from her father Charles. He was a voracious reader who spent what little money the family had on buying two or three newspapers a day.

Papa read everything within reach. If he saw a man passing out handbills, he would cross the street to get one and read it. The result was that, although he only finished the equivalent of fifth grade, he seemed to know a little about almost everything. (Chisholm, *Unbought and Unbossed*, 25)

From their father the children heard endless discussion of black heroes. These included Marcus Garvey, the Jamaican who in the 1920s said "black is beautiful" and became a hero to American black militants; and W.E.B. Du Bois who edited *Crisis*, the magazine of the National Association for the Advancement of Colored People. He also wrote many books and articles advocating complete equality for blacks.

Both mother and father encouraged Shirley and the other children to read, even when they did not want to.

We all had library cards and every other Saturday Mother took us to the library to check out the limit, three books each. Each of us had a dictionary, and our Christmas presents were books, often one of the endless "adventure" series such as the Nancy Drew or Bobbsey Twins stories. (Chisholm, *Unbought and Unbossed*, 31)

Being such a good student, Chisholm received scholarship offers from elite colleges, such as Vassar and Oberlin. But she went to Brooklyn College because her parents could not afford to pay living expenses at an out-of-town school.

While in college she joined the newly established Harriet Tubman Society, an all-black organization. The group met and discussed such topics as black racial consciousness, black pride, and white oppression of blacks.

Shirley had much to contribute—"more out of my reading than my experience."

I knew about Harriet Tubman and Frederick Douglass, W.E.B. Du Bois and George W. Carver, and I had managed to find some books in the public library about our African heritage that few people then studied or talked about; I knew about the Ashanti kingdoms, for instance. (Chisholm, *Unbought and Unbossed*, 24)

Since Shirley spent so much time in libraries, many boys thought she was just a bookworm. They were right in that she was an intellectual who loved books. They were surprised, however, when they saw her at parties and discovered that she was also fun loving and was a very good dancer.

Advocating that small children be taught to read and write, Chisholm dismissed the argument that they are not ready to learn such skills until later. She called such an argument "baloney."

In the primer class, I learned to read and write before I was five. Theoretically, my eye and hand muscles were not developed enough at that age. Psychological theories did not get much attention then from educators in the British West Indies. I have always believed that many teachers underestimate the powers of children. (Chisholm, *Unbought and Unbossed*, 8)

As an elected official Chisholm proposed and/or strongly supported a number of pieces of significant legislation that promoted the improvement of schools and libraries, especially in urban areas. Just one such project was SEEK (Search for Education, Elevation, and Knowledge), which granted scholarships enabling black and Puerto Rican students lacking necessary academic skills to enroll in state universities and receive remedial education.

The program recognized that not every bright high-school student was prepared for college work. Particularly in urban areas, high schools that enrolled large members of minority students did not offer college preparation. Not many of them had parents who could offer their children the support they needed as students. (Scheader, 66)

After retiring from Congress, Chisholm became a popular professor. In addition to classroom teaching, she met regularly with students and teachers after class at dinners or other gatherings for informal discussions of what they had studied. Her extensive knowledge of the topics gained both from experience and study and reading made her a superior teacher.

In her speeches and writings, Chisholm has demonstrated an extensive knowledge of history and current events, especially as related to civil rights and women's rights. She frequently has quoted or referred to the positions of Martin Luther King, Jr., Frederick Douglass, Robert Kennedy, Cesar Chavez, Harriet Tubman, Gloria Steinem, Christopher Lasch, and other leaders and scholars to strengthen her arguments.

She compared the modern civil rights movement to the experiences Frederick Douglass had had a century earlier. Like Douglass, African-American student activists were at first treated as "exhibition pieces" by well-meaning whites who led the civil rights movement. According to Chisholm, the black students of the 1960s began to achieve their goals only after they acted as a group, took leadership positions themselves, became more militant, and adopted "Black Power" as a motto.

To further bolster her belief that blacks can best improve their position in American society through collective action rather than individually, she quoted both Christopher Lasch and Ralph McGill, the famous editor of the Atlanta *Constitution*. Chisholm noted that Lasch, in his book *The Agony of the American Left* indicated that what "black power" means is that blacks should do for themselves "what other ethnic groups . . . have done" (Chisholm, *The Good Fight*, 143).

She noted that Ralph McGill, like some other white liberals, had at first been outraged by the Montgomery bus boycott, and he had denounced it. Later, in his book *The South and the Southerner*, however, he agreed that this group action had borne fruit.

He had to admit that it was "productive of the most change" of any tactic that had been tried. "No argument in a court of law could have dramatized the immorality and irrationality of a custom (so well)." (Chisholm, *The Good Fight*, 141)

Chisholm argued that America was never a "melting pot," a popular idea for many years. According to her, it has always been really a "mosaic" of elements that exist together but have never lost their identities. Thus minorities, including Irish, Germans, Italians, Jews, and others retained their group identity and achieved economic and political power. Blacks had to do the same.

Shirley Chisholm was born into a poor Brooklyn immigrant family. She learned to read at a young age and recommended that small children be taught reading skills when they are very young. Knowledge gained from reading undoubtedly contributed to her understanding of history, politics, and the race problem and to her effectiveness in providing leadership to improve American society.

IMPORTANT DATES IN SHIRLEY CHISHOLM'S LIFE

1924   Born in Brooklyn, New York.

1946   Received a bachelor's degree cum laude from Brooklyn College, later receiving an M.A. in early childhood education from Columbia University.

1959–1964   Educational consultant in the division of day care of New York City's bureau of child welfare. Participated in various political and social action groups, including the League of Women Voters and the Bedford-Stuyvesant Political League.

1960   Helped organize the Unity Democratic Club, a group that promoted the election of candidates to the New York State Assembly.

1964   Elected to the New York State Assembly.

1968   Elected to the United States House of Representatives.

1972   Made an unsuccessful bid for the Democratic Party's nomination for president, the first black woman to seek the nomination of a major political party.

1983   Appointed a professor at Mount Holyoke College.

1984   Co-founded the National Political Congress of Black Women, which in 1988 sent a delegation of more than 100 women to the Democratic National Convention.

SOURCES

Brownmiller, Susan. *Shirley Chisholm: A Biography*. Garden City, N.Y.: Doubleday & Co., 1970.

Chisholm, Shirley. *The Good Fight*. New York: Harper & Row, 1973.

Chisholm, Shirley. *Unbought and Unbossed*. Boston: Houghton Mifflin Co., 1970.

Fireside, Bryna J. *Is There a Woman in the House . . . or Senate?* Morton Grove, Ill.: Albert Whitman & Co., 1994.

Mueller, Michael E. "Shirley Chisholm," in *Contemporary Black Biography: Profiles from the International Black Community*, vol. 2, Barbara Carlisle Bigelow, ed. Detroit: Gale Research, 1992.

Scheader, Catherine. *Shirley Chisholm: Teacher and Congresswoman*. Hillside, N.J.: Enslow Publishers, 1990.

SANDRA CISNEROS
(1954-)

Sandra Cisneros was the first woman of Mexican American heritage (a Chicana) to receive a major publishing contract. She has become one of the most popular writers with American young people and has received many honors for her work. Cisneros was always a great reader. She read books of all kinds ranging from very light literature to serious writers.

Sandra Cisneros was born in Chicago on December 20, 1954. Her father was Mexican and her mother a Mexican-American. She led a rather lonely childhood, being the only girl in a family of six brothers. Moreover, the family, very poor, frequently moved to "neighborhoods that appeared like France after World War II—empty lots and burned out buildings" (Chavez, 99).

Sandra did not get a lot out of her grade and high school education. She felt the teachers were not much interested in the experiences of minorities. Going on to college, she received a bachelor's degree in English from Loyola University and studied at the University of Iowa's Writer's Workshop where she developed her writing skills.

Her ability began to be recognized in the early 1980s. *The House on Mango Street*, received the Before Columbus American Book Award. The book also brought Cisneros to the attention of Random House, and led to her contract with that publisher and the publication of *Woman Hollering Creek*.

Cisneros works have become classisc. They are widely available in bookstores and libraries and studied in classes by students in schools and colleges.

The Cisneros family was poor, but the children were fortunate in that their parents believed in education. Her mother was self-taught, and she made sure that all of her children had library cards. Her father insisted that they study hard. In an interview Cisneros said, "My father's hands are thick and yellow, stubbed by a history of hammer and nails and twine and coils and springs. 'Use this' my father said, tapping his head, 'not this' showing us those hands" (Chavez, 100).

The only girl in the family, Sandra buried herself in her books. She noted that if the family had stayed in one neighborhood long enough for her to make friends, she might not have needed to turn to books so much for pleasure.

Fortunately, she loved reading. Her school had only a small, poor selection of books, which Sandra read. They included lives of the saints, stodgy editions of children's stories published in the 1890s, and Horatio Alger-type stories. Even though she did not especially enjoy the stories, she liked them all the same because of their curious English, so different from what she was accustomed to. Many of the books Sandra loved were those she borrowed from the Chicago Public Library. She read them instead of doing housework, taking care of her younger brothers, or learning how to cook. Before going to college she was more of a reader than a writer, but reading was an important first step to becoming a writer. "I was reading and reading," she stated, "nurturing myself with books like vitamins, only I didn't know it then" (Cisneros, "From a Writer's Notebook," 74).

Sandra identified with characters in the various children's books she read. She enjoyed Hugh Lofting's *Doctor Doolittle* series, and she imagined being able to speak to animals. She loved *Alice in Wonderland* and *Through the Looking Glass* for the way in which everyday life was transformed into fantasy. She imagined that she was the sister in the "Six Swans" fairy tale, since she also was the only daughter in the family and her family name translated to "keeper of swans." *The Island of the Blue Dolphins* was another favorite, the story of a lonely girl who lives on an island.

Emily Dickinson was her favorite poet. When growing up in Chicago, she often thought about Dickinson, how she lived as a recluse never straying beyond her own house. When she died, however, she left a legacy of great poetry, some 1,775 poems.

I used to think of her and she gave me inspiration and hope all the years in high school and the first two in college when I was too busy being in love to write. Inside, some part of me secretly clung to the dream of becoming a writer. (Cisneros, "From a Writer's Notebook," 75)

Finally, Cisneros realized that Dickinson had a quite different life than she. Dickinson was rich, had servants, and lived alone. Cisneros, growing up, had none of these advantages. "Yet, like Dickinson, Cisneros has been able to take both the possibilities and the constraints of her unique situation and weave them into art." ("Sandra Cisneros," in *Elements of Literature*, 1158).

The Little House, by Virginia Lee Burton, was perhaps the most influential book in Cisneros' early life. As a child she read the book over and over, borrowing it from the library—sometimes borrowing it seven times in a row. Sandra and her brother once plotted on keeping the library book (pretending they lost it) and paying the fine. They would never have to be without it. Being honest people, of course, they did not keep it.

Sandra didn't realize people could buy books in stores. She thought books were so valuable that they were available only in libraries or schools, the only places she had ever seen them.

Sandra did some writing in high school, mainly poetry. A teacher encouraged her to write for a literary magazine, and eventually she became its editor.

A number of years later, while enrolled in the Iowa Writers Workshop, Cisneros realized that she too could write about a house. The class was studying Gustave Bachelard's *Poetics of Space*, and it suddenly dawned on Cisneros that she could write about her own type of house. It would not be a little rural house on a hill like the one in Burton's story, or an upper-class home such as the one Emily Dickinson lived in. It would be a house in a Chicano barrio like houses in the neighborhoods where Cisneros had spent her childhood, and it was the type of book no one else had written.

That's precisely what I chose to write: about third-floor flats, and fear of rats, and drunk husbands sending rocks through windows, anything as far from the poetic as possible. And this is when I discovered the voice I'd been suppressing all along without realizing it. (Olivares, 160)

Thus the idea for *The House on Mango Street* was born and became a best seller. Other books followed, and Cisneros was established as a major American writer as well as a spokesperson for Latino Americans.

Cisneros has used her own experiences as a young person, including her great love of reading, in her own books. The main character in *The House on Mango Street*, for example, is Esperanza, who loves books and dreams of one day having a nice house of her own. But she will not forget her roots.

One day I will pack my bags of books and paper. One day I will say goodbye to Mango. I am too strong for her to keep me here forever. One day I will go away.

Friends and neighbors will say, What happened to that Esperanza? Where did she go with all those books and paper? Why did she march so far away?

They will not know I have gone away to come back. For the ones I left behind. (Cisneros, *The House on Mango Street*, 110)

As a teacher, Cisneros enjoys helping many young people appreciate literature and writing. Even though she sometimes feels that teaching takes time away from her writing, she notes that she is willing to "work very hard for students that work hard for me." She also has stated that while teaching she gets "encouraged to be a writer" (Aranda, 77).

Cisneros' works have been used to interest students in literature. One ninth-grade teacher, Rodney D. Smith, wrote an article in which he noted how difficult it is to interest some students in classics, such as *The Great Gatsby* and *Death of a Salesman*. He and his colleagues had to fight parents and school board members to include works by minorities. Some charged that teachers would include low-quality works by blacks and other minorities.

Wouldn't this affirmative-action program in English class come at the expense of great literature? What multicultural author, whatever his or her race, sexual orientation, or gender, could match the works of F. Scott Fitzgerald, Mark Twain, or William Shakespeare? (Smith, 38)

Smith found that *The House on Mango Street* rose above such arguments. He wrote that its "use of voice, theme, and symbolism, as well as the honesty and clarity of the writing, rivals the best novels I have ever taught" (Smith, 38). He discovered that students who were uninterested in the classics and frequently skipped class were enthralled with Cisneros' work. Whenever he would stop reading from the book, students would plead with him to continue. "Normally, I'm the one who pleads with my students to read and finish a book" (Smith, 38).

Cisneros' reading started her on the road to becoming a major writer. Her books have added a new dimension to American literature, and have made readers of a whole new group of young people who found it difficult to relate to the classics of American and English literature. Once they realize how much they can learn and enjoy literature, however, perhaps many of them will learn to love some of the traditional writers, as Cisneros herself did when she was young.

IMPORTANT DATES IN SANDRA CISNEROS' LIFE

1954	Born in Chicago.
1976	Received Bachelor of Arts in English from Chicago's Loyola University.
1982 and 1987	Received National Endowment for the Arts fellowship in fiction and poetry.
1983	Published *The House on Mango Street*.
1985	Received Before Columbus Foundation, American Book Award for *The House on Mango Street*.
1987	Published *My Wicked, Wicked Ways*.
1991	Published *Woman Hollering Creek and Other Stories*.
1993	Received honorary doctorate from the State University of New York at Purchase.

SOURCES

Aranda, Pilar E. Rodriguez. "On the Solitary Fate of Being Mexican, Female, Wicked and Thirty-three: An Interview with Writer Sandra Cisneros," *Americas Review* 18 Spring, 1990.

Chavez, Andres. "Sandra Cisneros," in *Notable Hispanic American Women*, Diane Telgen and Jim Kamp, eds. Detroit: Gale Research, 1993.

Cisneros, Sandra. "From a Writer's Notebook," *Americas Review* 15 Spring, 1987.

Cisneros, Sandra. *The House on Mango Street*. New York: Vintage Books, 1984.

Cisneros, Sandra. *My Wicked, Wicked Ways*. Bloomington, Ind.: Third Woman Press, 1987.

Cisneros, Sandra. *Woman Hollering Creek and Other Stories*. New York: Random House, 1991.

Olivares, Julian. "Sandra Cisneros' *The House on Mango Street*, and the Poetics of Space," *Americas Review* 15 Fall–Winter, 1987.

"Sandra Cisneros," in *Elements of Literature: Fifth Course: Literature of the United States with Literature of the Americas*. Austin: Holt, Rinehart and Winston, 1997.

"Sandra Cisneros," in *Great Women Writers: The Lives and Works of 135 of the World's Most Important Women Writers, from Antiquity to the Present*, Frank N. Magill, ed. New York: Henry Holt and Co., 1994.

Smith, Rodney D. "All Brown All Around," *Progressive* 59 July, 1995.

EUGENE V. DEBS
(1855–1926)

Eugene Victor Debs was one of America's greatest leaders in the labor movement and also one of the nation's most important leaders of American socialism. One particular poem, Debs frequently told friends, had inspired him throughout his life. It was Henley's *Invictus*, which reads in part:

> It matters not how strait the gate,
> How charged with punishment the scroll,
> I am the master of my fate.
> I am the captain of my soul.

He also was inspired by and learned a great deal from the many classics he read beginning in childhood.

Eugene Victor Debs was born in Terre Haute, Indiana, on November 5, 1855. His parents, Jean Daniel and Marguerite Marie Bettrich Debs, had come to America from Alsace, France. They worked in the grocery business. As a child Gene worked in the store part time.

In his teens, Debs quit school and got a job on the railroad for a minimum wage. Although his work as a railroader lasted only a short time, it had a strong effect on him throughout his life. He saw firsthand the hard life of working men and the squalor in which they lived.

Debs joined the Brotherhood of Locomotive Firemen and rapidly rose to important positions in that union. When the American Railroad Union was founded, Debs became its president.

The union had some victories but also notable failures, such as the Pullman Strike initiated by harsh wage cuts decreed by the company. Management, allied with the courts, brought in strikebreakers, and the union was wrecked. Labor had suffered a major defeat and Debs was sentenced to serve prison time for violating a court order prohibiting union officials from communicating with striking workers.

While in jail Debs concluded that justice could not be brought to workers through strikes. This experience led him to believe that socialism was preferable to the capitalist system.

After his release from prison, Debs joined the Social Democratic Party, which later became the Socialist Party. He was its candidate for president several times.

In 1917 Congress passed the Espionage Act to enforce the draft. Debs made a long speech critical of conscription and United States participation in the World War. Although he did not advise draft resistance, he was arrested, convicted, and sentenced to ten years' imprisonment.

His years in prison were hard, but he was heartened by the many supporters who visited him and by the many sympathetic letters he received. He was released by presidential order after serving three years of his sentence.

Although in failing health, Debs, a popular figure, continued writing and made speaking tours throughout the nation.

Debs' father Jean Daniel loved romantic German and French literature so much that he named his first son after the famous writers, Eugene Sue and Victor Hugo. The latter became the younger Debs' favorite writer.

Young Debs had a wonderful memory and hungered for learning, but endless repetition of lessons taught in school—reading, writing, and ciphering—bored him. The best thing about school, he thought, was a little corner candy store located near by.

He preferred learning at home. His father would gather the children around him and read selections from the classics.

Gazing at the large busts of Voltaire and Rousseau, Eugene quietly listened to passages from Racine, Corneille, or the favorite, Hugo, and sometimes Goethe or Schiller. Thus he learned both French and German, and slowly absorbed the democratic traditions of Europe. He learned that men had hungered for freedom, written about it, fought and bled for it on a thousand dusky hills, long before the Civil War in America. (Ginger, 9)

He learned about the wretchedness and suffering of poor people when his father read passages from Hugo's masterpiece *Les Miserables*. He began to dream of ways that such poverty might be eliminated.

Gene realized that he needed to learn in order to help those who suffered. Education became the ruling passion of his life. He "squandered" his money on books. He bought himself a dictionary and a subscription to the New York *Tribune*. He also bought Appleton's *Encyclopedia*.

From Appleton's he gained detailed knowledge of American history. Accounts of the battles between the colonies and the British were fascinating. He found two new heroes: Patrick Henry and Thomas Paine. Debs noted that numerous times he found inspiration and strength from the words, "These are the times that try men's souls!" (Ginger, 25). Debs' father gave him a copy of Voltaire's *Philosophical Dictionary*. He spent months studying it.

Debs' interest in learning led him to found and to serve as president of the Occidental Literary Club in Terre Haute. A group of young men met regularly to discuss all kinds of topics, and prominent speakers were invited to address the group.

Debs invited the famous orator and agnostic Robert Ingersoll to be the first speaker. Club members raced throughout the town affixing posters announcing the Ingersoll speech on public buildings and even on churches. Despite bad weather, the large hall obtained by the club for the lecture was full, and considerable money was made. Debs was greatly impressed with Ingersoll, who figures "among the important influences of his life" (Currie, 19).

On one occasion in Indianapolis, Debs met the famous and colorful Indiana poet James Whitcomb Riley. Debs and Riley liked each other from the very beginning. Debs invited him to read his poems in Terre Haute. Riley, however, was not too popular with Terre Haute people, his humorous works were so different from the elegant phraseology of the poets of the day. Gene, on the other hand, was delighted by Riley's verses. Whenever Riley came to Terre Haute, he stayed with the Debs family. His poem about Terre Haute entitled *Regarding Terry Hut* delighted Gene.

> Take even statesmanship, and wit,
> And gineral git-up-and-git,
> Old Terry Hut is sound clean through!
> And there's Gene Debs—a man 'at stands
> And jest holds out in his two hands
> As warm a heart as ever beat
> Betwixt here and the judgment seat!

For years whenever Debs visited Indianapolis, he would get together with Riley. The two would talk poetry for hours and recite favorite verses. They would exchange opinions on old and contemporary poets, including Carl Sandburg whose poetry contrasted so much with the romanticism of the older poets.

Debs continued studying and reading throughout his life, even when working on the railroad and when in prison. While in prison he began serious study, which led him to embrace socialism as the way to bring economic justice to workers.

A Milwaukee socialist, Victor L. Berger, visited Debs in jail, gave him an impassioned talk on socialism, the first Debs had ever heard. He also presented him with a copy of Karl Marx's *Das Kapital*, a book which he cherished and which had much influence on him.

He received many more socialist books and pamphlets from his supporters while he was in prison. He was especially impressed by such utopian works as Lawrence Gronlund's *The Cooperative Commonwealth*, an attempt to domesticate Karl Marx; *Looking Backward* by Edward Bellamy; and the writings of Robert Blatchford, the English Socialist. The works of the European Marxist Karl Kautsky made an especially strong impression on Debs. He found Kautsky "clear and conclusive," and enabled him to move "out of darkness into light" (Radosh, 2).

Debs was a great orator and a prolific writer. Throughout his career he bolstered his speeches and writings by referring to the many works with which he was familiar. He had a phenomenal memory for what he had read, and was able to quote extensively from many sources. These included the Bible, the Declaration of Independence, and the writings of Jefferson, Thomas Paine, Marx, and others. He often quoted poets and novelists, including Shakespeare, Mark Twain, Longfellow, Thomas Lowell, Louisa M. Alcott, Wordsworth, and Victor Hugo.

In one work referring to his time in prison, he quoted or mentioned Longfellow, Patrick Henry, Aesop, Lowell, and especially Shakespeare. He noted, for example, that he had not been beaten and quoted Shakespeare, who wrote, "Sweet are the uses of adversity." In addition he indicated;

The immortal bard also wrote:

> This our life, exempt from public haunt,
> Finds tongues in trees, books in running brooks,
> Sermons in stones, and good in everything.

He argued that when he was in prison, "exempt from judicial persecution, the tongues of trees as well as the tongues of friends taught me that sweets could be extracted from adversity" (Debs, 17).

He ended by noting that "as Lowell sang":

> He's true to God who's true to man; wherever wrong is done,
> To the humblest and the weakest, 'neath the all-beholding sun.
> That wrong is also done to us, and they are slaves most base.
> Whose love of right is for themselves and not for all their race. (Debs, 20)

Debs was a strong proponent of women's rights and frequently spoke and wrote on the topic. In "Woman—Comrade and Equal," a pamphlet published by the Socialist Party, Debs referred to an article in the *London Saturday Review*, which argued that men were superior because they could keep women in subjection. He countered that statement by noting that it was "the snarl of the primitive," which should "kindle the wrath of every man who loves his wife or reveres his mother" (Debs, 453).

He also quoted famous writers who argued for the equality of women. He noted that the French writer Sardou contended that women were superior to men in almost every way, that they were full of noble instincts, and could almost always be trusted to do right. He wrote that Paolo Lombroso, one of the most perceptive students of the human mind, argued that even the most thoughtless, frivolous woman's soul has a spark of heroism. He referred to Shakespeare's characters. The bard "made his noblest women strong as men and his best men tender as women" (Debs, 455).

In an article entitled "Fantine in Our Day," Debs argued that society is wrong to condemn women it calls prostitutes. Like Fantine in Hugo's *Les Miserables*, such women are persecuted and shunned by a soulless society. He argued that Heine had such women in mind when he wrote "I have seen women on whose cheeks red vice was painted and in whose hearts dwelt heavenly purity" (393).

Although the American Railroad Union, of which Debs was president, failed and the Socialist Party declined, Debs left a lasting legacy for twentieth century United States. The ARU served as a model for modern labor unions. Major political parties were forced to adopt many of the reformist elements the Socialist Party had championed, including the abolition of child labor, minimum wage and maximum hour legislation, women's right to vote, and the graduated income tax.

Perhaps most important, his dedication to the alleviation of poverty, to social justice, and to peace has inspired other Americans in later generations and has contributed to the richness of American political life. (Sterling, 603)

IMPORTANT DATES IN EUGENE V. DEBS' LIFE

1855	Born in Terre Haute, Indiana.
1875	Joined and became secretary of a local of the Brotherhood of Locomotive Firemen.
1893	The American Railway Union (ARU) formed with Debs as president.
1894	ARU victorious in a strike against the Great Northern Railroad. Pullman strike failed. Debs arrested for his role in the strike and sentenced to prison.
1900, 1904, 1908, 1912, and 1920	Ran as Socialist candidate for president of the United States.
1918	After delivering an anti-war speech, Debs was indicted and sentenced to prison. While in prison (1920) ran for president and received more than 900,000 votes.
1926	Died in Elmhurst, Illinois.
1927	*Wall Bars*, his book about prison life, published.

SOURCES

Coleman, McAlister. *Eugene V. Debs: A Man Unafraid*. New York: Greenberg, 1930.

Currie, Harold W. *Eugene V. Debs*. Boston: Twayne Publishers, 1976.

Debs, Eugene V. *Writings and Speeches of Eugene V. Debs*, with introduction by Arthur M. Schlesinger, Jr. New York: Hermitage Inc., 1948.

Ginger, Ray. *The Bending Cross: A Biography of Eugene Victor Debs*. New Brunswick, New Jersey: Rutgers University Press, 1949.

Radosh, Ronald, ed. *Great Lives Observed: Debs*. Englewood Cliffs, New Jersey: Prentice-Hall, Inc., 1971.

Salvatore, Nick. *Eugene V. Debs: Citizen and Socialist*. Urbana, Illinois: University of Illinois Press, 1982.

Sterling, David L. "Eugene V. Debs," in *Great Lives from History: American Series*, vol. 2, Frank N. Magill, ed. Pasadena, Calif.: Salem Press, 1987.

CECIL B. DeMILLE
(1881–1959)

Cecil Blount DeMille was one of Hollywood's greatest directors and producers. Some of his best biblical film epics, such as *The King of Kings* and *The Ten Commandments*, had their origin in hearing his father read the Bible aloud. Cecil stored the tales in his memory and years later recalled how thrilling they were and what great movies they would make. DeMille got ideas for many other films from his extensive reading of a variety of books, old and new.

Cecil B. DeMille was born on August 12, 1881, in Ashfield, Massachusetts. He was the son of Henry deMille (Cecil was the first to capitalize the "D") and Matilde Beatrice Samuel. Both of Cecil's parents were involved in the theater. His father was a successful playwright, and after Henry's death, Cecil's mother became a theatrical agent in New York.

After graduating from the American Academy of Dramatic Arts, Cecil worked for a number of years as a stage actor, playwright, and theatrical manager. In 1913 he formed a motion picture firm, the Jesse L. Lasky Feature Play Company, with partners Lasky and Samuel Goldfish (later Goldwyn). Their first film, *The Squaw Man*, shot in Hollywood, was a great success both financially and critically.

In following years his reputation continued to grow as he directed expensive, elaborate feature films. They included society dramas, Westerns, comedies, war epics, and biblical extravaganzas. He is given credit for the switch from short productions to feature films for which Hollywood became so famous. A number of his most significant films are still popular and continue to be shown on television and are available on video. Some of his many noted movies include *The Plainsman, Samson and Delilah, The Ten Commandments, The King of Kings,* and *The Greatest Show on Earth.*

He also developed numerous movie stars. Only the great D. W. Griffith created as many stars as DeMille. DeMille is generally acknowledged as the person who more than anyone else helped Hollywood become the world's great film center. Some historians even go as far as calling him "the founder of Hollywood." His name became a household word long before the era of famous directors. Until his time only movie stars were so well known to the public.

When he was a small boy, Cecil was introduced to literature by his father Henry who read aloud the Bible and other stories to Cecil and his older brother every evening, first a chapter from the Old Testament and then one from the New Testament. After reading from the Bible, he would often read from English or American or European history or from the works of Thackeray, Victor Hugo, or other classic novelists, "dwelling with particular ripeness on the details of balls, parties, lavish coronations, and funerals," the kinds of activities that became so prominent in DeMille's movies (Higham, 5).

Many of DeMille's early films were based on famous novels and plays including *The Squaw Man, The Virginian,* and *The Call of the North.* All three were adapted from stage westerns. The latter two had been adapted from novels by Owen Wister and Stewart Edward White respectively.

According to one story, DeMille decided to do *The Ten Commandments* because of a *Los Angeles Times* contest. Readers were asked to suggest a story for a film. A huge amount of mail "poured in from fans eager to see a production with a religious theme" (Higashi, *Cecil B. DeMille and American Culture,* 179). With his knowledge of and love of the Bible, DeMille needed little prodding to produce his lavish production based on the Scriptures.

DeMille also used staff to do detailed research for such films. He made a habit of sending a secretary to the public library to get books with information that would lend authenticity to his movies. These included volumes on architecture, costume, gunnery, and other topics—whatever subjects were dealt with in a particular film.

Public libraries had one "irritating" requirement, however. They wanted their books back! Therefore DeMille decided to buy the needed volumes. The office soon became very crowded with books. DeMille realized that he would always need considerable research for the types of films he produced, particularly his historical dramas which needed authenticity. Therefore, he established a full-fledged research department, the first such department in the motion picture industry. As time went on, every major studio followed DeMille's lead and established their own research departments.

DeMille said he "cherished" the amusing verse written by an unknown author relative to his use of authentic history.

Cecil B. deMille,
Much against his will,
Was persuaded to keep Moses
Out of the War of the Roses. (Hayne, 116)

"The germ of *Unconquered* was born" on a Sunday afternoon when De-Mille was reading a book on American colonial history. He found that during the eighteenth century, white men and women worked not only as indentured servants but were also "bought and sold as slaves" (Hayne, 391). Fired up by the idea of doing a picture on the subject, he asked his researchers to do an in-depth study for the movie, which when released became a hit.

Needing constant research help, DeMille was fortunate in discovering an excellent researcher, Henry Noerdlinger.

From *Unconquered*, through such varied subjects as *Samson and Delilah, The Greatest Show on Earth*, and *The Ten Commandments* . . . Henry Noerdlinger has been the most thorough and accurate research consultant I have ever had, making himself as much at home among the pyramids of the Pharaohs as in the tinsel and spun-candy world of the circus. (Hayne, 393)

Noerdlinger's book, which documented the research done for *The Ten Commandments*, was published by the prestigious University of Southern California Press. In the book Noerdlinger recounts the extensive work done in order to lend authenticity to the film. He and his assistants "consulted some 1,900 books and periodicals, collected nearly 3,000 photographs, and used the facilities of 30 libraries and museums in North America, Europe, and Africa" (Noerdlinger, 2).

Despite his demanding schedule, DeMille read for pleasure as well as for professional purposes, often before going to sleep at night. (He almost never slept more than five hours.) The Bible remained a favorite book throughout his life. According to his niece, Agnes De Mille, he kept a copy of the Scriptures by his bedside (Agnes De Mille, *Speak to Me, Dance with Me*, 223).

One lesson that can be learned from DeMille's life is the importance of reading to small children. DeMille argued that some of his greatest successes were due to his father's reading to him when he was a child.

IMPORTANT DATES IN CECIL B. DeMILLE'S LIFE

1881   Born in Ashfield, Massachusetts.

1900   Began appearing on the stage in New York and on the road.

1913   Formed with his partners the Jesse L. Lasky Feature Play Company.

1914	*The Squaw Man,* a "colossal film" by the standards of the time, released. Established DeMille as a noted director in Hollywood, which was not yet the great film capital it would become.
1915	*The Cheat* released. It contained the type of sexy situations and independent women that audiences craved. A big success, it was followed by films with similar themes.
1923	*The Ten Commandments* released. Became one of Hollywood's greatest successes. Other religious epics followed, including *The King of Kings* and *The Sign of the Cross.* Although religious in nature, they also included many sexual images and situations.
1929–1956	DeMille directed fewer than twenty of his seventy films, perhaps because so much of his time was taken up in conservative political activities.
1950	Appeared in *Sunset Boulevard.*
1953	Received an Academy Award for *The Greatest Show on Earth.*
1959	Died in Los Angeles. His autobiography published posthumously.

SOURCES

De Mille, Agnes. *Speak to Me, Dance with Me.* Boston: Little, Brown and Company, 1973.

Hayne, Donald, ed. *The Autobiography of Cecil B. DeMille.* Englewood Cliffs, N.J.: Prentice-Hall, 1959.

Higashi, Sumiko. *Cecil B. DeMille and American Culture: The Silent Era.* Berkeley: University of California Press, 1994.

Higashi, Sumiko. *Cecil B. DeMille: A Guide to References and Resources.* Boston: G. K. Hall, 1985.

Higham, Charles. *Cecil B. DeMille.* New York: Charles Scribner's Sons, 1973.

Noerdlinger, Henry S. *Moses and Egypt: The Documentation to the Motion Picture* The Ten Commandments. Los Angeles: University of Southern California Press, 1956.

FREDERICK DOUGLASS (1817?–1895)

Frederick Douglass was a slave, and it was illegal for slaves to learn to read. Douglass was determined, however, to become literate despite the repressive law. He realized that reading and writing were not mere skills. They were a way out of slavery.

Douglass was born in Maryland, a slave state, probably in 1817, although historians are not certain of the exact date. His mother, a slave named Harriet Bailey, named him Frederick Augustus Washington Bailey. He never knew anything about his father.

Very early in his life he learned the brutalizing effects of slavery, being beaten himself and witnessing the barbaric treatment of other slaves, both men and women. In 1838 he escaped to the North. He realized he would need to change his surname in order to avoid being caught and sent back to Maryland. He chose the name of a hero called Douglas in Sir Walter Scott's *Lady of the Lake*. He spelled it with two s's, however—Douglass—as prominent black families spelled it.

In Boston he was employed as an agent of the Massachusetts Anti-Slavery Society. He was an attractive, commanding figure and became one of the most noted speakers and writers for the cause of freedom for African Americans and also for women's rights.

In 1845 Douglass set sail for England in order to avoid being caught and returned to slavery. While in Britain he became a popular orator speaking out against slavery, in favor of women's rights, freedom for Ireland, and other liberal causes.

He returned to America with money to buy his freedom and established *North Star*, a newspaper for American blacks. During the Civil War, he assisted in recruiting blacks for Massachusetts Colored Regiments.

After the Civil War, he continued a busy schedule of writing and speaking. He also held important political positions from then until late in his life, including United States Minister to Haiti.

Douglass first learned to read when at the age of eight years he was sent to live in Baltimore with Hugh and Sophia Auld as companion to their son Tommy. He persuaded Mrs. Auld, a kind, pious woman, to teach him to read the Bible. He was a fast learner and quickly mastered the alphabet and the spelling of some words. Hugh Auld was enraged when he found Frederick was learning to read. He thundered that reading was illegal for slaves and would spoil him. He might even try to run away!

Sophia Auld never taught him again, but Frederick found other ways to further his education. He bribed, coaxed, and tricked white boys to share their lessons with him. He tried to read everything he could find, including scraps of newspapers he found in the streets. When he was about twelve, he managed to get fifty cents and bought his first book, *The Columbian Orator*. It was a standard rhetoric book, used in schools. It contained short speeches by famous orators and dialogues to be memorized by the students.

The exercises in the *Orator* taught Frederick how to be an effective speaker. He would always remember reading those speeches in the *Orator* given by champions of liberty, those who argued that truth and beauty would triumph over ignorance and cruelty. They included Charles James Fox, Richard Brinsley Sheridan, the younger William Pitt, and the great champion of Irish freedom, Daniel O'Connell.

He read it assiduously.

Every opportunity I got, I used to read this book. Among much of other interesting matter, I found in it a dialogue between a master and his slave. The slave was represented as having run away from his master three times. . . . In this dialogue, the whole argument in behalf of slavery was brought forward by the master, all of which was disposed of by the slave. . . . The conversation resulted in the voluntary emancipation of the slave on the part of the master. (Douglass, 41–42)

He also read newspapers, including the *Baltimore American*, and from them he learned about abolitionists and their attempts to do away with slavery. The papers also reported Nat Turner's insurrection in Virginia and "he sensed an unspoken fear on the part of the Southern journalists" who wrote about it (Huggins, 7).

When he was about fifteen, Douglass was forced to leave the city and return to a country plantation. He must have been heartbroken. Unlike the vast majority of plantation slaves, Frederick had learned to read and write in the city and had experienced "a liberty of thought and action wholly alien to a country slave's imagination" (Huggins, 8).

After arriving in the country, however, Frederick jumped at the chance to help a man named Wilson teach a Sabbath school for black children. They had a few Bibles and some old spelling books to work with. The second meeting, however, was broken up by a mob of white men.

Not long after, Frederick started another school, this time meeting secretly in the woods. He taught reading and the Bible to both slaves and free blacks. Within a year he had a number of students, at one time more than forty. They proved to be good pupils, many of them learning to read. Douglass and his charges became good friends. When looking back on his life, he stated that none of his employments gave him more satisfaction than teaching those slaves. His attachment to them was very deep and permanent, and his parting from them was "intensely painful" (Douglass, 601).

After escaping North, Frederick married and worked at odd jobs to support himself and his family. Then a momentous event occurred. He discovered the weekly abolitionist paper, the *Liberator* and became a regular subscriber. He read it carefully every week. It contained scathing denunciations of the practice of slavery and of slaveholders and expressed sympathy for the persecuted slaves: "Its powerful attacks upon the upholders of the institution—sent a thrill of joy through my soul, such as I had never felt before" (Douglass, 96).

Douglass was more successful in his condemnation of slavery than other speakers and writers because of who he was. It was his personal story and his ability to so movingly describe that story which made him irresistible. Most abolitionists were white or freed blacks who did not have firsthand experience of slavery. Douglass himself had been there, and he described his own experiences of being treated as sub-human. Others could speak out without great danger to themselves.

Frederick Douglass, however, had escaped, was a fugitive still, and but for his master's ignorance of his whereabouts would be at once returned to slavery. Douglass's story therefore was even more fascinating because he stood in defiance of the law, and because the telling of it took a rare kind of courage. (Huggins, 2)

Douglass read many of the great writers of the time. They included Alexandre Dumas the Elder, Charles Dickens, Harriet Beecher Stowe, and John Greenleaf Whittier. He often quoted such authors in his own speeches and writings.

Referring to famous authors who shared abolitionist sentiment lent strength to his own arguments. He cheered anti-slavery societies with such statements as the following:

Scholars, authors, orators, poets, and statesmen give it [abolition] their aid. The most brilliant of American poets volunteer in its service. Whittier speaks in burning verse to more than thirty thousand, in the National Era. Your own Longfellow whispers, in every hour of trial and disappointment, "labor and wait." James Russell Lowell is reminding us that "men are more than institutions." (Douglass, 449)

He often quoted Whittier, the great American anti-slavery poet who wrote poems such as the following in which a slave bemoans that his children have been sold into the Deep South.

> Gone, gone, sold and gone
> To the rice swamp dank and lone,
> Where the slave-whip ceaseless swings,
> Where the noisome insect stings,
>
> Woe is me, my stolen daughters! (Douglass, 48)

He credited Harriet Beecher Stowe for lighting "a million camp fires in front of the embattled host of slavery, which not all the waters of the Mississippi, mingled as they are with blood, could extinguish"(Douglass, 449).

He referred to Charles Dickens when arguing that all the methods of torture used on slaves in the West Indies were also used, even more cruelly, in the United States: starvation, the gag, the whip, the thumb screw, the dungeon, the bloodhound. If some doubted his word, he indicated they should "read the chapter on slavery in Dickens's Notes on America" (Douglass, 401). Reading had helped set Douglass free. In turn his own speeches and best selling books and articles played a major role in freeing all of America's slaves.

IMPORTANT DATES IN FREDERICK DOUGLASS' LIFE

1817?	Born in rural Maryland.
1825	Sent to live with Hugh and Sophia Auld to be a companion to their son Tommy. Mrs. Auld began to teach him to read.
1838	Escaped from slavery.
1838	Married Anna Murray.
1841	Employed as an agent for the Massachusetts Anti-Slavery Society. In time became one of America's greatest orators.
1845	Published his first autobiography *Narrative of the Life of Frederick Douglass*. Published two additional autobiographies in succeeding years.
1845–1847	Lived in England to avoid being captured and returned to slavery. Spoke widely throughout Britain.
1847	Returned to America and founded a newspaper, the *North Star*.
1860s	Assisted in recruiting colored regiments in the Civil War.
1889	Appointed United States Minister to Haiti.
1895	Died in Washington, D.C.
1994	The Library of America published *Frederick Douglass Autobiographies*, including all three autobiographies with a detailed chronology and extensive notes by Henry Louis Gates, Jr. (See below for complete citation.)

SOURCES

Douglass, Frederick. *Autobiographies: Narrative of the Life of Frederick Douglass, an American Slave; My Bondage and My Freedom; Life and Times of Frederick Douglass.* New York: Library of America, 1994.

Hagler, D. Harland. "Frederick Douglass," in *Great Lives from History: American Series,* vol. 2, Frank N. Magill, ed. Pasadena, Calif.: Salem Press, 1987.

Huggins, Nathan Irvin. *Slave and Citizen: The Life of Frederick Douglass.* Boston: Little, Brown and Co., 1980.

McFeely, William S. *Frederick Douglass.* New York: W. W. Norton & Co., 1991.

Quarles, Benjamin. *Frederick Douglass.* New York: Atheneum Publishers, 1968.

BOB DYLAN
(1941–)

The *Encyclopedia of Rock* named Bob Dylan "the most influential singer-songwriter of the rock era" (Hardy and Laing, 152). He excelled in folk songs and rock and is considered one of our finest poets, his songs really being poems set to music. Dylan became one of America's most famous and most socially conscious singers and writers of songs. His songs called attention to the plight of the dispossessed, the alienated, and the poor. He read widely those writers whose works similarly expressed compassion for underdogs, and his reading has considerable influence on his own work.

Robert Allen Zimmerman was born in Duluth, Minnesota, on May 24, 1941. When he was six, his family moved to Hibbing, Minnesota, a town of high unemployment, which had been the scene of many bitter strikes. Many iron ore miners had been injured, some killed by police and others by scabs shipped in by mine owners. It is widely felt that Bob's experience with such persecuted workers had a strong influence on him and on his writing and singing.

He began writing poems and songs and playing his guitar when he was in school, and he formed several folk song groups then. After enrolling at the University of Minnesota, he changed his name to Bob Dylan, possibly in honor of the Welsh poet Dylan Thomas.

In 1961 Bob went to New York, and embarked on the road to fame as a folk singer and later as a leading rock musician. He achieved international fame, and a number of his songs were among the most popular of the time. Many were recorded not only by himself but by other noted singers. "Blowin' in the Wind," "Mr. Tambourine Man," "Like a Rolling Stone," and "Desolation Row" are just a few of his very popular songs.

Dylan has been the subject of many biographical and musical studies. He has received numerous awards for his music, has been inducted into the Rock and Roll Hall of Fame, and has received an honorary doctorate from Princeton University. He also received a Lifetime Achievement Award at the 1991 Grammy awards ceremony. Long after other popular singers have disappeared from public notice, Dylan continues to be a top entertainer. For example, at the 1998 Grammy ceremony, he received awards for Best Album, Best Contemporary Folk Album, and Best Male Rock Performance.

Young Bob was "annoyed and depressed" by school. He was not against reading and studying, he just did not like the school curriculum nor the reading required in his classes. He preferred more realistic works, especially those of John Steinbeck.

Bob's discovery of Steinbeck, who wrote so movingly about the suffering of poor farmers and laborers, was a real revelation for him. First he read *Cannery Row*, then everything else by that author. According to a high school girlfriend, Bob "identified with all the people in the books" (Scaduto, 31). He came over to her house with a copy of *Cannery Row* in his hand:

"This is a great book," he told her, excitedly describing the novel. "Steinbeck is a great writer." And, with that boyish enthusiasm that many would find so infectious, Bob read everything of Steinbeck's. "Hey, hey, do you know Steinbeck wrote *East of Eden* that James Dean movie?" he once shouted. (Scaduto, 31)

Bob also became familiar with both country and urban folk songs while leading musical groups during high school. He was especially impressed by the words and music of the protest songs depicting the struggles of working-class people, including those by Aunt Mollie Jackson and her sister, Sarah Ogan Gunning.

They wrote and sang songs about labor violence and bitter class feelings that existed in their region, the coal fields of Kentucky. Their protest songs became so popular they were "almost taken over by northern urban groups" (Scaduto, 34).

Dylan also discovered a number of beat and symbolist poets. They became a major influence on his own writing. He said:

I didn't start writing poetry until I was out of high school. I was eighteen or so when I discovered Ginsberg, Gary Snyder, Philip Whalen, Frank O'Hara and those guys. Then I went back and started reading the French guys, Rimbaud and Francois Villon. (Heylin, 97)

In 1960 a friend, David Whitaker, introduced Dylan to the autobiography of Woody Guthrie, the Oklahoma song writer, folk singer, and folk hero. Guthrie became famous singing about the struggles of people during the great depression. Whitaker told Bob he really had to read it. Guthrie was from Oklahoma, the Dust Bowl. He rode the rails and moved about with the Okies when they were forced off their farms and had to move to California.

They had some difficulty locating Guthrie's *Bound for Glory*, since neither the library nor any local bookstores had it in stock. Finally, they found that a university faculty member had a copy, and they borrowed it. Dylan read it over and over. He sat in the Scholar (a coffee-shop hangout for University of Minnesota students) all day one day and read it. "He was just amazed at it. He fell in love with Woody Guthrie right away" (Scaduto, 50).

Bob carried *Bound for Glory* around with him for weeks. Whenever the chance arose, he would stop his friends and read passages from it.

After arriving in New York City in 1961, Dylan met Suze Rotolo. He liked that fact that she was intellectual, pretty, cultural, and passionate. They were quickly drawn to each other and loved being by themselves and shutting out the rest of the world. They spent their time going to movies and reading. Suze's interest in literature "uncovered a whole new fascination for Bob" (Spitz, 154).

Rotolo had collections of Edna St. Vincent Millay, Dylan Thomas, Emily Dickinson, Rimbaud, Brecht, and Byron, and they went through them together. "In essence, Suze was a mirror image of Bob, dowered by all the knowledge and savvy he longed to absorb. And which, in time, he would" (Spitz, 154).

Although Bob was very well read, he did not talk much about his reading, sometimes even denying that he knew particular writers. Apparently he thought it might tarnish his image as an unlettered country singer. A musician friend, Dave Van Ronk, said that when Bob was asked whether he had heard of Dylan Thomas or Arthur Rimbaud, writers who had undoubtedly influenced some of Bob's own writing, he assiduously avoided answering.

In fact when asked about Rimbaud, Bob simply said "Who?" Later, Van Ronk looked over the collection of books in Bob's apartment.

On his shelf I discovered a book of translations of French symbolist poets that had obviously been thumbed through over a period of years! I think he probably knew Rimbaud backward and forward before I even mentioned him. I didn't mention Rimbaud to him again until I heard his "A Hard Rain's A-Gonna Fall," his first symbolist venture. I said to Bob: "You know, that song of yours is heavy in symbolism, don't you?" He said: "Huh?" (Shelton, 99–100)

In addition to Guthrie, Steinbeck, and Rimbaud, critics have pointed to the influence of Alan Ginsberg, T. S. Eliot, and Berthold Brecht in Dylan's writing. As noted by Mellers, "while Dylan's originality is his strength, his art has roots, and these are a strength also" (Mellers, 112).

Dylan was well versed in the Bible, and many of his songs reflect biblical words and situations. In one album alone, *John Wesley Harding*, there are at least sixty-one biblical allusions to the Old Testament or New Testament (Heylin, 184). To cite just one example, the very moving song "Long Ago and Far Away" refers to the persecution of Jesus who preached brother-hood and peace. Sadly he was then crucified.

Dylan's songs are reminiscent of earlier ages. Like the bards of old, Dylan sang poems. The *Guardian* called him "Homer in Denim," arguing that his work put him in a league with "Pound, Auden and MacNeice" (Shelton, 229). Numerous scholars consider Bob Dylan to be a very important poet. A number of conferences of academics have been held to discuss his work, and his influence is sometimes compared favorably with some of history's greatest writers.

Poet Kenneth Rexroth stated,

Probably the most important event in recent poetry is Bob Dylan. . . . [He] is the American beginning of a tradition as old as civilization in France, and some of his stuff is surprisingly good read over in hypercritical cold blood. This Dylan break-through is another great hope for poetry" (Shelton, 227).

Another critic argued that the Beatles began to legitimize rock among students and the intelligentsia. "Dylan takes it further, using rock 'n' roll to express complex personal visions, parables with messages like a sermon—moralizing, judgmental" (Rinzler, 48).

Dylan's influence on future performers was perhaps best summarized by Bruce Springsteen when he spoke at Dylan's induction into the Rock and Roll Hall of Fame in 1988. He said that Dylan "freed your mind the way Elvis freed your body."

He showed us that just because the music was innately physical did not mean it was anti-intellectual. He had the vision and the talent to make a pop song that contained the whole world. (Heylin, 401)

Springsteen also noted that Dylan had changed rock and roll forever. He argued that without Dylan many great songs would never have been written or performed. He claimed that numerous great artists owed a debt to Dylan, including the Beatles, the Beach Boys, the Sex Pistols, Marvin Gaye, and Springsteen himself. "To this day," Springsteen said, "wherever great rock music is being made, there is the shadow of Bob Dylan" (Heylin, 402).

IMPORTANT DATES IN BOB DYLAN'S LIFE

1941   Born Robert Allen Zimmerman in Duluth, Minnesota.

1959–1960   Student, University of Minnesota. While there he took the name of Bob Dylan.

1961   Established himself as a folk singer in New York writing and performing protest songs.

1962	Wrote "Blowin' in the Wind," immediately recognized by Pete Seeger as one of the greatest folk songs ever written.
Mid-1960s	Was moving out of the protest song vein and becoming a recognized rock/blues singer.
1970	Received an honorary doctor of music degree from Princeton University. Published a novel, *Tarantula*.
1988	Inducted into Rock and Roll Hall of Fame.
1991	At the Grammy awards ceremony, Dylan received a Lifetime Achievement Award.
1998	Won Grammy awards for Best Album, Best Contemporary Folk Album, and Best Male Rock Performance.

SOURCES

Hardy, Phil, and Dave Laing. *Encyclopedia of Rock*. New York: Schirmer Books, 1987.

Heylin, Clinton. *Bob Dylan: Behind the Shades*. New York: Summit Books, 1991.

McKeen, William. *Bob Dylan: A Bio-Bibliography*. Westport, Conn.: Greenwood Press, 1993.

Mellers, Wilfrid. *A Darker Shade of Pale: A Backdrop to Bob Dylan*. New York: Oxford University Press, 1985.

Rinzler, Alan. *Bob Dylan: The Illustrated Record*. New York: Harmony Books, 1978.

Scaduto, Anthony. *Bob Dylan*. New York: NewAmerican Library, 1973.

Shelton, Robert. *No Direction Home: The Life and Music of Bob Dylan*. New York: Beech Tree Books, William Morrow, 1986.

Spitz, Bob. *Dylan: A Biography*. New York: McGraw-Hill, 1989.

Williams, Paul. *Performing Artist: The Music of Bob Dylan*, vol. 1. Novato, Calif.: Underwood-Miller, 1990.

THOMAS A. EDISON
(1847–1931)

Thomas Alva Edison transformed the world with many landmark inventions, some original and others major practical improvements in things previously invented. He held an enormous number of patents, nearly 1,100. Much of his reading was related to his scientific interests. He also, however, loved general reading of novels, stories, poetry, history, and newspapers.

Thomas A. Edison was born on February 11, 1847, in Milan, Ohio. He did not do well in school partly because of his increasing deafness, and he attended school for fewer than four years. He was therefore largely self taught beginning with the lessons his mother taught him at home.

By the time he was ten years old, Edison spent much of his time doing chemical experiments and selling vegetables and newspapers. During the Civil War and later, from 1863–1868, he became a telegraph operator in various parts of the country. During that time he became interested in electricity and invented an electronic vote recorder.

In 1869 Edison arrived in New York with hardly any money. He got a job with a Wall Street firm and invented an improved stock ticker. That invention and additional improvements to stock tickers technology brought him a great deal of money.

Several years later Edison established his research and development laboratory in Menlo Park, New Jersey. It became a prototype for many such laboratories established since that time.

Edison's invention of the incandescent electric light vastly improved and transformed electrical technology. A few of his additional inventions include the phonograph, the motion picture camera, the storage battery, and the microphone.

While teaching young Edison at home, his mother avoided forcing or prodding him. Instead "she made an effort to engage his interest by reading him works of literature that she had learned to love." Most women of the 1850s, if they read to their children, would read simple children's stories.

> But Nancy Edison had superior taste. Believing that her son, far from being dull-witted, had unusual reasoning powers, she read to him from such books as Gibbon's *Decline and Fall of the Roman Empire*, Hume's *History of England*, or Sears's *History of the World*; also literary classics ranging from Shakespeare to Dickens. (Josephson, 21)

Edison was not at all bored by these serious works. He was fascinated by them. By the time he was nine years old, he was reading such books himself and became a very fast reader thus making it fairly easy to read many, many books in his self-education.

He also liked the romantic Waverly novels by Sir Walter Scott. Like so many other young people of all generations, he loved the adventures related in Scott's *Ivanhoe*, *Rob Roy*, and *The Heart of Midlothian*. He also enjoyed *Robinson Crusoe* and even thought of duplicating the feats of the wonderful man in the book. There also was *Pilgrim's Progress*, which detailed Pilgrim's long struggle to resist temptation. Dickens' works, including *Oliver Twist*, were also favorites. *Oliver Twist*, *David Copperfield*, and *Dombey and Son* were then new books at the public library (Miller, 51–52).

Edison's mother also made him study the Bible and took him to church every Sunday. In church he was told that hellfire was the punishment for all kinds of sins, "some of which he seemed to have a knack for committing" (Conot, 6). Such religious experience did not have a lasting effect on Edison. A turning point came when his father gave him a copy of Tom Paine's *Age of Reason*, and the work turned out to be one of the most important pieces he ever read. Paine, the radical Revolutionary War hero and freethinker wrote that his religion was "doing good." Edison agreed with that idea. "I can still remember the flash of enlightenment that shone from his pages," Edison wrote long afterward (Josephson, 23).

Edison's interest in science was awakened by his reading of scientific books. His mother gave him a copy of R. G. Parker's *School of Natural Philosophy* when he was nine years old. The book described and illustrated a number of scientific experiments which could be done at home, and Edison read and tested every experiment in the book.

His mother also found an old *Dictionary of Science* for him. Edison pored over the book, learning more and more about science. As he grew, he continued to read many scientific books and articles.

Learning became a game that he loved. He spent all of his pocket money on chemicals, which he arranged in bottles on shelves in his room. He continued to read scientific books and articles at home and after he set out on his own. He would frequently get himself excused from work and head to the library.

> In the library stacks, Tom tracked down Dionysius Lardner's classic work on the *Electric Telegraph*, as well as his *Handbook of Electricity, Magnetism and Acoustics*. He read Richard Culley's *Handbook of Practical Telegraphy*. Charles Walker's *Electric Telegraph Manipulation*, and Robert Sabine's *History and Practice of the Electric Telegraph*. (Baldwin, 42)

Edison's pocket notebooks "bear witness to his assiduous research and to the wide spectrum of his interests" (Baldwin, 42). One great scientist who became a role model for Edison was the Englishman Michael Faraday. Edison read Faraday's journals, and he said that was one of the decisive events in his life. Like Edison, Faraday had risen from an obscure family in England, got much of his education through his individual study and reading. Faraday, for example, read through the *Encyclopedia Britannica*, and he, like Edison, kept a notebook with quotations from and questions about what he had read.

When he was fifteen, Edison became one of the first members of the newly reorganized Detroit Public Library.

> My refuge was the Detroit Public Library. I started, it now seems to me, with the first book on the bottom shelf and went through the lot, one by one. I didn't read a few books. I read the library. Then I got a collection called "The Penny Library Encyclopedia" and read that through.
>
> I read Burton's "Anatomy of Melancholy"—pretty heavy reading for a youngster. It might have been, if I hadn't been taught by my deafness that almost any book will supply entertainment or instruction. (Runes, 45)

Edison discovered Victor Hugo's masterpiece *Les Miserables* shortly after it had been translated from French into English. He identified with the noble characters in the book. They included Jean Valjean who served in prison and was pursued by police for years because of a minor crime. He also sympathized with the boy Gavroche and other lost, homeless children whose struggles to live were so graphically portrayed in the novel. He so loved and spoke so glowingly about Hugo's work that some of his friends called him "Victor Hugo" Edison.

For the rest of his life, Edison was a passionate reader of fiction as well as scientific works. He would divide his days between his business affairs and "reading marathons."

In addition to works mentioned above, he loved the novels of Dickens, Hawthorne, George Eliot, James Fennimore Cooper, and Mark Twain; as well as works by Darwin, Disraeli, Longfellow, and Virgil. He read the *Encyclopedia Britannica* "to steady his nerves." He also often read detective stories and the *Police Gazette*, a racy magazine which appealed to men who wanted something funny and sexually titillating. He might be reading a heavy scientific tome one moment, and then for recreation pull out a copy of the *Gazette*. "He was an omnivorous reader who maintained a charge account at Bretano's and bought books by the shelf" (Conot, 226). He also read numerous newspapers and magazines. He read two morning newspapers and three evening newspapers and "all the principal magazines" (Runes, 56).

Edison had five children, and he strongly encouraged their reading, just as his parents had encouraged him to read years earlier. In addition to reading novels and plays together, the children were required to read and memorize sections of encyclopedias and science reference books. The children also often helped Edison by poring through "volume upon volume of science reference books" and finding citations which he could use in his work (Baldwin, 287).

He was once asked what a man over seventy can do to keep busy. He responded:

The trouble is, that a man who can't keep busy [in his seventies] didn't take an interest in a great number of things when he was mentally active in his younger years. If he had done so, he would find plenty to occupy his time in reading, observing and watching people. (Runes, 57)

Thomas A. Edison, one of the greatest men of his time, was not educated in prestigious schools and great universities. He had very little schooling, and taught himself by observing people and by reading extensively throughout his life—novels, poetry, newspapers, and, of course, many scientific works. He showed that dedication and hard work can often lead to great success, even for someone with a serious handicap, such as his deafness.

IMPORTANT DATES IN THOMAS A. EDISON'S LIFE

1847	Born in Milan, Ohio.
1863	Began work as a telegraph operator.
1869	Patented his first invention, the electrographic vote-recorder. Invented improvements for stock tickers.
1876	Established his research and development laboratory at Menlo Park, New Jersey.
1879	Issued his first patent on the incandescent electric light.
1879–1931	Invented numerous devices and took out almost 1,100 patents.
1928	Received Congressional Medal of Honor.
1931	Died in West Orange, New Jersey.

SOURCES

Baldwin, Neil. *Edison: Inventing the Century*. New York: Hyperion, 1995.

Clark, Ronald W. *Edison: The Man Who Made the Future.* New York: G. P. Putnam's Sons, 1977.

Conot, Robert. *A Streak of Luck.* New York: Seaview Books, 1979.

Josephson, Matthew. *Edison.* New York: McGraw-Hill, 1959.

Miller, Francis Trevelyan. *Thomas A. Edison: Benefactor of Mankind: The Romantic Life Story of the World's Greatest Inventor.* Philadelphia: John C. Winston Co., [1931].

Runes, Dagobert D., ed. *The Diary and Sundry Observations of Thomas Alva Edison.* New York: Philosophical Library, 1948.

ALBERT EINSTEIN
(1879–1955)

German-born American scientist Albert Einstein is one of the most important scientists of the ages. He ranks with Galileo, Copernicus, and Newton for making one of the greatest contributions to human understanding of the universe. His theory of relativity fundamentally changed humankind's understanding of the physical world. When he was very young Einstein read books about science and mathematics. The books inspired him, and thus began his truly great scientific career.

Albert Einstein was born the son of moderately prosperous Jewish parents in Ulm, Germany, on March 14, 1879. During his early childhood, he did not exhibit any special gifts. He did not learn to speak until he was three years old, and for a number of years he did not speak very well. Even at nine, he still stumbled over words.

He attended gymnasium school in Munich but showed little interest in his studies there and disliked the regimentation and authoritarian atmosphere at the school. Much of his education took place at home. He later studied in Switzerland and became a Swiss citizen.

Einstein received a doctorate from the University of Bern, and in 1905 he published three major scientific papers. One of them contained his theory of relativity, which in time brought him great acclaim throughout the world.

When Adolf Hitler came to power in Germany in 1933, Einstein determined never to return to that country. He accepted a position at Princeton University, became an American citizen, and remained at Princeton for the rest of his life. In 1939 he wrote a letter to President Franklin Roosevelt and alerted him to the military potential of atomic energy and to the fact that Germany might try to make such a bomb. The letter helped push the United States to emphasize atomic research.

In addition to his scientific eminence, Einstein became a very effective spokesman on various social issues. He was a leading advocate of world peace. He spoke out strongly in favor of freedom of speech during the McCarthy era when scientists and others were attacked for expressing opinions unpopular with right-wing elements.

He also worked tirelessly on behalf of Zionism, which he saw as a way for European Jews to survive. He received an offer to become the second president of Israel. Although deeply moved by the offer, he declined because he felt that he was unsuited to fulfill the duties of such an office.

Einstein received many awards and honors for his work, including the Nobel Prize for Physics.

Albert Einstein's father introduced him to literature when he was a child. The family was not religious in the traditional sense. Albert's father Hermann considered Jewish dietary laws an ancient superstition.Instead of reading the Bible, he would gather the family around him in the evening and read the great German poets Schiller and Heine. According to biographer Philipp Frank, "[T]heir preference for the dramas and poems of Schiller, replete with moral pathos, was a substitute for the reading of the Bible." (Frank, 7).

Although Albert detested the authoritarian school he attended, he appreciated one dedicated teacher named Reuss who taught the classics. Albert, having a strong feeling for the artistic and for ideas that brought him closer to nature, developed a strong attachment to Reuss.

[Reuss] aroused in him a strong interest in the German classical writers, Schiller and Goethe, as well as in Shakspere. The periods devoted to the reading and discussion of *Hermann and Dorothea*, Goethe's half-romantic, half-sentimental love story written in a period of the greatest political unrest, remained deeply engraved in Einstein's memory. (Frank, 12)

According to Clark, however, "the influence that led Einstein onto his chosen path" did not come from school. It came from Max Talmey, a young Jewish medical student, who lent young Einstein the technical books that had a such a profound effect on him. Talmey was introduced to the happy Einstein home and met Albert, "a pretty, dark-haired boy." He found that Albert was interested in physics.

I gave him therefore as reading matter A. Bernstein's *Popular Books on Physical Science* and L. Buchner's *Force and Matter*, two works that were then quite popular in Germany. The boy was profoundly impressed by them. Bernstein's work especially, which describes physical phenomena lucidly and engagingly, had a great influence on Albert, and enhanced considerably his interest in physical science. (Clark, 15)

Then Albert showed an interest in mathematics. Talmey gave him a copy of a popular math textbook by Spieker *Lehrbuch der eben Geometrie* and recommended additional books to the boy. Albert showed tremendous mathematical talent. He solved the problems in the books very quickly. His mathematical talent was so great that Talmey could not keep up with him.

Albert's reading also had a strong influence on his religious beliefs. As an adolescent he underwent a strong religious phase. He became very conscious of and proud of his Jewishness. He read the Bible and other religious books avidly. He even composed religious songs and sang them on his way to school.

That phase did not last long, however. His scientific reading convinced him that much of what he had read in the Bible and other religious works clashed with scientific knowledge and could not be true. He became an agnostic and did not believe in a personal God. To him God stood for the rational connections and laws which governed the behavior of the universe.

Einstein's lifelong love of philosophy began when Talmey recommended that he read Kant's *Critique of Pure Reason*. Although Kant was very difficult for most people to comprehend, and Albert was only a child of thirteen years old, he understood the work very well. Kant became his favorite philosopher.

In his teens and early twenties, he immersed himself in the study of philosophy, as well as the study of science. It is probably fair to say that he considered himself as much a philosopher as a scientist.

While in Switzerland in the early part of the century, Einstein became the center of a group of young students. They met on a regular basis and discussed science, mathematics, philosophy, and literature.

Einstein's love of literature lasted throughout his life.

He loved Shakespeare's poetic form and wonderful feeling for characterization. Don Quixote was rich in fantasy and full of beautiful characters and stories. He often identified himself in a lighthearted way with the ill-fated knight. (Sayen, 134)

He was enthralled with the novels of Tolstoy, *War and Peace*, *Anna Karenina*, and *Resurrection*. He admired Tolstoy's moral leadership and at one time claimed that he was the most important prophet of the time. He disagreed, however, with Tolstoy's emphasis on sexual abstinence.

Dostoevsky was another favorite. He noted that Dostoevsky "gives me more than any scientist. . . . It is the moral impression . . . the feeling of elevation, that takes hold of me when the work of art is presented" (Sayen, 134–135).

Einstein loved to read aloud just as his father had done. In the evenings he would gather family and friends around and read poetry and fiction to them.

His sister Maja, whom he always considered his closest friend, suffered a stroke in 1946. Although physically incapacitated, her mind remained sharp. Einstein read to her from Bernard Shaw, Bertrand Russell and many other favorite authors until her last days when she died in 1951. Although saddened by her passing, he wrote, "But there was also much that was beautiful . . . in those evening hours in which I read to her from the most excellent books of all peoples through the ages" (Sayen, 231).

Einstein had a special interest in Freud. Although he never completely agreed with Freud's theories, he read his work in order to gain a better understanding of his younger son Eduard who suffered from schizophrenia and was confined to a home in Switzerland for a long time.

Einstein's adult writings are full of references to literature and philosophy. In his autobiographical work, *Out of My Later Years*, for example, he used his knowledge of many writers to explain his own outlook on life.

In a discussion of his religious beliefs, he referred to the Bible, Spinoza, Buddha, Darwin, and Galileo. He noted that conflict arises between religion and science when a religious group "insists on the absolute truthfulness of all statements recorded in the Bible" (Einstein, 25). In a discussion of Judaism, he referred to Moses, Spinoza, and Karl Marx. He noted they were Jews who were very different from each other, but all of them "lived and sacrificed themselves for the ideal of social justice" (Einstein, 249).

He also argued that freedom was necessary to produce great people. Without it, he claimed, there would have been no great poets, such as Shakespeare and Goethe.

Einstein remains an important role model for our time. Although one of history's greatest scientists, he was not narrowly dedicated to his profession. He was also a noted humanist inspired by the great literature he had studied. He expended much time and effort on social causes, including world peace, freedom of expression, and the establishment of the State of Israel.

IMPORTANT DATES IN ALBERT EINSTEIN'S LIFE

1879	Born in Ulm, Germany.
1888	Attended the Luitpold Gymnasium school in Munich. Disliking the regimentation, he left without a diploma in 1895.
1900	Passed an examination that allowed him to teach.
1901	Became a Swiss citizen. Published his first scientific paper.
1905	Published three landmark scientific papers, including the paper on the theory of relativity.
1909	Became associate professor of physics at the University of Zurich.
1920s	Traveled widely lecturing. Hailed as a creative genius.
1921	Received the Nobel Prize for Physics.
1933	When the Nazi leader Hitler came to power, he resolved never to return to Germany. He accepted a position at Princeton University where he remained for the rest of his life.

1930s and   Worked tirelessly to assist Jewish victims of Nazi persecution.
1940s

1939   Wrote his landmark letter to President Roosevelt on the threat of Germany's potential for making an atomic bomb. Letter helped to initiate the American Manhattan Project to create such a bomb.

1940s and   Devoted himself to world peace, freedom of speech, and Zionism.
1950s

1955   Died in Princeton, New Jersey.

SOURCES

Bernstein, Jeremy. *Einstein*. New York: Viking Press, 1973.

Clark, Ronald W. *Einstein: The Life and Times*. New York: World Publishing, 1971.

Einstein, Albert. *Out of My Later Years*. New York: Philosophical Library, 1950.

Frank, Philipp. *Einstein: His Life and Times*. Translated by George Rosen; edited and revised by Shuichi Kusaka. New York: Da Capo Press Paperback [1989] c1947.

Highfield, Roger, and Paul Carter. *The Private Lives of Albert Einstein*. New York: St. Martin's Press, 1993.

Sayen, Jamie. *Einstein in America: The Scientist's Conscience in the Age of Hitler and Hiroshima*. New York: Crown Publishers, 1985.

White, Michael, and John Gribbin. *Einstein: A Life in Science*. New York: Dutton, 1993.

BENJAMIN FRANKLIN
(1706–1790)

Benjamin Franklin was the greatest early American leader never to become president of the United States, but he served in many other crucial positions for the colonies and the American government. He was a great reader and did more to promote books and reading among the public of his time than any other person born within what became the United States. He founded a social library open to association members; he published his own works and books by others; he founded and published newspapers.

Unlike many other colonial leaders, Franklin was egalitarian, tolerant, believed strongly in democracy, and was a rabid opponent of slavery, long before such ideas were common or acceptable in most social circles. Franklin also had an almost religious belief in the value of the written word.

Benjamin Franklin was born in Boston on January 17, 1706. After attending school for a brief period, he went to work full time. He hated his first job, making candles and soap. He then became a printer's apprentice to his brother James.

The brothers did not get along, however, and Ben, almost penniless, ran away to Philadelphia. Fortunately, he quickly got a job as a printer and did very well in that work.

In 1727 he established the Junto, a club for young men devoted to the discussion of natural philosophy, politics, and morals. He also published a newspaper called *The Pennsylvania Gazette*, and began *Poor Richard's Almanack*, which contained common sense and witty sayings and quickly gained a large circulation.

Franklin undertook important missions for the colonies. He made several trips to England on behalf of the colonies during which he tried to reconcile the differences between the British and the Americans. When it became evident that reconciliation was impossible, Franklin served as a member of the committee drafting the Declaration of Independence.

He then traveled to France to negotiate a treaty with the French who assisted the colonies in their fight against the British. Fluent in French and very interested in French culture, he became immensely popular there. After the colonies won their independence in 1783, he served as United States minister to France.

Franklin also achieved fame for his invention of many useful objects, including the Franklin Stove, bifocal glasses, the lightning rod, and a device for removing books from high shelves. He never received any profit from his inventions.

Ben learned to read when he was very young. In his *Autobiography*, Franklin, in the language which seems somewhat archaic to modern readers, described his early love of books and reading. "From a child I was fond of Reading, and all the little Money that came into my Hands was ever laid out in Books" (Labaree, 57). It was this bookish inclination that encouraged Ben's father to make him a printer.

As he grew a little older, he realized that having had little schooling, he had great gaps in his education. He therefore embarked on a serious program of reading, which he continued for the rest of his life. He became better educated than many who had gone to school for years.

Ben read all the books in his father's little library, but many of them were polemical theological works which he did not find very interesting. He indicated that he had often regretted that "at a time when I had such a Thirst for Knowledge, more proper Books had not fallen in my Way" (Labaree, 58).

Becoming a printer's apprentice had one great advantage for twelve-year-old Ben: access to good books. Customers and friends would bring books he could read, and booksellers' apprentices would lend him their employers' books, which he would take home and read until late at night.

Essays to Do Good, by Cotton Mather, had a lasting effect on Franklin. Years after first reading it, he wrote a letter to Mather's son in which he stated that the book had an influence on his conduct throughout his life. He noted that he had "always set a greater Value on the Character of a *Doer of Good*, than on any other kind of Reputation." He further claimed that "if I have been, as you seem to think . . . a useful Citizen, the Publick owes the Advantage of it to that Book" (Labaree, 18).

Another favorite book was John Bunyan's *Pilgrim's Progress*. Young Ben enjoyed it so much that he then read a collection of Bunyan's works. When finished, he sold those books and bought some works entitled *Historical Collections* thought to be the work of R. Burton. The collections were random pieces of biography, history, travel, fiction, and science.

He also enjoyed Plutarch's *Lives*. He thought the time spent reading the charming, vivid stories of ancient people was time spent to great advantage.

When he was about sixteen years old, Franklin became a vegetarian after reading Thomas Tryon's *The Way to Health*, a book recommending a vegetable diet. He proposed to his brother James that he would prepare his own vegetable meals if James would give him half the money he paid for board. The money he saved "became an additional fund for buying books" (Van Doren, 16).

Ben was determined to improve his language skills. Fortunately, he discovered James Greenwood's *An Essay towards a Practical English Grammar*. He studied it assiduously, and was so favorably impressed with the work that years later he recommended that it be adopted for an academy he proposed establishing in Pennsylvania.

Young Franklin composed poems, and achieved some success by having some published. His father, however, a devotee of the stately Psalms of David, was appalled at the "literary deformities" composed by his son, and put a stop to such writing.

In his teens Franklin read books that attempted to disprove the system of rational, humanistic thought called deism. They had the opposite effect on him, however. The arguments in favor of deism seemed stronger to him than the refutations. He was especially impressed by Shaftesbury's *Characteristics*, a deist Bible, and "his skepticism became irrevocably entrenched" (Aldridge, 10).

He also studied Bacon's essays, and read Blaise Pascal's *Les Lettres Provinciales*. He especially enjoyed Pascal's work and re-read it on various occasions.

Franklin, being a lover of books, undertook various activities that made books and reading available to the colonists who previously had very limited access to such materials. He organized a discussion group, the Junto, with friends with whom he liked to talk. At club meetings various philosophical and political questions were discussed. The members were almost all great readers.

Franklin proposed that the members pool their books so that each one would have access to the books owned by all the others. They were therefore set up on a wall in the room where the club met. He wrote, "by thus clubbing our Books to a common Library, we should, while we lik'd to keep them together, have each of us the Advantage of using the Books of all the other Members, which would be nearly as beneficial as if each owned the whole" (Labaree, 130).

The Junto's book collection was disbanded after a relatively short time, however, because the members were dissatisfied that the books were not properly cared for. Franklin then proposed organizing a library that would be open to Junto members and other citizens. Any "gentleman" could read the books, but only those who would pay a fee could take books out. Thus was established "the Mother of all"—American subscription libraries (Labaree, 130).

Books were imported from London and a librarian was hired to care for the collection. Books were carefully selected, and included many classic and modern works on a wide variety of topics. Following Franklin's lead, local leaders throughout the colonies established many similar libraries.

Franklin also opened a bookshop. He printed *Poor Richard's Almanac* and other works by himself as well as those written by others. In 1744 he printed Samuel Richardson's *Pamela*, "the first novel published in America" (Labaree, 72).

He also printed a German hymnbook for German Americans, the first such book printed in America. He started the first German-American newspaper, *Die Philadelphische Zeitung*.

Franklin's wide reading provided maxims, epigrams, and proverbs for *Poor Richard's Almanack*. A large proportion of these sayings were culled from such English and European writers as Rabelais, Sterne, Swift, Dryden, Pope, Bacon, and LaRochefoucauld.

Biographer Esmond Wright argues that although many of the proverbs are very old, "Franklin gave them vigor, clarity and punch, and transformed them in the process" (Wright, *Franklin of Philadelphia*, 54).

The English proverb "God restoreth health and the physician hath the thanks" he changed to "God heals and the doctor takes the fee." . . . He aimed at balance and brevity. "The greatest talkers are the least doers" became "Great talkers, little doers." (Wright, *Franklin of Philadelphia*, 54)

Franklin did not pretend all the sayings were original. "Why should I give my readers bad lines of my own, when good ones of other people's are so plenty?" (Wright, *Benjamin Franklin: His Life*, 98).

Some interesting and sometimes amusing events, related to writers, books, and reading occurred to Franklin. When on a boat trip near Long Island, for example, a Dutch passenger fell overboard and Franklin rescued him. The Dutchman took a book out of his pocket. Franklin saw that it was *Pilgrim's Progress* by a favorite author, John Bunyan, and in Dutch. He was pleased when he found it had been translated not only into Dutch but into most European languages and probably had been read more than any other book except perhaps the Bible. Franklin especially appreciated "Honest John" Bunyan. He was the first he knew of who mixed narration and dialogue, "a Method of Writing very engaging to the Reader" (Labaree, 72).

Franklin admired and wanted to meet Edward Gibbon, the author of the *Decline and Fall of the Roman Empire*. According to one story, Gibbon refused to meet him since he did not want to speak with an American rebel. Franklin apparently wrote Gibbon a note indicating he still had the greatest respect for the noted historian. He also stated sarcastically that he would be happy to supply Gibbon with material whenever the latter undertook writing about the decline and fall of the British empire.

During his years serving as an American representative in England and France, Franklin socialized with a number of writers and scholars, some of whom he had admired and who had admired him. He met David Hume, James Boswell, LaRochefoucauld, and Voltaire.

He spent several pleasant weeks in Scotland with David Hume, who had praised Franklin as the first American philosopher and writer to whom Britain was indebted. Hume wrote:

America has sent us many good things, gold, silver, sugar, tobacco, indigo, etc.; but you are the first philosopher, and indeed the first great man of letters, for whom we are beholden to her. (Van Doren, 290)

Franklin was received with great enthusiasm in France even though the British ambassador said they should not receive an emissary of the Americans. The French hoped to find someone who combined "the reason and wit of Voltaire with the primitive virtues celebrated by Rousseau, and they were sure they had found their hero in Franklin" (Van Doren, 570).

Franklin was entertained royally by LaRochefoucauld. His meeting with Voltaire was most touching. The public demanded that they kiss in the French manner, and they did.

In his old age Franklin continued to read and study. He had a prodigious memory for things he had read years before.

Ben Franklin has always been an inspiration and role model for generations of Americans. From humble beginnings he became a great man. No matter how famous he became, however, he always retained his sense of humor and his love of mankind, and his love of philosophy, books, and reading.

IMPORTANT DATES IN BENJAMIN FRANKLIN'S LIFE

1706   Born in Boston.

1718   Apprenticed to his brother James, a printer.

1721   Contributed pieces to *The New England Courant*. Became a freethinker.

1723   Broke from his printer's apprenticeship in Boston and moved to Philadelphia.

1727   Organized the Junto.

1729   Became editor of the *Pennsylvania Gazette*.

1732   Began publishing *Poor Richard's Almanack*.

1742   Invented the "Franklin" stove.

1744   Established the American Philosophical Society.

1752   Experimenting with a kite, discovered lightning is an electrical discharge.

1776	Served on committee to draft the Declaration of Independence.
1776	Sent to France as agent of the colonies.
1779	Appointed Minister Plenipotentiary to France.
1787	Delegate to the Constitutional Convention.
1790	Died in Philadelphia.

SOURCES

Aldridge, Alfred Owen. *Benjamin Franklin: Philosopher and Man*. Philadelphia: Lippincott, 1965.

Crane, Verner W. *Benjamin Franklin and a Rising People*. Boston: Little, Brown and Co., 1954.

Labaree, Leonard W. et al., eds. *The Autobiography of Benjamin Franklin*. New Haven, Conn.: Yale University Press, 1964.

Van Doren, Carl. *Benjamin Franklin*. New York: Viking, 1938.

Wright, Esmond, ed. *Benjamin Franklin: His Life as He Wrote It*. Cambridge, Mass.: Harvard University Press, 1990.

Wright, Esmond. *Franklin of Philadelphia*. Cambridge, Mass.: Harvard University Press, 1986.

BILL GATES
(1955–)

Bill Gates, head of the world's largest computer software company, became the richest man in the world. As a young man he was noted for his broad knowledge of all kinds of topics gained from reading. A college friend said you couldn't win an argument with Gates.

You couldn't win an argument with the guy! No matter what the subject, it seemed like he'd read everything about it. For every point you made, he would have a fact or figure to prove you wrong. (Zickgraf, 8)

Bill Gates was born in Seattle, Washington, on October 28, 1955, and named William Henry Gates III. His father William Henry Gates, Jr., was a prominent attorney, and his mother Mary Maxwell Gates was a former schoolteacher who participated widely on community boards and in charitable activities.

His family was loving and well educated, had high ideals, and had a strong influence on Gates' philosophy of life. While enjoying dinner, they often carried on animated discussions on a variety of topics.

As a student Bill loved science and math, and he was thrilled when his school introduced the computer. While still in school, he and a school friend formed a company that used computers to analyze traffic for small towns. The summer before his high school graduation he worked in Washington, D.C. as a page in the United States Senate, a highly educational experience for any young person.

Bill attended Harvard University for a short time to study law. He is remembered there as a skinny boy with glasses and long, shaggy hair. One friend, a dorm neighbor, said Gates was sort of a "crazy guy" at school. He didn't put sheets on his bed. When he went home for Christmas, he left "the door to his room open, lights on, money on his desk, and Bill was in Seattle" (Zickgraf, 8). But he was also remembered as a brilliant guy. He had fantastic knowledge and a great memory.

After abandoning law, he devoted himself to developing computer technology. Within a few years Microsoft Corporation was born with Gates as chairman of the board.

The rest is history. Microsoft became a leading computer company. By 1990 its annual revenues were more than $1 billion and its business continued to grow rapidly.

Despite such phenomenal success, Gates and his Microsoft colleagues retained high ideals, concerned about human rights issues and government decisions. For example, in 1986 Microsoft announced that it would support the anti-apartheid movement in South Africa by refusing to sell computer products to that country.

Another example of Gates' concern for the less fortunate is his becoming a large benefactor of public libraries located in poor areas.

Typical, in many ways, of other youths, Bill Gates participated in boys' activities: riding a bicycle, playing tennis, dating, going to Boy Scouts, and singing in his church choir. But he also spent long hours alone thinking and reading. He read light literature, including Edgar Rice Burroughs' *Tarzan* and Martian stories. But he also devoured biographies of famous people.

In school Gates excelled, usually at the top of his class. He had a remarkable memory. According to a high school English teacher, he once memorized a three-page soliloquy for a school play in one reading.

When he was eight years old, Bill Gates began reading his family's set of *World Book Encyclopedia*. He had a great time and "determined to read straight through every volume" (Gates, 116). Later he discovered the *Encyclopedia Britannica* and read much of it.

He loved reading the encyclopedias and learned a great deal from them. He realized later, however, that they had the limitation of being strictly alphabetical with related topics often scattered throughout the volumes. Modern CD-ROM encyclopedias, he argued, give the reader quick access to related topics in a way that a paper-based encyclopedia could never do.

Bored with his studies at Harvard, Gates spent hours playing poker and sitting in his room trying to figure out what to do with his life. During that period he also read a lot of fiction, and he especially enjoyed such books as J. D. Salinger's *Catcher in the Rye* and John Knowles' *A Separate Peace* "because they dealt with the reality of growing up even when you don't want to" (Ichbiah and Knepper, 14–15).

One magazine article had a phenomenal effect on Gates when he was still a sophomore at Harvard. He had been playing poker and losing. He and a friend picked up a copy of *Popular Electronics* and found an article on the world's first personal computer, and he was overcome by a sense of excitement and purpose he hadn't felt for a long time. He described the experience as follows:

As we read excitedly about the first truly personal computer, Paul and I didn't know exactly how it would be used, but we were sure it would change us and the world of computing. We were right. The personal-computer revolution happened and it has affected millions of lives. It has led us to places we had barely imagined. (Gates, xi)

As an adult Gates has enjoyed reading biographies, just as he did as a teenager. He has read just about everything about certain heroes—Franklin D. Roosevelt, Leonardo da Vinci, and Napoleon. He also has searched out new biographies about important inventors and business people. Such biographies have helped him understand how such people think and have given him ideas about how to run his own company.

He noted, for example, that Edison understood that to sell electricity "he had to demonstrate its value to consumers." Edison realized that "people would pay to bring electric power into their homes so that they could enjoy a great application of electric technology—light" (Gates, 68).

He cited Albert Sloan's *My Years at General Motors* as one of the best books of all time "because it explains how the company completely redefined the world of automobiles" (Ichbiah and Knepper, 223).

Gates' career is similar to that of people such as Sloan. Innovative and inventive, they all realized the value of public information. Gates knew that he would have to convince people of the value of his products before they would spend money to purchase them.

He, therefore, attempted "to adapt the successful strategies of other great entrepreneurs to the realm of software" (Ichbiah and Knepper, 223).

In 1997 Bill Gates announced that he and his wife Melinda, wanting to assist the information poor, established the Gates Library Foundation. Its major purpose is to provide computer hardware and software to public libraries in poor areas, whose users normally do not have access to all the wonderful electronic reading material and other information available to the affluent. Totaling $400,000,000 in cash and computer equipment and software, it is the largest grant for library purposes since the Carnegie grants of many years ago paid for the construction of public library buildings.

Gates described the purpose of his foundation in a videotaped message delivered at an annual conference of the American Library Association.

Since I was a kid, libraries have played an important role in my life. In the past couple of years I have had the opportunity to visit many libraries and see firsthand how people are using personal computers and the Internet to do anything from look for a job to research a term paper. . . . Witnessing the empowerment this technology has given people underscores my belief that computers can really make a difference in the lives of others. (Kniffel, 14–15)

He noted the foundations's goal is equal opportunity for all.

The ALA Council voted to recognize and celebrate Bill and Melinda Gates for establishing the Gates Library Foundation and for specifically targeting the neediest communities for this type of assistance.

Bill Gates, a reader and lover of books, libraries, and information, has made access to information materials readily available to millions of people throughout the world. The more affluent have access through the Internet. And his $400 million gift to public libraries has assisted those who have less money to obtain the information they need. Much more needs to be done for the latter group, but it is hoped that Gates' gift will inspire others to donate funds and materials to provide everyone, regardless of their economic status, with access to needed information.

IMPORTANT DATES IN BILL GATES' LIFE

1955   Born in Seattle, Washington.

1970   Formed a company with Paul Allen that used computers to analyze traffic for small towns.

1973   Graduated from high school and attended Harvard University for a year.

1975   Formed the company called Microsoft.

1980   Microsoft chosen by IBM to write the basic program for its new PC.

1985   Microsoft introduced *Windows*, the program designed to make PCs more useful and easier to use.

1986   At thirty years of age, Gates had become one of the world's richest men.

1990   Microsoft's annual revenues topped $1 billion.

1997   Created the Gates Library Foundation, a nonprofit organization dedicated to bringing computer information to public libraries in low-income neighborhoods.

SOURCES

Gates, Bill. *The Road Ahead*. New York: Viking, 1995.

Ichbiah, Daniel, and Susan L. Knepper. *The Making of Microsoft: How Bill Gates and His Team Created the World's Most Successful Software Company*. Rocklin, Calif.: Prima Publishing, 1991.

Kniffel, Leonard. "Gates Foundation to Invest $400 Million in Libraries," *American Libraries* 28, August, 1997.

Wallace, James. *Hard Drive: Bill Gates and the Making of the Microsoft Empire*. New York: Wiley, 1992.

Zickgraf, Ralph. *William Gates: From Whiz Kid to Software King*. Ada, Okla.: Garrett Educational Corporation, 1992.

ROBERT GODDARD
(1882–1945)

As a boy, Robert Hutchings Goddard dreamed of sending rockets into space. He never forgot his dedication to rocket science and became the great American pioneer of rocketry—"the father of the Space Age."

As the deviser of the first successful liquid-fuel rocket and as a tireless explorer of the theoretical and practical problems of rocketry decades before the subject gained substantial support in the United States, Goddard stands as the great American pioneer of space travel. (Ellis, 124)

When he was a teenager, Goddard climbed a tree and imagined a spaceship that might travel to Mars. On descending from the tree, he was a different boy. For the rest of his life, he devoted himself to the study of rocketry.

Robert Goddard was born in Worcester, Massachusetts, on October 5, 1882. His father was Nahum Goddard, a bookkeeper, and his mother was Frances Hoyt Goddard.

Robert suffered from poor health. He had various bronchial ailments which necessitated his frequent absence from school and not graduating from high school until he was in his twenties. He later attended Worcester Polytechnic Institute and Clark University, and received a Ph.D. in physics from the latter institution. Poor health plagued him all his life. Nonetheless, he made enormous contributions to rocket science.

Goddard launched his first rocket from a farm in Massachusetts. In succeeding years, he launched a number of larger rockets.

Only after his death did Goddard's achievements begin to be realized. Many awards were given to him posthumously, including the Congressional Gold Medal.

Goddard was a reader from his earliest years. His reading played an important role in stimulating his interest in space.

He not only enjoyed books but also found relief from his childhood illnesses in reading. When he was sixteen, he found a story, which became crucial in his development as a rocket scientist.

In the Boston *Post*, he came on a provocative fiction series and shortly obtained the novel, *The War of the Worlds*, in which he was soon absorbed. He would re-read it many times through the years, often around Christmas, as a rather extraordinary Yuletide gift to himself. (Lehman, 22)

He was fascinated by the author's (H. G. Wells) description of Martians. According to the author, they were very intelligent, warlike, frightful beings who had traveled 14,000,000 miles, and, unbeknownst to mankind, were watching human affairs very carefully.

The story affected Goddard very deeply. He began to think of "possible ways and means of accomplishing the physical marvels" described in the book (Lehman, 23).

Years later Goddard wrote Wells telling him that when he was a teenager he read his *War of the Worlds* and it had made a deep impression on him. He decided that "what might be called 'high altitude research' was the most fascinating problem in existence" (Lehman, 23). (Unfortunately, Wells' reply was very brief and disappointing to Goddard. Wells simply wrote a thank you note stating that he appreciated the sort of greeting Goddard sent him.)

Goddard was also influenced by Jules Verne's book *From the Earth to the Moon*. He also read Verne's biography.

He read Rudyard Kipling's works for inspiration and enjoyment. He wrote to Kipling:

I have enjoyed your writings for many years, and there seems to me no one who has such versatility. . . . Although I have never been in India, your stories of India have a particularly strong appeal here in New Mexico, where I am engaged in research work over a period of several years. We have the dust, the insects, and the heat . . . and yet we can see, sixty miles away, the cool mountains covered with tall pine trees. (Goddard and Pendray, vol. 2, 823–824)

Goddard began reading technical, scientific works in his youth. One he discovered was Sir Isaac Newton's *Principia Mathematica*. Newton's Third Law on action and reaction was especially significant to him, and he read it many times.

To every action there is always opposed an equal reaction: or the mutual actions of two bodies upon each other are always equal, and directed to contrary parts.

On reading the third law, Goddard had accidentally stumbled upon the key to motion in space. He wrote:

The Third Law was accordingly tested, both with devices suspended by rubber bands and by devices on floats, in the little brook back of the barn, and the said law was verified conclusively. It made me realize that if a way to navigate space were to be discovered, or invented, it would be the result of a knowledge of physics and mathematics. (Lehman, 32)

Goddard realized he needed to study physics at the university. This study assisted him in becoming the great "father of rocketry."

Robert Goddard's reading inspired him to become a pioneer in rocketry. It might even be argued that he might never have pursued his study of rocketry had he not read *The War of the Worlds* and other imaginative works about space. His experience should inspire countless other young people to read and to find the role they would like to pursue in life.

IMPORTANT DATES IN ROBERT GODDARD'S LIFE

1882	Born in Worcester, Massachusetts.
1899	Climbed a cherry tree and imagined how a space ship might travel to Mars. When he descended, he was a different boy, and he devoted the rest of his life to rocket research.
1899–1901	Kept from school because of illness. Then returned to high school.
1911	Received a Ph.D. in physics from Clark University.
1919	Published an article which would become a classic: "A Method of Reaching Extreme Altitudes." At the time, it met with great skepticism, and he henceforth worked in anonymity.
1926	Launched the first successful liquid-propellant rocket near Auburn, Massachusetts.
1929	Upon Charles Lindbergh's recommendation, received a $50,000 grant from Harry Guggenheim for his research.
1930s and 1940s	Continued rocket research in New Mexico.
1945	Died in Baltimore, Maryland.
1960s	His monumental contributions to rocket science began to be recognized. He received many awards and honors posthumously. A Robert H. Goddard airmail stamp was issued.

SOURCES

Ellis, Robert P. "Robert H. Goddard," in *The Great Scientists*, vol. 5, Frank N. Magill, ed. Danbury, Conn.: Grolier Educational Corporation, 1989.

Goddard, Esther C., and G. Edward Pendray, eds. *The Papers of Robert H. Goddard Including the Reports to the Smithsonian Institution and the Daniel and Florence Guggenheim Foundation*, 3 vols. New York: McGraw-Hill, 1970.

Lehman, Milton. *This High Man: The Life of Robert H. Goddard*. New York: Farrar, Straus and Co., 1963.

Verral, Charles Spain. *Robert Goddard: Father of the Space Age*. Englewood Cliffs, N.J.: Prentice-Hall [1963].

Winter, Frank H. *Prelude to the Space Age: The Rocket Societies, 1924–1940*. Washington, D.C.: Smithsonian Institution Press, 1983.

HELEN HAYES
(1900–1993)

"I cannot imagine life without books."

So stated actress Helen Hayes, the "First Lady of the American Theatre."

I have had a longstanding love affair with the world between hard covers. Becoming eligible for my first library card is a most vivid childhood memory. Loving books starts early. Preschool. Prekindergarten. Prenatal? Some think it does; intense young mothers-to-be now read *Alice in Wonderland* to their gestating future bookworms. (Hayes with Gladney, 56)

Helen Hayes was born in Washington, D.C. on October 10, 1900, the daughter of Francis Van Arnum Brown and Catherine Estelle (Essie) Hayes. Francis was descended from a family that had come to America before the Revolution, and his mother thought he had married beneath him when he took Essie Hayes, the daughter of Irish immigrants, as his bride. Helen Hayes described the Hayes family: "The Hayeses were scamp Irish. . . . There are the careful, thrifty Irish and there are the other kind. We were the other kind" (Hayes with Dody, 24). Nonetheless, it was from the "scamp Irish" side of the family that Helen got her love of reading as well as her love of the theater.

Little Helen began acting in small parts in Washington when she was only five. Then in 1909 she made her Broadway debut playing Little Mimi in Victor Herbert's musical *Old Dutch*. The producer thought Helen Hayes Brown was too long for a theater marquee. "We'll call her Helen Hayes," he said.

The rest is history. Helen played many roles throughout the remainder of her adolescent and teenage years. In time she would receive many awards for her acting and become one of the most famous actresses in the world. Although she appeared in a number of films and received awards for such work, she never cared much for being a movie star. Her love was the theater, and she spent most of her professional life appearing on the stage, not on the screen.

Hayes always loved reading, being read to, and attending plays—literature performed on the stage. One of her fondest memories of childhood was being read to at bedtime. Another was sharing Sunday newspaper stories with family members.

One person who influenced Helen's love of reading was her "scamp Irish" grandfather Patrick Hayes. He had immigrated from Ireland during the potato famine. He was a "terrific reader." He read everything he saw, even scraps of newspaper he found on the street. One of his greatest ambitions was to translate Shakespeare into Gaelic. He could easily recite Shakespeare from memory, "especially when he was in his cups." "His main dream in life," Hayes wrote, "was to translate Shakespeare into Gaelic." "I never learned if he achieved this ambition," she added. "His curiosity and love of reading," she noted, "were traits that ran in the family and were passed on to me as well" (Hayes with Hatch, 3).

Both of Helen's parents were frequently away from home. Francis was a traveling salesman, and Essie might be on tour with a "fifth rate" theatrical company pursuing her unsuccessful dream of becoming a famous actress. While her parents were away, Helen was left in charge of her grandmother Hayes whom she called "Graddy." Graddy would often tell her "hair-raising" stories. Helen would sit on the floor at Graddy's knee and listen raptly to the tales. One chilling story she always remembered was about a bride who died at the altar. About to be lowered into the grave, she suddenly sat up, not dead at all but "only in a coma."

Now that we hear complaints about all the violence on television that children are exposed to, I remember Graddy's tales; they were just as scary, but I lapped them up. (Hayes with Hatch, 8)

Both Essie and Graddy were theater lovers and they frequently took Helen to plays. They would "scrape together" the money for seats in "the peanut gallery," and attended a variety of performances—Shakespeare, operettas, and even Sarah Bernhardt performing in French.

Her favorite early theater experience was a performance of Franz Lehar's operetta, *The Merry Widow*.

I was exhalted by it, hypnotized. When the curtain fell on the last act and the audience began to leave, I kept staring at the stage. I didn't budge from my seat. Mother tried to move me, but I wouldn't leave. Finally, a gentleman who saw she was having trouble picked me up bodily and began to carry me out.

I began to scream—this is my mother's story—"I won't leave! I won't leave the theatre!" And of course, I never did. (Hayes with Hatch, 6)

During her years in the theater, Helen Hayes pursued her "addiction for anything with words on it":

It was lucky for me that I fell in with good company there at an early age, good playwrights whose lines I learned as a job, friends who pressed good books on me. . . . These people filled my head with literature that was often beyond my capacity—but whether or not I understood what I was reading, I was acquiring a taste for good words. (Hayes with Funke, 12–13)

Illustrative of Hayes' love of literature is a story she recounts of meeting a dying woman on a train whose only joy was examining the many jewels various men had given her. Hayes was wearing her entire jewel collection: an engagement ring and a wedding band. But she was not jealous of the other woman's large collection of expensive gems. She had a great fortune inside her head. "[T]he gifts from Shakespeare, Shaw, Max Anderson, and James M. Barrie—these were only a few. I'd had to learn their words as a job—but I had hung on to them" (Hayes with Funke, 14).

In the books she wrote, Helen Hayes invariably noted the value of reading. In *A Gift of Joy* she mentioned that we rely on philosophers, poets, and playwrights to "articulate what most of us can only feel, in joy or sorrow."

Whenever I feel my courage wavering I rush to them. They give me the wisdom of acceptance, the will and resilience to push on. They enable me to see that I am not alone, that others have known similar problems. I'm so grateful for this inheritance, this legacy—this gift of joy —that makes me feel as rich as Croesus and enables me to say with Emerson:

I am the owner of the sphere,
Of the seven stars and the solar year,
Of Caesar's hand, and Plato's brain,
Of Lord Christ's heart, and Shakespeare's strain.
(Hayes with Funke, 15)

In *Loving Life*, published when she was in her eighties, she wrote even more clearly about the importance of books and reading:

Since I've been a member of the performing arts for eighty years, you might assume that I am delighted that people prefer to receive their entertainment and education by being spectators. But I am all too aware of the importance of reading. . . . I, like most of my contemporaries, was read to when I was very young —and even later on, when studying theatrical roles. My love for literature started then. (Hayes with Gladney, 59)

Hayes felt that reading is very important for our society, and deplored the fact that so many people read so little. "Not reading means not thinking clearly," she wrote. "When the respect for language is lost," she continued, "an inadequate working vocabulary makes it virtually impossible to formulate a point of view, much less defend it in dialogue. It impairs the ability to reason" (Hayes with Gladney, 58).

She wrote that some teachers, not properly equipped to teach literature, spoiled the great writers for children. She deplored the pervasiveness of television and recommended that people turn off the TV set and read Dickens, Twain, or Shakespeare.

She also wrote that she agreed with such writers as Jonathan Kozol and John Hersey that listening to condensed recorded versions of our literary heritage is a poor substitute for actually reading the work. Once works are condensed, much important material is lost. She wrote:

Listening is toil free—no effort, no time to stop and think, to reread. What about sweet, soothing solitude and the "silence that surrounds reading?" (Hayes with Gladney, 61)

Helen Hayes' love of literature began when she was a small child, and that "love affair with the world between hard covers" continued throughout her long life. She always tried to convey her love of books and reading to others, recommending that they become frequent readers. She strongly believed that reading brings much joy and also makes it possible for people to think and reason clearly.

IMPORTANT DATES IN HELEN HAYES' LIFE

1900	Born in Washington, D.C.
1905	Made her stage debut in an amateur theatrical.
1909	Made her Broadway debut.
1928	Married playwright Charles MacArthur (died 1956).
1931	Received Academy Award, best actress, for *The Sin of Madelon Claudet*.
1936	Drama League of New York Award for *Victoria Regina*.
1947	Antoinette Perry (Tony) Award, best dramatic actress, for *Happy Birthday*.
1952	Emmy Award.
1958	Antoinette Perry (Tony) Award, best dramatic actress, for *Time Remembered*.
1959	A Broadway theater was named after her. After it was demolished in 1982, another Broadway theater was named after her.
1970	Academy Award, best supporting actress, for *Airport*.
1988	Received National Medal of Arts. Presented by President Reagan.
1993	Died in Nyack, New York.

SOURCES

Barrow, Kenneth. *Helen Hayes: First Lady of the American Theatre*. Garden City, N.Y.: Doubleday, 1985.

Hayes, Helen, with Sandford Dody. *On Reflection: An Autobiography*. New York: M. Evans and Co., 1968.

Hayes, Helen, with Lewis Funke. *A Gift of Joy*. New York: M. Evans and Co., 1965.

Hayes, Helen, with Marion Glasserow Gladney. *Loving Life*. Garden City, N.Y.: Doubleday, 1987.

Hayes, Helen, with Katherine Hatch. *My Life in Three Acts*. San Diego: Harcourt Brace Jovanovich, 1990.

Murphy, Donn B., and Stephen Moore. *Helen Hayes: A Bio-Bibliography*. Westport, Conn.: Greenwood Press, 1993.

ZORA NEALE HURSTON (1891–1960)

Zora Neale Hurston is one of America's best writers. She is considered the finest African-American woman writer in the first half of the twentieth century. Hurston, publishing in the 1920s through the 1940s, is noted not only for her own work but also because she was the major inspiration for modern black feminist writers. Her works, nearly forgotten for years, were rediscovered in the 1970s and have become extremely popular. They are read and studied in schools and colleges throughout the United States and abroad.

From her early childhood, Zora loved reading and listening to tales told by black neighbors. Through those experiences she gained an excellent command of language as well as ideas for her own work.

Zora Neale Hurston was born in Eatonville, Florida, in 1891, probably on January 7 of that year, but the exact date is disputed. She was one of eight children. Zora was a tough child. Because she knew how to fight, the boys let her play with them.

Unlike many small Southern towns, Eatonville was a self-governing all-black community, which made it possible for her to develop a strong sense of individuality and self-worth.

Zora's father was a minister and three-term mayor of Eatonville who tried to suppress Zora's exuberant spirit. Zora loved her mother Lucy Ann Potts who encouraged the girl's independence. When Zora was thirteen, Lucy Ann died, and Zora's world fell apart.

When her father remarried, Zora could not get along with her stepmother. She lived with various relatives, worked at different jobs, including housekeeper, nanny, and waitress, and could not attend school. After a number of years, however, she got a job that enabled her to finish high school and get a college degree from Howard University. Her further study of anthropology gave Hurston additional information to return to the South to study the stories told by Southern blacks, which were often continuations of African oral storytelling.

Zora's first story "John Redding Goes to Sea" was published in 1921, and her writing career was launched. In the following years she won critical acclaim for her short stories, plays, and novels. She is credited with saving many southern black folk tales, tales she heard as a child or discovered in her research, stories which might otherwise have been lost forever.

Hurston was unique for her time in that she concentrated her writing on the everyday life of American blacks. It was an age when many blacks thought they should conform to the middle-class ideas of whites.

Far from being ashamed of the lower classes, she knew that their expressions—black folklore, blues, and spirituals—were those of a people who were healthy minded and who had survived slavery through their own creative ingenuity. (Howard, 953)

Hurston published her last book *Seraph on the Suwanee* in 1948. For the rest of her life she lived in obscurity working as a teacher, librarian, maid, and reporter. She never made much money and died in poverty and was buried in an unmarked grave.

More than ten years later, the Pulitzer prize winning author Alice Walker discovered Hurston's grave. She erected a stone which reads:

Zora Neale Hurston
"A Genius of the South"
Novelist, Folklorist, Anthropologist

Thus began a great revival of interest in Hurston's work.

Zora learned to read before she went to school. Fortunately for her, her mother, a former school teacher, encouraged Zora's love of books and reading and provided her with much to read.

Zora would often slip under the porch and read a book. Zora also enjoyed going to Joe Clark's store in Eatonville where people sat on the porch and told stories. She loved hearing those tales, and thus began her lifelong interest in black folk stories.

These tales were passed down orally from generation to generation, but no one in the African-American community thought to record them on paper. After Zora left Eatonville, she never forgot those "lying tales," and later she traveled around the state and country in order to collect and record these precious stories. (Yanuzzi, 16)

For days when her mother was ill, Zora sat by her bedside and told her the stories she had heard at the store. Before she died, Lucy Ann told Zora always to remember the tales. Her mother told her that the stories kept their people alive. As long as the stories were told, they would remember Africa in their hearts.

Zora attended school until she was thirteen. She excelled in reading and the teachers always encouraged her in that activity. She devoured books by popular white authors, including Rudyard Kipling, Robert Louis Stevenson, and Hans Christian Andersen.

Upper class white ladies from the North sometimes visited Zora's school. According to Hurston, they were not just curious to see what a Negro school was like, they were also kind and sympathetic towards the children.

One particular such visit was especially important to Zora. Two young white women just popped in unexpectedly, and the teacher Mr. Calhoun had his fifth grade class stand in a line in front of the room and read for them. The story was of Pluto and Persephone, and it was especially difficult for most of the children who stumbled along when they read their parts. It was very easy for Zora, however. She had read it several times and was "exalted by it."

Zora read her paragraph beautifully. Mr. Calhoun and the two ladies, Mrs. Johnstone and Miss Hurd, were very impressed with Zora's reading ability.

The next day they sent Zora three books. They were *The Swiss Family Robinson*, a book of fairy tales, and an Episcopal hymnbook. Hurston wrote later, "A month or so after the two young ladies returned to Minnesota, they sent me a huge box packed with clothes and books" (Hurston, 60).

the books gave me more pleasure than the clothes. I had never been too keen on dressing up. It called for hard scrubbings with Octagon soap suds getting in my eyes, and none too gentle fingers scrubbing my neck and gouging in my ears. (Hurston, 53)

The box contained books of Greek and Roman myths, Grimm's fairy tales, the story of Dick Whittington, and books by Hans Christian Andersen and Rudyard Kipling. It also included Norse tales. Hurston indicated she loved the Norse stories best of all. She could imagine seeing Thor swinging his mighty hammer as he sped across the sky and Odin who went to the well of knowledge to drink.

Of the Greek tales, she liked the Hercules stories best. The tales of other gods and goddesses "left her cold."

The ladies had also included little religious books about little girls who gave up their lives to Christ and good works. They usually died, preaching as they passed away. Hurston was utterly indifferent to their deaths because she could not understand death. Also they were unbelievable, they had "no meat on their bones." (Hurston, 54)

Zora began reading the Bible when she was quite young. She especially liked the Old Testament because it was much more exciting than the New

Testament. She was fascinated with the stories of David because he was such an active man who went about smiting those God told him to smite. She also liked Leviticus because it taught about the facts of life, facts the old folks would not have told a child.

In later years she undertook a serious study of religion and philosophy. She studied the great religions of the world. After such intense study, she developed her own philosophy of life. She concluded that humans cannot understand God's mind, and if he had a plan for the universe, it would be folly to try to comprehend it. Therefore, she did not pray, but would never "by word or deed, attempt to deprive others of the consolation" provided by prayer (Hurston, 279).

Describing the value of her early reading, Hurston wrote:

In a way this early reading gave me great anguish through all my childhood and adolescence. My soul was with the gods and my body in the village. People just would not act like gods. Stew beef, fried fat-back and morning grits were no ambrosia from Valhalla. . . . I wanted to be away from drabness and to stretch my limbs in some mighty struggle. (Hurston, 56)

After leaving home, Zora traveled from town to town and worked at a variety of jobs. Her life was poor and dreary, but she continued to dream about having a better life. Her reading lifted her up. She would often stretch out in the woods and read. One time she found a copy of Milton's complete works in a trash heap.

The back was gone and the book was yellowed. But it was all there. So I read Paradise Lost and luxuriated in Milton's syllables and rhythms without ever having heard that Milton was one of the greatest poets of the world. I read it because I liked it. (Hurston, 127)

In her early twenties Zora published a story which impressed Charles S. Johnson, the editor of *Opportunity* magazine. Johnson sponsored literary contests, and he published two of Zora's stories in his magazine. She quickly found herself a respected writer in what was called the Harlem Renaissance.

Hurston was fortunate in meeting the popular novelist Fannie Hurst. Hurst was a sincere liberal whose novel, *Imitation of Life*, explored race prejudice in America. Hurst employed Zora as secretary, chauffeur, and companion. They became close friends. Hurston did not feel at all awed by the famous novelist, and freely made recommendations to her about her writing. Hurst, in turn, took Hurston's recommendations seriously.

Langston Hughes, the black poet who was also a prominent member of the Harlem Renaissance, became one of Hurston's favorite writers. Hurston and Hughes were close friends for a number of years until they had a falling out over a play they were writing together, each accusing the other of stealing ideas for the work. In any case Hurston long admired Hughes' art which she thought could be truly communicative. On her trips South in which she gathered black folk tales, she would bring his latest book of poetry to group meetings and read aloud. "Boy, they eat it up," she reported to him one time. She noted that he was being quoted wherever black people congregated (Hemenway, 116).

Hurston's work was unique. Unlike other black writers of her time whose fiction carried strong political and social messages, Hurston simply told lyrical, poetic stories about her people. She is considered the "black foremother" of modern black feminist authors.

The craft of Alice Walker, Gayl Jones, Gloria Naylor, and Toni Cade Bambara bears, in markedly different ways, strong affinities with Hurston's. Their attention to Hurston signifies a novel sophistication in black literature: They read Hurston not only for spiritual kinship inherent in such relations but because she used black vernacular speech and rituals, in ways subtle and various, to chart the coming to consciousness of black women, so glaringly absent in other black fiction. (Gates, 286)

IMPORTANT DATES IN ZORA NEALE HURSTON'S LIFE

1891   Born in Eatonville, Florida.

1904   Lucy Ann Potts Hurston, Zora's mother, died.

1919   Enrolled in Howard University.

1921   Published her first story "John Redding Goes to Sea."

1927   Took a folk tale collecting trip to Florida.

1934   Published her first book of fiction, *Jonah's Gourd Vine*.

1935   Published *Mules and Men*.

1937   Published *Their Eyes Were Watching God*.

1942   Published *Dust Tracks on a Road*, her autobiography.

1960   Died in poverty and buried in an unmarked grave in Fort Pierce, Florida.

1973   Writer Alice Walker, the person who became most responsible for creating a revival of interest in Hurston's work, found Hurston's grave and bought a headstone to mark it.

1991   Eatonville, Florida, held its first Zora Neale Hurston festival.

SOURCES

Gates, Henry Louis, Jr. "Afterword," in *The Complete Stories: Zora Neale Hurston*. New York: HarperCollins, 1995.

Hemenway, Robert E. *Zora Neale Hurston: A Literary Biography*. Urbana: University of Illinois Press, 1977.

Holloway, Karla F. C. *The Character of the Word: The Texts of Zora Neale Hurston*. Westport, Conn.: Greenwood Press, 1987.

Howard, William L. "Zora Neale Hurston," in *Great Lives from History: American Women Series,* vol. 3, Frank N. Magill, ed. Pasadena, Calif.: Salem Press, 1995.

Hurston, Zora Neale. *Dust Tracks on a Road: An Autobiography.* Philadelphia: J. B. Lippincott, 1971.

McKissack, Patricia, and Fredrick McKissack. *Zora Neale Hurston: Writer and Storyteller.* Hillside, N.J.: Enslow Publishers, 1992.

Miller, William. *Zora Hurston and the Chinaberry Tree.* New York: Lee & Low Books, 1994.

Yannuzzi, Della A. *Zora Neale Hurston: Southern Storyteller.* Springfield, N.J.: Enslow Publishers, 1996.

THOMAS JEFFERSON
(1743–1826)

All readers and library users owe the third president of the United States a special debt of gratitude. After the British had burned the Library of Congress during the War of 1812, Jefferson made his collection of books available to reestablish the library. It grew into the largest library in the world.

Jefferson was also one of the strongest advocates of the freedom to read, and, in addition, he was one of the first to call for the establishment of public libraries throughout the land. Millions of Americans annually benefit by using the books and other information materials available through the Library of Congress and in their own free public libraries.

"I cannot live without books," Thomas Jefferson wrote to John Adams. The statement has been quoted many thousands of times to indicate how greatly he depended on books and reading.

Thomas Jefferson was a man of many accomplishments in addition to his advocacy of books and reading. He made important contributions in science, education, agriculture, law, politics, and architecture.

Jefferson was born at Shadwell, Virginia, on April 13, 1743. He graduated from William and Mary College, studied law, and was admitted to the bar in 1767. He served as a member of the Virginia legislature called the House of Burgesses, participated in the Continental Congress, and authored the Declaration of Independence.

He served as United States minister to France, and was elected to two terms as president of the United States. Major accomplishments during his tenure as president included expansion of the United States through the Louisiana Purchase, repeal of unpopular excise taxes, and the Lewis and Clark Expedition. Bothered by the regal trappings of the nation's capital, he also instituted a democratic simplicity in Washington.

In retirement he provided leadership in the founding of the University of Virginia, drew up architectural plans for the university, and founded its library. He also continued his activities as a philosopher-statesmen, scientist, and architect.

Jefferson's father Peter Jefferson had a small but select library, including much-read editions of Shakespeare and the Bible. Young Jefferson early developed a passion for books and reading that would last throughout his life.

When his father died, Thomas inherited his library. There were approximately forty books. The collection included a Bible and prayer book and works of history, astronomy, and geography, as well as several volumes by Addison.

The forty volumes he is known to have inherited constituted an insignificant library in the light of his mature standards, but they formed the nucleus of his first collection. (Malone, vol. 1, 32)

Jefferson read a wide variety of literature. Much can be learned about his reading from the notebooks he began to keep when he was about twenty-one years old that contain many comments on books he read.

The classical writers were favorites. They delighted him "throughout life and were the chosen companions of his old age" (Malone, vol. 1, 104).

He read Greek and Latin works, including those of Homer, Euripides, Aeschylus, and Virgil. He especially valued the maxims of Seneca and the republican ideas of Cicero. He also read Plato, but did not care for him. He thought his *Republic* was filled with "puerilities" and "unintelligible jargon" (Mayo, 300).

Jefferson immersed himself in English writing—prose and poetry. He bought Milton's works when he was twenty-one and copied many extracts from Milton in his notebook. At a later period, he recommended that young people "read the best of the poets" (Malone, vol. 1, 104).

Shakespeare was always a favorite. He appreciated his observation of human nature and his unequaled use of the English language. Jefferson also loved live performances. He "rarely missed a chance to attend the theater in Williamsburg" (Malone, vol. 1, 105).

He had amassed a significant library by his mid-twenties. Unfortunately, he lost it all in a fire when his house was burned to the ground. He immediately began building up a second library. By 1783 he had 2,640 volumes, a very large library for the time.

He continued collecting books until his was probably the largest personal library in the country. He "elaborately cataloged" the collection according to the scheme devised by Sir Francis Bacon.

Throughout his more than eighty-three years of life, the indefatigable Virginian never stopped buying books, lending books to friends, and advising both acquaintances and relatives on worthy books to read. (Nash, 15)

While serving as ambassador to France, he spent many afternoons going through the bookstores in Paris "in search of treasures." He was especially interested in anything "relating to America" (Nash, 15).

As a leading jurist, Jefferson was often asked for advice by aspiring lawyers. In a letter to one such person, Jefferson noted that it is generally assumed that the best way to learn the law is by apprenticing oneself to a successful lawyer. He noted that one could learn that way. He argued, however, that all that is really necessary for a student is access to a good library, and directions on the order in which books should be read.

He then listed a large number of books that the student should study, and recommended the method of study.

I will arrange the books to be read into three columns, and propose that you should read those in the first column till 12 oclock every day; those in the 2d. from 12. to 2. those in the 3d. after candlelight, leaving all the afternoon for exercise and recreation, which are as necessary as reading. (Koch and Peden, 498)

He listed all the legal types of books recommended. He also noted that study of nonlegal materials was essential, especially science and history. And he advised works that should be read so the lawyer would master a good writing style. These latter included poetry and grammar and lectures on rhetoric.

He offered to allow the student to use his books, but cautioned him to be sure to take care of them since many of the books he had lent to readers had never been returned. Guard them and do not "lend them to anybody else," he advised (Koch and Peden, 499).

In 1814 the British burned Washington, and the Congressional Library was destroyed. Jefferson promptly offered his library of almost 6,500 books as a replacement. He was paid $23,950 for the best collection of books in the land. It was undoubtedly worth much more. "By one noble stroke," wrote Nash, "the Library of Congress rose from its ashes in doubled size and acquired a breadth of holdings that foretold its emergence as a truly national library" (Nash, 21).

Jefferson spent considerable time preparing his collection for the trip to Washington. Many of his books were on loan and had to be recalled and placed in their proper locations in the collection. The books were loaded onto wagons that carried them to Washington.

In advancing what was for his time a "radical idea," that public libraries be established throughout America, Jefferson wrote:

Nothing would do more extensive good at small expense than ... a small circulating library in every county, to consist of a few well-chosen books to be lent to the people . . . such as would give them a general view of other history and particular view of that of their own country, a tolerable knowledge of geography, the elements of natural philosophy, of agriculture and mechanics. . . . My services in this way are freely at . . . command. (Mayo, 292)

He argued that nobody "more sincerely wishes the spread of information among mankind than I do, and none has greater confidence in its effect towards supporting free and good government" (Mayo, 292).

Jefferson's defense of the freedom of speech and the related freedom to read is legendary. In 1814, shortly before he sold his library to Congress, Jefferson wrote in defense of a Philadelphia bookseller who was being prosecuted for selling a particular book. He indicated that he was mortified that a book could become the subject of a criminal investigation. He argued that if one felt a book to contain false facts, the facts should be disproved, but both sides should be heard (Bestor, 9).

His ideas about free access to books and information, even the most controversial, were far ahead of his time. Instead of recommending censorship, as did many of his contemporaries, he believed that even books containing ideas repugnant to many should be protected by government.

"Permit the books to circulate freely," he maintained, "but encourage the most searching criticism of them and work vigorously to bring the criticisms to public attention" (Bestor, 16).

Jefferson had mixed feelings about Montesquieu's *Spirit of Laws*. He believed it had many truths but also a number of errors. He was especially upset by Montesquieu's reverence for the British system and his suspicion of democracy. He found an antidote not in censorship but in a book by a Frenchman, Count Destutt de Tracy. In its English translation it was entitled *Commentary and Review of Montesquieu's Spirit of Laws*. Jefferson recommended it as an important work for American students, and persuaded the College of William and Mary to adopt it. A copy was also placed "cheek by jowl" next to Montesquieu's work in the library of the new University of Virginia (Bestor, 16).

Another example of Jefferson's reaction to books containing ideas repugnant to him was his method of dealing with David Hume's *History of England*, probably the most noted history of England at that time. He felt Hume's treatment was too slanted towards Tory conservatism, too favorable to monarchy, and menacing to republics, to the democratic ideals which Jefferson espoused. He recommended reading Hume but also reading books that strongly upheld democratic ideals.

When Jefferson retired to his beloved Monticello, he continued involvement in his many activities in architecture, science, philosophy, and agriculture. He continued to read and study and to add to his library until the end of his life. He also personally selected, cataloged, and classified the collection of books for the library of the University of Virginia during his last few years.

Not only did he personally select the university's first library—6,680 separate items—he also classified every single one of them and drew up the regulations for their use. His method of classification endured for more than eighty years. (Nash, 21)

In advanced age, Jefferson confessed that he still had a "canine appetite for reading." He considered it an antidote to the problems of growing old. "I see in it a relief against the taedium senectutis . . . a lamp to lighten my path through the dreary wilderness of time before me" (Malone, vol. 6, 190).

IMPORTANT DATES IN THOMAS JEFFERSON'S LIFE

1743   Born in Virginia.

1767   Admitted to the bar.

1769   Admitted to the House of Burgesses.

1774   Served as a Delegate to the Continental Congress.

1776   Drafted the Declaration of Independence.

1779   Elected Governor of Virginia.

1785   Succeeded Franklin as Minister to France.

1800   Chosen third president of the United States. He was later elected to a second term.

1815   Offered his library to Congress after the congressional library had been burned by the British.

1826   Died at Monticello on July 4 while fellow Americans were celebrating the fiftieth anniversary of the Declaration of Independence.

SOURCES

Bestor, Arthur. "Thomas Jefferson and the Freedom of Books," in *Three Presidents and their Books: The Reading of Jefferson, Lincoln, Franklin D. Roosevelt.* Urbana: University of Illinois Press, 1955.

Koch, Adrienne, and William Peden, eds. *The Life and Selected Writings of Thomas Jefferson.* New York: Modern Library, 1944.

Malone, Dumas. *Jefferson and His Time,* 6 vols. Boston: Little, Brown and Co., 1948–1977.

Mayo, Bernard, ed. *Jefferson Himself: The Personal Narrative of a Many-Sided American.* Charlottesville: University Press of Virginia, 1942.

Nash, George H. *Books and the Founding Fathers: A Lecture to Commemorate the Year of the Reader,* Delivered on November 1, 1987. Washington, D.C.: Library of Congress, 1989.

HELEN KELLER (1880–1968)

Reading is one of the most difficult skills for children to learn. For Helen Keller, who was both blind and deaf, it was many times more difficult than for most youngsters. How could such a person read? Words were spelled out into her hand by her teacher, as noted below; and when she learned Braille, she could read for herself by running her fingers over the embossed pages.

Even learning a simple word was a great challenge for young Helen. In one of her books she explained how she, who could neither see nor hear, learned her first word—the word for water—when her private teacher Anne Sullivan spelled out the word in her hand.

Some one was drawing water and my teacher placed my hand under the spout. As the cool stream gushed over one hand she spelled into the other the word *water*, first slowly, then rapidly . . . and somehow the mystery of language was revealed to me. I knew that "w-a-t-e-r" meant the wonderful cool something that was flowing over my hand. That living word awakened my soul, gave it light, hope, joy, set it free! (Keller, *The Story*, 36)

That same day Helen learned several other words, including father, mother, sister, and teacher.

Helen Keller was born in Tuscumbia, Alabama, on June 26, 1880, a normal healthy child. She became gravely ill, however, in February of 1882, and was left blind and deaf.

When she was seven years old, her parents employed twenty-one-year-old Anne Sullivan to teach Helen. Sullivan herself was partially sighted. Helen made amazing progress, learning to read and eventually learning to speak.

When of college age, Helen entered Radcliffe College and graduated with honors. She became the world's foremost spokesperson for the blind, lecturing throughout the world, and writing many articles and a number of books on the problems and opportunities of those with handicaps such as her own.

When Helen was small, Anne Sullivan read fairy tales and poetry to her. These included Hans Christian Andersen's tales, and the poetry of Oliver Wendell Holmes and John Greenleaf Whittier.

Once Helen learned to read Braille, she became an inveterate reader. She read her first story in May, 1887, when she was seven years old, and "from that day" she devoured everything "that has come within the reach of my hungry finger tips."

At first I had only a few books in raised print—"readers" for beginners, a collection of stories for children, and a book about the earth called "Our World." I think that was all; but I read them over and over until the words were so worn and pressed I could scarcely make them out. (Keller, *The Story*, 91)

She loved *Little Lord Fauntleroy*. Anne Sullivan read it to her, then Helen read it again and again. Throughout her childhood Keller thought of that work as a sweet, gentle companion.

During her adolescence Helen read many, many books at her home and during her visits to the world renowned Perkins Institute for the Blind in Boston. She stated she could not remember them all:

But I know that among them were "Greek Heroes," LaFontaine's "Fables," Hawthorne's "Wonder Book," "Bible Stories," Lamb's "Tales from Shakespeare," "A Child's History of England" by Dickens, "The Arabian Nights," "The Swiss Family Robinson," "The Pilgrim's Progress," "Robinson Crusoe," "Little Women," and "Heidi," a beautiful little story which I read afterward in German. (Keller, *The Story*, 93)

She did not read, study, or analyze the books and stories nor did she read them to learn a moral. Like so many other children, she simply read them for pleasure.

Helen also loved Kipling's *Jungle Book* and another book entitled *Wild Animals I Have Known*. She felt a real interest in the animals because they were real animals and not just fictional "caricatures of men" (Keller, *The Story*, 94). She sympathized with "their loves and hatreds," laughed about their funny adventures, and wept "over their tragedies. . . . And if they point a moral, it is so subtle that we are not conscious of it" (Keller, *The Story*, 94).

Helen also developed a deep love of Greek literature—Greek poetry, the *Iliad*, fabulous stories about nymphs, heroes, and demigods, tales about Greek gods and goddesses. She imagined the gods and goddesses still walked on earth, talked with humans, and she secretly within her heart built shrines to some whom she especially loved.

Helen loved the Bible all her life with a passion, more than any other book. She read it for years, and was inspired by it. She cherished such inspiring stories as those of Esther and Ruth. She came to believe, however, that many Bible stories were mere myths similar to the mythical Greek and Roman literature she had been reading. Moreover, she did not like parts of the Bible she found ugly and even barbarous, and she thought it might be better if they were eliminated from the book, which she found otherwise so beautiful.

Helen could not remember a time—since she had become "capable of loving books"—that she did not love Shakespeare. Favorite plays were *Macbeth, The Merchant of Venice,* and *King Lear.* When she came to the part in *King Lear* in which "Gloster's eyes" were put out, she was seized with anger. She sat rigid for a time, her fingers unable to move, the blood throbbing in her temples.

She fell in love with Walt Whitman's work. At one point she encountered much self-doubt and felt isolated.

It was Walt Whitman who restored her self-confidence and courage. "When I read *The Song of the Open Road* . . . my spirit leaped up to meet him." Later she was to say at a Whitman dinner, "He has opened many windows in my dark house." (Brooks, 44)

An unusually gentle and tolerant person, Keller could never condemn Shylock nor even Satan whom she associated with Shylock, but she was sorry for them. She felt they could not be good "because no one seemed willing to help them or give them a fair chance."

There are moments when I feel that the Shylocks, the Judases, and even the Devil, are broken spokes in the great wheel of good which shall in due time be made whole. (Keller, *The Story,* 97)

Keller's progress at the Perkins Institute in Boston was so great, that she was becoming internationally famous. The first blind deaf mute who had come into contact with the outer world lived at Perkins. She was Laura Bridgman, already elderly when Helen first met her. Unlike Miss Bridgman, who never developed significant intelligence, Helen was destined to make rapid progress and become an intelligent, well adjusted adult.

Beginning when Helen was an adolescent, Anne took her to Perkins almost every year. The institute director Michael Anagnos considered Helen "the Eighth Wonder of the World." It was while at the institute that Helen was taken to visit the local homes of the great writers—Emerson, Hawthorne, and Alcott—and to correspond with such famous people as John Greenleaf Whittier, Oliver Wendell Holmes, and the theologian Phillips Brooks.

She wrote Whittier, a favorite poet, explaining that she could neither see nor hear, but that she loved his poetry.

I think you will be surprised to receive a letter from a little girl whom you do not know, but I thought you would be glad to hear that your beautiful poems make me very happy. (Lash, 111)

By the time Helen was ten she was reading German, Latin, and French. When she was ten she wrote, without assistance, a long letter in French to Anagnos who was in Greece at the time.

When twelve years old, Helen was asked what book she would like to take on a long trip. She replied, *Paradise Lost*. At that time she was reading the French writers Racine and La Fontaine, and "chuckling over" the funny incidents in Moliere's *Le Medecin Malgre Lui* "as her fingers moved slowly over the raised-print lines" (Brooks, 25).

Anne took Helen to New York in 1894 to the Wright-Humason School for the Deaf to further her studies and to learn to speak. It was one of her major disappointments that although she learned to speak, she was disappointed that her speech was only passably understandable.

While in New York, in addition to reading many books, Helen enjoyed reading *The New York Times* because it helped her keep track of current events. Also while in New York she met another favorite author, Mark Twain, at a party. He was very pleasantly surprised at her perceptiveness and noted:

Without touching anything, of course, and without hearing anything, she seemed quite well to recognize the character of her surroundings, She said,"Oh, the books, the books, so many, many books. How lovely!" (Lash, 193)

They formed a life-long friendship, and Twain called her a "miracle," a term used many times since then when describing Helen in books and films.

In 1896 Helen enrolled in a school for young ladies to prepare herself for her entrance to Radcliffe College. The instructors there had no experience in teaching any but ordinary pupils. Helen had some difficulties there because Miss Sullivan could not always spell out into Helen's hand all the books required, and the text-books she needed could not always be embossed into Braille by the time she needed them. Nonetheless, she did well in her studies there.

Helen entered Radcliffe College in 1900. She pursued a generally humanities course: English literature, French, German, history, the Bible, government, philosophy, and economics. Sullivan tapped out the lectures into Helen's hand. She became the first deaf-blind person to graduate from that college, and she graduated *cum laude*.

In her studies Helen was comforted by the fact that some great writers were blind, just as she was. Homer and Milton, although blind, wrote great poems.

There are two prominent examples of the crucial role books played in Helen's life. One was her joyful acceptance of the Swedenborgian religion. The other was her joining the Socialist Party.

Helen had been brought up in traditional Christianity. She especially cherished the religion of love taught to her by Bishop Phillips Brooks, that is, God is Love and the Light of All Men. She was confused, however, and felt that he never could answer to her satisfaction her questions about spirit and the relationship between divine love and the physical world.

She made these discoveries by herself. During her college days Helen had grown increasingly bewildered by the subject. Then a momentous event occurred while she was sitting in the library. Helen was overcome with the distinct feeling that she had been far away. Anne Sullivan asked her what had happened. "I have been in Athens," Helen replied.

Scarcely were the words out of my mouth when a bright amazing realization seemed to catch my mind and set it ablaze. I perceived the realness of my soul. . . . It was clear to me that it was because I was a spirit that I had so vividly "seen" and felt a place thousands of miles away. (Lash, 781)

A Swedenborgian friend, John Hitz, gave Helen a Braille copy of the book *Heaven and Hell* by the Swedish scientist and mystic Emanuel Swedenborg. The book explained the concept of a spiritual world to Helen's satisfaction. Before she had finished it, she had found her faith. She was "radiant." She had found her religion, "a religion that . . . enriched her life ever since" (Waite, 187–88). She continued to read Swedenborg's words as well as the Bible. She felt that the Swedish writer's works deepened her sense of God's presence and gave her a richer understanding of scripture.

For many years Helen was distressed by the plight of poor workers. "Why is it," she asked, "that so many workers live in unspeakable misery? With their hands they have builded great cities and cannot be sure of a roof over their heads" (Keller, *Out of the Dark*, 13). Such feelings led her to become a socialist. To questions about her becoming a socialist, she replied, "How did I become a socialist? By reading. The first book I read was Wells's 'New Worlds for Old.' . . . Mr. Wells led to others" (Keller, *Out of the Dark*, 20).

In addition to books on socialism she read periodicals. One was a German Socialist periodical in Braille—"The other socialist literature that I have read has been spelled into my hand by a friend who comes three times a week to read to me whatever I choose to have read" (Keller, *Out of the Dark*, 21). The friend read to Keller both the *National Socialist* and the *International Socialist Review*.

When Helen publicly proclaimed herself a socialist, some of her supporters were afraid that her association with the socialists would seriously damage her credibility. However, Helen seemed to lead a charmed life. Although public hysteria often destroyed the careers of others who announced that they were socialists, Keller seemed impervious to such attack, and her popularity and influence continued unabated.

Throughout her adult life Keller made many speeches that raised large sums of money for the blind. Although she personally considered her deafness a worse handicap than the blindness, she constantly worked so that the blind could gain education and self-reliance. She recruited many celebrities to help solicit funds for Braille and talking books.

She lobbied United States presidents and other politicians, traveling to Washington to testify on behalf of legislation to assist the blind. She became a close friend and ally of Eleanor Roosevelt, another person who worked for the poor and handicapped.

Her public appearances and several books, which became best sellers, also alerted the public to the problems and opportunities of blind people. Her own personal story, told so movingly, was most effective in gaining the attention and sympathy of leading citizens and the public at large.

Books and reading had always been important to Helen Keller, even greater in importance to her than to sighted people. She had always depended on books not only for the pleasure and wisdom they bring to all readers but also for the transmittal of knowledge and information that others have received through their eyes and ears.

In a word, literature is my Utopia. Here I am not disenfranchised. No barrier of the senses shuts me out from the sweet, gracious discourse of my book-friends. (Keller, *The Story*, 100)

IMPORTANT DATES IN HELEN KELLER'S LIFE

1880   Born a normal healthy child in Tuscumbia, Alabama.

1882   Left blind and deaf after a serious illness.

1887   Anne Sullivan became Helen's tutor. She taught her to communicate with the outside world.

1900   Entered Radcliffe College.

1903   Published her autobiography *The Story of My Life*, which became a best seller.

1904   Graduated with honors from Radcliffe.

1904–1960s For most of her adult life Keller lectured throughout the world on behalf of the blind and raised funds for organizations for the blind. Published a number of additional books, including *The World I Live In; Out of the Dark; My Religion; Helen Keller's Journal; Teacher;* and *The Open Door.*

1931–1960s Received honorary doctorates from a number of universities, including Temple University; University of Glasgow; University of Witwatersand, South Africa; University of Delhi; and Free University of Berlin.

1968　　Died at home. Her ashes were interred in the National Cathedral in Washington, D.C.

SOURCES

Brooks, Van Wyck. *Helen Keller: Sketch for a Portrait.* New York: E.P. Dutton & Co., 1956.

Keller, Helen. *Out of the Dark: Essays, Letters, and Addresses on Physical and Social Vision.* Garden City, N.Y.: Doubleday, Page & Co., 1914.

Keller, Helen. *The Story of My Life.* Garden City, N.Y.: Doubleday, 1954. (Original copyright, 1902.)

Lash, Joseph. *Helen and Teacher: The Story of Helen Keller and Anne Sullivan Macy.* New York: Delacorte Press/Seymour Lawrence, 1980.

Waite, Helen Elmira. *Valiant Companions: Helen Keller and Anne Sullivan Macy.* Philadelphia: Macrae Smith Co., 1959.

JOHN F. KENNEDY
(1917–1963)

John F. Kennedy was the first Catholic to be elected president of the United States. He was also one of the youngest and most intellectual of all presidents, the only one in recent memory who made literature such an important part of his public life. Kennedy's associates "spearheaded the groundwork for capturing the party's nomination by exploiting his reputation as a writer and historian, as an intelligent, devoted, and sincere student of the American past and present" (Parmet, 479). In speeches Kennedy, an avid reader, would often quote writers, ancient and modern. He published many articles and several books on political and historical subjects.

John Fitzgerald Kennedy was born on May 9, 1917, in Brookline, Massachusetts. He was the descendant of Irish immigrants who had become an important political and financial family. His father, Joseph Kennedy, was a wealthy business executive who served for a time as ambassador to Great Britain. His mother, Rose Fitzgerald Kennedy, was the daughter of John Fitzgerald, "Honey Fitz," who had been a United States congressman and mayor of Boston.

"Jack" Kennedy participated in sports with the rest of his family, but he also was often ill as a child, spending much time in bed. While at Harvard, he received a serious back injury that plagued him for the rest of his life. He also was stricken with Addison's Disease, a condition which reduces a person's immunity to illness.

Jack Kennedy attended public schools in Brookline, the Riverdale School in New York, and the Choate Preparatory School in Connecticut. He graduated from Harvard with honors. While there he wrote a thesis detailing Britain's unpreparedness for war. His book *Why England Slept* was based on that thesis.

After graduating from Harvard, Kennedy tried to enlist in the army but was rejected because of his back injury. He spent months in strengthening exercises, and was then allowed to enlist in the United States Navy shortly before the Japanese attacked Pearl Harbor. Kennedy commanded a PT boat, which was rammed and sunk. Kennedy was credited with extreme heroism saving the lives of three of his crew members. For his conduct he was awarded a Purple Heart and a Navy and Marine Corps Medal.

Kennedy's career as an elected official began in 1946 when he was elected to the United States House of Representatives from Massachusetts' Eleventh District. He served in that body for a number of years, and then was elected to the U.S. Senate.

Kennedy was elected president in 1960. America had never had a Catholic president, and many non-Catholics feared that the policies of someone of that faith would be dominated by the church. Kennedy successfully convinced the populace that he was a free agent and would follow the United States Constitution.

Unfortunately, the new president served only three years. He was assassinated in 1963 by Lee Harvey Oswald. Since then countless numbers of books and articles have been published about his presidency and about the assassination. Many of the latter argue that his assassination was a conspiracy of some group, not simply the work of one person.

Among other accomplishments, Kennedy and his wife Jacqueline Bouvier Kennedy will be remembered for inspiring millions with their interest in literature, music, and art. Frequently, prominent novelists, poets, musicians, and other artists were invited to perform at the White House. They left a legacy of legend, named Camelot by admirers.

Rose Kennedy read aloud to her children at bedtime. She noted that Jack of all the children was the most receptive to reading. Books became a very important part of his life.

One time Nathan Pusey, president of Harvard University, asked her why Jack read so much. It was partly because, she remarked, he had been sick so much as a child. He participated in sports, but he also had to spend long periods in bed when others were outdoors playing. He learned to love reading, and always read constantly.

He especially loved adventure stories. His childhood favorite was *King Arthur and His Knights*. He also enjoyed *The Arabian Nights* and John Bunyan's *Pilgrim's Progress*. His grandmother Fitzgerald bought him a copy of *Billy Whiskers*, a story about a goat, that Jack also enjoyed.

Within a few years, his reading became almost entirely dominated by nonfiction, especially history and biography.

Ideas became important for their relevance to current problems; fantasies began to lose their charm. History and biography, and particularly those that described outstanding leadership, dominated his reading. (Parmet, 17)

He was the most intellectual in the family. His sister Eunice said he was the brightest of all his siblings. Whenever questions arose, Jack would be the one to go and look up the answer.

Friends and acquaintances were often surprised not only at how much he read but at the profundity of his reading material as a teenager. When only fifteen, while in Massachusetts General Hospital, young Kennedy was surrounded by books. They included such serious works as Winston Churchill's *The World Crisis*.

Churchill became one of Jack's favorite writers. He read everything the British statesman had written, even things which appeared in *Hansard*, the British version of the American Congressional Record. He also was deeply interested in American presidents. He read almost every book written about them.

At Harvard, the future president undertook a serious honors program under the guidance of his professors. He spent many hours in the library and was often seen around campus with an armload of books. He read extensively about the various "isms" undermining democracy worldwide including communism, fascism, imperialism, militarism, and nationalism. Much of what he learned he used in his first book, *Why England Slept*.

After his election to political office, Kennedy continued his habit of reading serious material, mainly American and English history and biography. While dressing in the morning, "he would prop open a book on his bureau and read while he put on his shirt and tied his necktie" (Schlesinger, 105).

He read about Lincoln, Marlborough, John Quincy Adams, Calhoun, Talleyrand, and other important political/historical figures. He also occasionally read poetry. Shakespeare and Byron are quoted in a notebook he kept from 1945 to 1946.

The first book he gave his wife, Jacqueline, was Marquis James' *The Raven*, a biography of Sam Houston. She could not remember his reading novels at all except for some Ian Fleming thrillers. It had been reported that he was addicted to Ian Fleming's James Bond novels, but that was really a publicity gag, according to Kennedy biographer Arthur Schlesinger, Jr. (Schlesinger, 105).

He did, however, read most of Hemingway and some contemporary fiction, including *The Deer Park*. He listed Stendahl's *The Red and the Black* as a favorite book. He was undoubtedly the only modern American politician who quoted Madame de Stael, a rather obscure French essayist, on "Meet the Press."

Notebooks he kept from 1945 to 1946 shed light on the depth of his reading. They contain sayings from many great figures. For example:

Aeschylus—"In war, truth is the first casualty."

Jefferson—"Widespread poverty and concentrated wealth cannot long endure side by side in a democracy."

Burke—"Our patience will achieve more than our force."

Dante—"The hottest places in hell are reserved for those who, in a period of moral crisis, maintain their neutrality."

He even quoted Huck Finn on *Pilgrim's Progress*: "The statements are interesting—but steep" (Schlesinger, 105–106).

John Buchan's *Pilgrim's Way* was a favorite book. It dealt with the untimely death of a young, talented Briton.

He loved his youth, and his youth became eternal. Debonaire and brilliant and brave, he is now part of that immortal England which knows not age or weariness or defeat. (Schlesinger, 87)

Jacqueline Kennedy later said that the reality of men dying young haunted Jack.

Kennedy's inauguration in January, 1961, became a celebration for American artists. Robert Frost was invited to speak, the first poet in memory to read a poem at a presidential inauguration. He recited his poem "The Gift Outright" from memory. In addition fifty leading artists, writers, and composers were invited to attend the inaugural. They included W. H. Auden, Alexis Leger, Paul Tillich, Robert Lowell, John Hersey, John Steinbeck, Allen Tate, and Jacques Maritain. Politicians who were "hoarding tickets" to the event were annoyed, but Kennedy did not mind. Auden called the invitation "as thrilling as it was surprising." "What a joy," said Steinbeck, "that literacy is no longer prima facie evidence of treason" (Schlesinger, 731).

Numerous writers and other artists, including those who could not be present at the inaugural, were proud and grateful to the new president. Archibald MacLeish, for example, wrote:

No country which did not respect its arts has ever been great and ours has ignored them too long. . . . I heard the inaugural address on an uncertain short-wave set in . . . the Windwards. It left me proud and hopeful to be an American—something I have not felt for almost twenty years. (Schlesinger, 732)

Thus began the Kennedy practice of inviting leading writers and other artists to the White House. Such exposure gave the arts a level of prestige they had not enjoyed before.

Kennedy's extensive reading provided him not only information for his writing but also a fine literary style. His book, *Profiles in Courage*, received glowing reviews, and he was awarded the Pulitzer Prize for that work. He published numerous articles in popular magazines and newspapers, including such prestigious publications as *Foreign Affairs*, *The New York Times Magazine*, *The Washington Post*, and *The Progressive* (Parmet, 480).

Like other politicians, Kennedy used ghostwriters. However, his own role in such writing is still critical, as noted by biographer Herbert Parmet.

For the general public, there was no way to distinguish between Kennedy and his ghostwriters. Once one realizes the latters' involvement, the danger exists of ignoring Kennedy's personal role, thereby depriving him of credit for at least spiritual and intellectual inspiration. (Parmet, 480)

It is obvious that Kennedy had extensive historical and political knowledge gained through reading, and reading was an important factor in making it possible for him to reach the heights. Although born into wealth, he had to become independent of his family. He developed a depth of knowledge and feeling far beyond his family, but he always continued to love them.

His potential was recognized by many. Professor William G. Carleton of the University of Florida, for example, spent an evening discussing world affairs with the Kennedys in Palm Beach in 1941. He found that John Kennedy "had a far better historical and political mind than his father or his elder brother [Joseph]."

John's capacity for seeing current events in historical perspective and for projecting historical trends into the future was unusual. (Schlesinger, 80)

IMPORTANT DATES IN JOHN F. KENNEDY'S LIFE

1917	Born in Brookline, Massachusetts.
1939	Took a six-month leave from Harvard to serve as secretary to his father who was United States ambassador to Great Britain.
1940	Graduated *cum laude* from Harvard University.
1940	Published *Why England Slept*. The book, based on his thesis at Harvard, received laudatory reviews.
1941–1945	Served in the United States Navy. Decorated with U.S. Navy and Marine Corps medal, Purple Heart.
1946	Elected to the United States House of Representatives, one of the youngest men ever elected to that body.
1952	Elected to the United States Senate.
1953	Married Jacqueline Bouvier.
1956	Published *Profiles in Courage*.
1957	Awarded Pulitzer Prize for biography for *Profiles*.
1960	Elected president of the United States, the first Catholic to be elected to that office.
1963	Assassinated in Dallas, Texas.

SOURCES

Brogan, Hugh. *Kennedy*. London and New York: Longman, 1996.

Hamilton, Nigel. *J.F.K.: Reckless Youth*. New York: Random House, 1992.

Kennedy, John, F. *Profiles in Courage*. New York: Harper & Brothers, 1956.

Kennedy, John, F. *Why England Slept*. New York: W. Funk, 1940.

Manchester, William. *Remembering Kennedy: One Brief Shining Moment*. Boston: Little, Brown and Co., 1983.

Parmet, Herbert S. *Jack: The Struggles of John F. Kennedy*. New York: Dial Press, 1980.

Reeves, Richard. *President Kennedy: Profiles of Power*. New York: Simon & Schuster, 1993.

Schlesinger, Arthur M., Jr. *A Thousand Days: John F. Kennedy in the White House*. Boston: Houghton Mifflin, 1965.

Sorensen, Theodore C. *Kennedy*. New York: Harper and Row, 1965.

MARTIN LUTHER KING, JR.
(1929–1968)

Dr. Martin Luther King, Jr., is considered the most influential American civil rights leader of the century. He was very well versed in the Bible and widely read in the works of great thinkers—American, European, and Asian. He often made references to what he had read in his phenomenally successful speeches and writings.

Martin Luther King, Jr., was born January 15, 1929, into one of Atlanta's elite black families. His father was the prominent, well-to-do pastor of the Ebenezer Baptist Church, and his mother was the daughter of the minister who had preceded King's father as pastor of that church.

Although most of Atlanta's black population was poor, it included a small but prosperous upper class, partly the product of segregation. They were business people, ministers, and professionals who catered to black families, who were often not welcome in white areas.

Young King was small but very athletic and intellectually curious. He enjoyed competitive sports as well as words and ideas.

King was an above-average student in school. In later years, however, he bemoaned the fact that his education in segregated schools had been very poor. One of his greatest early childhood disappointments was that he was not allowed to attend the same school as a close boyhood friend who was white. When he tearfully asked his parents the reason, they told him about the "race problem" in America.

King entered Morehouse College at the age of fifteen, and several years later he was ordained a Baptist minister. He graduated with honors from the mostly white Crozer Theological Seminary, and received a Ph.D. in theology from Boston University.

He married Coretta Scott in 1953. Within a year he took the position of minister of Dexter Avenue Baptist Church in Montgomery, Alabama.

In 1955 Rosa Parks, a local black seamstress, was arrested in Montgomery for refusing to go to the back of a bus. A meeting was called at which King made an inspired speech encouraging a boycott against the bus company. He stressed the boycott would be totally nonviolent. The crowd rose en masse, roaring their approval when asked to support the boycott.

The year-long boycott ended in victory when the Supreme Court declared that segregated bus systems were illegal. The successful boycott, which demonstrated the power of nonviolent resistance, gave King national prominence as a civil rights leader. A year after that victory, King and associates founded the Southern Christian Leadership Conference to organize civil rights activities throughout the south.

From then until his death, King led civil rights demonstrations and campaigns all over the south. He also turned his attention to de facto segregation in the north and organized activities to bring together people of all races to fight against poverty.

In 1968 King went to Memphis to support a sanitation workers' strike. While standing on a balcony of the Lorraine Motel in that city, he was shot to death. His murder shocked Americans, and more than 100,000 people attended his funeral in Atlanta. His tombstone expressed King's vision. It was inscribed:

> Free at last, free at last,
> Thank God almighty I'm free at last.

King's work has been carried on by his widow, Coretta Scott King, through the Martin Luther King, Jr. Center for Social Change in Atlanta.

The youthful King had a great memory, loved words, and treasured books. Even before he could read, by the age of five, he could sing entire hymns and recite long biblical passages from memory. "You just wait and see," he told his parents, "When I grow up I'm going to get me some big words" (Oates, 9). "Even before he could read," his father boasted, "he kept books around him, he just liked the idea of having them" (Oates, 9). When still an adolescent, he gathered books from throughout the house and arranged them on a secretary desk. That collection became his "library."

In addition to the words he read, the young Martin was fascinated by the power of the words he heard spoken by his father and other ministers. He learned much from both the preachers' oratorical manner of speaking and the idea of deliverance from oppression which had been prevalent in the black slave culture for many years. He dreamed of being a great speaker himself.

While in college King went far beyond what his professors taught him. On his own he undertook an intensive study of the works of great philosophers, including Rousseau, Hobbes, Bentham, Mill, Locke, Nietzsche, and

Marx. He was on "a serious quest for a philosophical method to eliminate social evil" (Oates, 25).

He was impressed with Karl Marx, and spent his 1949 Christmas vacation reading *Das Kapital, The Communist Manifesto,* and other works about communism. He rejected Marx's materialism, but agreed with the exposure of the evils of capitalism.

One who had great influence on him was the nineteenth-century theologian Walter Rauschenbusch, the leading exponent of the Social Gospel. Rauschenbusch gave to American Protestantism a sense of social responsibility that has had a lasting influence on many Christians. King read his work avidly and found in him the kind of Christian activism he longed for.

In *Christianity and the Social Crisis* and other books, Rauschenbusch blamed capitalism for all the poverty and squalor throughout the land. He damned business as "the last entrenchment of autocracy," capitalism as "a mammonistic organization with which Christianity can never be content." He urged Christians to build a new social order—a truly Christian order, "in which moral law would replace Darwin's law of the jungle" (Oates, 25).

King realized that Christian love alone could not bring about necessary change. His study of history convinced him that love could be impotent. Love had not brought an end to slavery in America. It took a war to do that. Nor had it prevented the Holocaust in Europe. However, he concluded that armed rebellion could not help.

His study of the history of slavery convinced him that armed rebellion would be suicidal. American blacks, a minority, and their supporters could never defeat a heavily armed majority.

He was thus faced with a dilemma. If neither Christian love nor armed rebellion would bring about justice, how could justice be accomplished? Gandhi's teachings provided the answer.

Gandhi influenced King probably more than any other figure. Gandhi taught that nonviolent resistance meant not cooperating with evil. Gandhi himself had been influenced by the American philosopher Thoreau whose essays on civil disobedience had made a strong impression on him.

One Sunday King attended a lecture on Gandhi given by Mordecai W. Johnson, the president of Howard University. Johnson contended that Gandhi had made love and truth into a powerful method of gaining social change. He maintained that the Gandhian type of nonviolence could improve race relations in America.

King had heard of Gandhi, but Johnson's message was so profound and electrifying that he left the meeting and bought a half-dozen books about Gandhi's life and works. The most important were Louis Fischer's work and Gandhi's own *Autobiography.*

As he read about Gandhi, King became deeply interested in his campaign of nonviolence. Studying further, he realized "the Christian doctrine of love operating through the Gandhian method of nonviolence was one of the most potent weapons available to oppressed people in their struggle for freedom" (King, "Pilgrimage to Nonviolence," 440).

King was especially impressed with the sense of community preached by Gandhi. In Gandhi's emphasis on nonviolence and love, King discovered the best method for social reform. He believed Gandhi "was probably the first person in history to lift the love ethic of Jesus above mere interaction between individuals to a powerful effective social force on a large scale" (Oates, 32).

During the bus boycott in Montgomery, he "became more and more convinced of the power of nonviolence" (King, "Pilgrimage to Nonviolence," 440).

King's great oratory, speeches, and writings were influenced and strengthened by quotes from or references to the Bible and to a great variety of philosophers and poets he had studied.

After Rosa Parks was arrested in Montgomery, King was concerned that blacks would use the same kind of violent tactics used by the white citizens' councils organized to preserve segregation. They were "the methods of open and covert terror, brutal intimidation, and threats of starvation" (Washington, 428).

Serving as spokesman for the movement, King insisted that it be nonviolent. His mind "was driven back to the Sermon on the Mount and the Gandhian method of nonviolent resistance" (King, "Pilgrimage to Nonviolence," 440).

In his most famous speech, "I Have a Dream," King included references to the Bible, the Declaration of Independence, the United States Constitution, the Emancipation Proclamation, and phrases from "My Country 'Tis of Thee." He ended by reciting the Negro spiritual which begins "Free at last, free at last" (Washington, 217–220).

In the notable speech, "I See the Promised Land," he mentioned Plato, Aristotle, Socrates, Euripides, Aristophanes, Jesus, Martin Luther, and Abraham Lincoln. In that manner he brought together thinkers from different cultures and ages to make particular points. He ended the speech, given on the eve of his assassination, with a prophetic reference to the famous hymn.

I'm not fearing any man. Mine eyes have seen the glory of the coming of the Lord. (Washington, 286)

On another occasion he argued "we shall overcome," because Carlyle said, "no lie can live forever," and William Cullen Bryant claimed, "truth crushed to earth shall rise again." In addition, he noted:

We shall overcome because there is something in this universe that justifies James Russell Lowell in saying, truth forever on the scaffold, wrong forever on the throne. Yet the scaffold sways the future, and behind the dim unknown standeth God within the shadows keeping watch above His own. (Washington, 52–53)

During the twelve years of his public life, from his days in Montgomery until his assassination in 1968, King led civil rights campaigns. He gave many hundreds of speeches and published numerous articles and a number of books. He also encouraged others leading such campaigns, including students who organized sit-ins at segregated lunch counters and other facilities. He was frequently asked for advice to help in the struggle, and he always encouraged nonviolence and love. He noted:

At the center of nonviolence stands the principle of love. In struggling for human dignity the oppressed people of the world must not allow themselves to become bitter or indulge in hate campaigns. To retaliate with hate and bitterness would do nothing but intensify the hate in the world. Along the way of life, someone must have sense enough and morality enough to cut off the chain of hate. This can be done only by projecting the ethics of love to the center of our lives. (Washington, 8)

IMPORTANT DATES IN MARTIN LUTHER KING, JR.'S LIFE

1929	Born in Atlanta, Georgia.
1953	Married Coretta Scott.
1955	Received doctorate from Boston University. Led successful boycott of the Montgomery bus system.
1956	Supreme Court ruled segregated bus systems were illegal.
1957	Helped found the Southern Christian Leadership Conference.
1958	Survived an attempted assassination in New York City.
1959	Visited India to study Gandhi's techniques of nonviolence.
1960s	Led sit-ins and freedom rides. Was often jailed.
1963	Wrote his famous "Letter from Birmingham Jail" encouraging clergy to support the civil rights movement.
1963	Gave his electrifying "I Have a Dream" speech at the Lincoln Memorial during the March on Washington attended by about 250,000 people.
1964	President Lyndon Johnson signed the Civil Rights Act. King was awarded the Nobel Peace Prize.
1965	Led a voter registration drive in Selma, Alabama. People came from all over America to support the right of blacks to vote. President Johnson signed the Voting Rights Act. Malcolm X assassinated.
1968	Organized a "Poor People's Campaign" to fight against poverty of poor people of all races.
1968	Assassinated in Memphis, Tennessee.

SOURCES

Ansbro, John J. *Martin Luther King, Jr.: The Making of a Mind.* Maryknoll, N.Y.: Orbis Books, 1982.

Fairclough, Adam. *Martin Luther King, Jr.* Athens: University of Georgia Press, 1995.

Garrow, David J. *Bearing the Cross: Martin Luther King, Jr., and the Southern Christian Leadership Conference, a Personal Portrait.* New York: William Morrow, 1986.

King, Martin Luther, Jr. "Pilgrimage to Nonviolence," *Christian Century* 77 April 13, 1960.

King, Martin Luther, Jr. *Stride Toward Freedom: The Montgomery Story.* New York: Harper & Row, 1958.

King, Martin Luther, Jr. *Strength to Love.* New York: Walker and Co., 1963.

Oates, Stephen B. *Let the Trumpet Sound: The Life of Martin Luther King, Jr.* New York: Harper and Row, 1982.

Washington, James Melvin, ed. *A Testament of Hope: The Essential Writings of Martin Luther King, Jr.* San Francisco: Harper & Row, 1986.

STEPHEN KING
(1947–   )

Stephen King, a master storyteller, revived the genre of horror fiction in the latter half of the twentieth century. He became "one of the most influential American writers" of his genre and "is certainly the most popular" (Barth, 843). He is frequently referred to as "the dean of American horror fiction."

By the early 1990s King had become "a publishing marvel with nearly one hundred million copies of his works in print worldwide." He was also the first writer to have three, four, and finally five titles appear simultaneously on the *New York Times* best-seller list.

Reading exerted a powerful influence on King's writing. He became an avid reader of fantasy and horror stories as a child and continued such reading in adulthood.

Reading was the key to King's love of writing. "My mother read to me. I became a writer by becoming a reader. I love imaginative fiction. I just sit in my office at night and kick back and read a book. The dog lies down by the footstool!" (*The Guinness Book of World Records*, 177)

King also encouraged young people to experience the joys of reading. "If you read, then you are never bored" (*The Guinness Book of World Records*, 177).

Stephen King was born in Portland, Maine, the son of Donald and Ruth King on September 21, 1947. When Stephen was two years old, his father went out to buy a pack of cigarettes, did not come back, and was never seen again.

King was born not long after the end of World War II and grew up in the 1950s. The destructive capabilities of the atomic bomb, which had ended the war, cast a terrifying shadow over the land for many years. Some of King's interest in terror came from his experiences as a child. He wrote:

We were fertile ground for the seeds of terror, we war babies; we had been raised in a strange circus atmosphere of paranoia, patriotism, and national *hubris*. (King, 23)

King's mother worked in various low paying jobs. The family lived a lower middle class life.

King went to local schools and then to the University of Maine on a scholarship. He majored in English and graduated in 1970. He was married a year later. They were "poor as church mice" (Beahm, *The Stephen King Companion*, 25).

Unable to get a teaching job, King worked at a variety of low-paying occupations, including that of pressing sheets in a laundry and pumping gas in a filling station. His wife worked in a doughnut shop. Finally, he got a position teaching English.

King sold some short stories to small-circulation magazines. With the publication of *Carrie*, he quickly became an internationally renowned writer. The movie based on the book was equally popular.

A number of additional King works have been adapted successfully to the screen. They usually have been directed by internationally noted directors and star major movie actors.

King's mother loved to read. It provided an escape from her life of drudgery. She also enjoyed reading to her children.

Young Stephen's earliest memories of written stories were those his mother read to him and his brother. She read "Classics Illustrated" comics which were adaptations of classical works of literature. She also read some of the actual classics, such as *Treasure Island*.

Stephen was influenced by radio and movies, as well as books. When he was four years old he heard a radio adaptation of Ray Bradbury's story "Mars Is Heaven." He had to listen through the door because his mother did not want him to hear the horrific story. It scared him, and that night he slept where he could see the light from the bathroom.

His first exposure to horror movies was the 1954 film *The Creature from the Black Lagoon*. He knew the creature was not real but thought it might visit him in his dreams. Even when viewing the same film many years later with his son, the film still affected him.

One day Stephen's mother brought home a book from the library. King recognized it as a library book because it was dull on the outside, unlike the colorful books and comics he was used to. However, it was, like many other library books, interesting on the inside. She said he would not like the story, *The Strange Case of Dr. Jekyll and Mr. Hyde*, because it was too scary. Stephen asked her to read it to him anyway. She protested but not very hard because she loved it. Stephen also loved it.

I lived and died with that story, with Mr. Utterson and with poor Dr. Jekyll, and particularly with Dr. Jekyll's other side, which was every vestige of pretense of civilization thrown away. I can remember lying in bed, wakeful after that night's reading was done, and what I usually thought of was how Mr. Hyde walked over the little girl, back and forth, breaking her bones; and it was such a terrible image and I thought, *I have to do that; but I have to do that worse.* (Beahm, *The Stephen King Story*, 17)

On his own Stephen read Dr. Seuss books. Seuss's grim comedy, *The 500 Hats of Bartholomew Cubbins*, made a strong impact on him. He was especially impressed by the fact that ordinary people could suddenly be struck with very frightening, weird situations for no reason at all. "It was an idea that, years later, would become the cornerstone of virtually all of his major fiction" (Beahm, *The Stephen King Story*, 17).

Stephen discovered another author who would remain a favorite with him. While exploring a relative's attic, he found a box of books that had belonged to his father. One of the books was an anthology of horror stories by a master of such fiction, H. P. Lovecraft. It gave him an introduction to serious fantasy-horror literature.

So that book, courtesy of my departed father, was my first taste of a world that went deeper than the B pictures which played on Saturday afternoon or the boys' fiction of Carl Carmer and Roy Rockwell. When Lovecraft wrote "The Rats in the Walls" and "Pickman's Model," he wasn't simply kidding around or trying to pick up a few extra bucks; he *meant* it, and it was his seriousness as much as anything else which that interior dowsing rod responded to, I think. (King, 102)

When he was in high school King divided books between "works of literature like *Hamlet* and *Moby Dick* that teachers assigned him to read ("Gotta Read") and the works of popular literature he read on his own volition ("Wanna Read")." In the latter category he placed Shirley Jackson, Wilkie Collins, Ken Kesey, Tom Wolfe's essays, Jack London, Agatha Christie, Andre Norton, Margaret Mitchell's *Gone with the Wind*, and numerous comic books.

Other youthful favorites were Steinbeck's *The Grapes of Wrath*; John D. MacDonald's *The End of Night*; John Fowles' *The Collector*; *Jude the Obscure* by Thomas Hardy; William Golding's *Lord of the Flies*; *Hot Rod* by Henry G. Felsen; and Richard Matheson's *I Am Legend*. King noted that many ideas for his books came from what he had read.

I've never considered myself a blazingly original writer in the sense of conceiving totally new and fresh plot ideas.... What I try to do ... is to pour new wine from old bottles. ... *The Shining* was influenced by Shirley Jackson's marvelous novel *The Haunting of Hill House*; *The Stand* owes a considerable debt to both George R. Stewart's *Earth Abides* and M. P. Shiel's *The Purple Cloud*; and *Firestarter* has numerous science fiction antecedents. *Salem's Lot*, of course, was inspired by and bears a fully intentional similarity to . . . Bram Stoker's *Dracula*. I've never made any secret of that. (Beahm, *The Stephen King Companion*, 39)

King's love of reading played an important role in his becoming such a famous writer. He loved to read, and also recommended that others experience the joys of reading, arguing that "if you read, then you are never bored" (*The Guinness Book of World Records*, 177).

IMPORTANT DATES IN STEPHEN KING'S LIFE

1947   Born in Portland, Maine.

1949   His father left home and was never heard from again.

1959–1960   Very significant event occurred: King found and read a box of fantasy-horror books.

1970   Graduated from the University of Maine with a major in English.

1971   Married Tabitha Spruce. Supported family by working in a variety of menial jobs.

1974   His first published novel, *Carrie*, is released.

1976   Release of film version of *Carrie*, which became a great success.

1977–   Many more of his books published, including *The Shining, The Stand, Pet Sematary, The Tommyknockers, Needful Things,* and *Misery*. A number were made into successful films.

SOURCES

Barth, Melissa E. "Stephen King," in *Encyclopedia of World Authors II*, vol. 3, Frank N. Magill, ed. Pasadena, Calif.: Salem Press, 1989.

Beahm, George. *The Stephen King Story*. Kansas City: Andrews and MacMeel, 1991.

Beahm, George, ed. *The Stephen King Companion*. Kansas City: Andrews and MacMeel, 1989.

The Guinness Book of World Records. Stamford, Conn.: Guinness Media, 1997.

King, Stephen. *Danse Macabre*. New York: Everest House, 1981.

Russell, Sharon A. *Stephen King: A Critical Companion*. Westport, Conn.: Greenwood Press, 1996.

Saidman, Anne. *Stephen King: Master of Horror*. Minneapolis: Lerner Publications, 1992.

ROBERT E. LEE
(1807–1870)

Robert E. Lee was commander of the Confederate forces during the Civil War and one of the greatest military strategists in American history. Lee hated slavery, secession, and thought war would be a disaster. Nonetheless, he chose to lead the South in the war. He was guided by his reading of the Bible and his loyalty to the South, his native region.

He looked to the Bible for guidance, and found it there, especially in Paul's first letter to Timothy: "But if any provide not for his own, and especially for those of his own house, he hath denied the faith, and is worse than an infidel."

In addition to being a great military leader, Lee had an extensive knowledge of literature. Having studied it from his youth, he was equally familiar with both ancient and modern works.

Robert E. Lee was born in Stratford, Virginia, on January 19, 1807, the fifth of the seven children of Colonel Henry "Light-Horse" Harry Lee and Ann Hill Carter Lee. Both of his parents belonged to aristocratic Virginia families. "Light Horse" Harry Lee had served as a cavalryman in the Revolutionary War and as governor of Virginia.

Robert attended local schools in Alexandria where the family had moved when he was four years old. He later enrolled at the United States Military Academy at West Point, was an excellent student, and graduated second in his class.

After graduation Lee held a number of important positions as an army engineer, as a field officer during the Mexican War, and as superintendent at West Point. In 1860 he assumed command of troops in Texas.

When Texas seceded from the Union, Lee dutifully obeyed orders to return to Washington. The Lincoln administration offered him the command of Union forces at the outbreak of the Civil War. After much soul searching, Lee turned down that offer, resigned his commission, and was given command of the Virginia Militia. Within a short time he became brigadier general in the new confederate army.

He led his troops to many victories. The Union's forces, however, were considerably larger and better equipped, and defeated the Confederacy. On April 9, 1865, Lee surrendered to General Grant at Appomattox Court House.

His later years were spent as president of Washington College in Lexington, Virginia, where he distinguished himself as a respected, able college administrator. After his death, the college was renamed Washington and Lee in his honor.

Robert E. Lee's reading was fairly typical of upper-class youths of his time. As an educated youngster, he read the ancient Greek and Latin writers Homer, Longinus, Tacitus, and Cicero.

He became so well-grounded in Latin that he never quite forgot the language, though he did not study it after he was seventeen. Later in life, he expressed deep regret that he had not pursued his classical course further. (Freeman, vol. 1, 36)

After completing his early schooling, Robert was not at all sure about what to do with his life, and certain books may have had a significant impact on his decision to enter the military. One was "Light-Horse" Harry Lee's *Memoirs of the War in the Southern Department of the United States,* which gave details of the Revolutionary War in the South. The second was a book by Judge William Johnson, *Sketches of the Life and Correspondence of Samuel Greene.* Johnson argued that Light-Horse Harry's book contained some inaccuracies. The third was *The Campaign of 1781 in the Carolinas* by Henry Lee the younger, which contained a defense of *Memoirs of the War.*

Lee biographer Douglas S. Freeman notes that the books were discussed at length by the Lees and that "an hereditary fondness for a career of arms was thereby strengthened in Robert" (Freeman, vol. 1, 37).

At West Point Robert excelled in French. French books about military strategy, especially that of Napoleon, were considered essential for those who would have leadership positions in the American army. One of Lee's most critical readings in French was Gourgaud's and Montholon's *Mémoires pour servir à l'histoire de France sous Napoleon, ecrits a Sainte-Hélène.* Other volumes included Napoleon's lengthy notes, some of the emperor's "most discerning observations on defensive war."

To manoeuver incessantly, without submitting to be driven back on the capital which it is meant to defend or shut up in an intrenched camp in the rear. (Freeman, vol. 1, 354)

Freeman speculates that this particular book had a lasting effect on Lee. "It is easy to trace the parallel," Freeman wrote, "between what Napoleon here advised and what Lee undertook in the campaign from the Rapidan to the James in 1864. Analogies between his operation and those of Napoleon in 1796 readily suggest themselves" (Freeman, vol. 1, 355).

In addition to studying Napoleon at West Point, Lee studied the American Revolution very carefully. He borrowed a number of books on the topic from the library including the lives of Benedict Arnold and Ethan Allen.

Lee did a great deal of independent study while at West Point. In the spring of 1828, for example, he withdrew fifty-two books from the library. They covered a wide field of subjects: navigation, travel, strategy, biography, and history. Books he borrowed and read on his own at that time include the French edition of Rousseau's *Confessions, Life of Paul Jones,* Hamilton's *Works,* Atkinson's *Navigation,* Ferguson's *Astronomy,* and Machiavelli's *Art of War.*

Throughout his career Lee continued to study. He read the Bible almost every day. He also read biography, history, military strategy, and other topics. Reports of his reading include the following works:

The *Iliad*

Goldsmith's *Rome*

A two-volume biography of Goethe

Goethe's *Faust*

Shakespeare

Macaulay's *England*

Dickens' *Bleak House*

The Vicar of Wakefield

Kane's *Arctic Expeditions*

Many anthologies of English poetry

Many issues of current literary magazines

Thomas A. Kempis' *Imitation of Christ*

In thanking the person who sent him a copy of the *Imitation,* he noted: "I have read some of your favourite chapters, & hope I may derive from the perusal of the book, the good you desire" (Sanborn, 303).

He rarely read much fiction, in fact he considered most of it narcotic. He read poetry, however, and remembered favorites, knowing "more poetry than most soldiers" (Freeman, vol. 1, 353).

While serving as president of Washington College, Lee impressed the faculty enormously with his knowledge. They were awed by his "familiarity with Latin and Greek, the literary classics, ancient and modern, and with French and Spanish, both language and literature" (Sanborn,

277–278). "It seemed to them that his knowledge was universal, for he was conversant in any department" (Sanborn, 278).

During his last days Lee read about the Franco-Prussian War, "and all his sympathies in that contest were with the French."

"No," he wrote a kinswoman, not long before Sedan, "I am not 'glad that the Prussians are succeeding.' They are prompted by ambition and a thirst for power. The French are defending their homes and country." In that he saw the struggle of his own Southland. (Freeman, vol. 4, 485)

The Bible remained a comfort to Lee until the end of his life. He stated that he preferred it to any other book. One time some English admirers sent him a beautiful edition of the Bible. Typical of Lee's regard for the scriptures was the response he wrote to their spokesman: "The Bible is a book in comparison with which all others in my eyes are of minor importance, & which in all my perplexities has never failed to give me light & strength" (Sanborn, 303).

On September 28, 1870, not long before his death, Lee arose early for morning prayers and read the Psalter for the day as was his practice. "Praise the Lord," the passage began. "Praised be the Lord out of Sion: who dwellest at Jerusalem," it ended (Freeman, vol. 4, 485).

The Psalter's lines for that evening were quite prophetic.

Though I walk in the midst of trouble, yet shalt thou refresh me: thou shalt stretch forth thy hand upon the furiousness of mine enemies, and thy right hand shall save me.

The Lord shall make good his loving kindness toward me: yea, thy mercy, O Lord, endureth for ever; despise not then the work of thine own hands. (Freeman, vol. 4, 485–486)

IMPORTANT DATES IN ROBERT E. LEE'S LIFE

1807   Born in Stratford, Virginia.

1825   Entered West Point.

1829   Graduated from West Point second in his class.

1834   Appointed assistant to chief engineer of United States Army.

1847   Made lieutenant colonel in Mexican War.

1852   Became Superintendent at West Point.

1856   Began service on frontier duty in Texas.

1861   Appointed chief of Virginia forces.

1865   Elected president of Washington College.

1870   Died in Lexington, Virginia.

SOURCES

Connelly, Thomas L. *The Marble Man: Robert E. Lee and His Image in American Society*. New York: Knopf, 1977.

Freeman, Douglas Southall. *R. E. Lee: A Biography*, 4 vols. (The Pulitzer Prize Edition). New York: Charles Scribner's Sons, 1948.

Lee, Robert Edward. *Recollections and Letters of General Robert E. Lee by His Son Capt. Robert E. Lee*. 2nd ed. Garden City, N.Y.: Doubleday, Page, and Co., 1924.

Sanborn, Margaret. *Robert E. Lee: The Complete Man [1861; 1870]*. Philadelphia: J. B. Lippincott Co., 1967.

Thomas, Emory M. *Robert E. Lee: A Biography*. New York: W. W. Norton & Co., 1995.

DOUGLAS MACARTHUR (1880–1964)

Douglas MacArthur, the general who commanded American troops in the Pacific during World War II, is considered by many historians to be the greatest American military strategist of the century. Lloyd J. Graybar, for example, wrote the he "had a greater impact on American military history than virtually any other officer in the twentieth century" (Graybar, 1425). William Manchester argued that he was "the only allied general who had proved that he knew how to fight the Japanese" (Manchester, 250).

MacArthur was also a great reader, perhaps the best read of any American military leader in modern history. Even in the midst of battle, he always had his books with him, for learning, to get ideas for his communiques and speeches, and for relaxation.

He was also a man of many paradoxes, controversial, temperamental, imperious. He won many honors, but also was cited for insubordination on a number of occasions. He never went to church himself, but he read the Bible every day, and considered himself one of the two greatest defenders of Christianity, the other being the Pope.

As commander of the American military occupation of Japan after the war, he introduced democratic reforms, including women's rights, civil liberties, labor unions, and land reform. Back home he became the darling of far right reactionaries.

Unlike most great military leaders, he quarreled bitterly and sometimes publicly with the Joint Chiefs of Staff, President Truman, General Eisenhower, and others. At the Republican National Convention, he unsuccessfully tried to deny Eisenhower the nomination for president.

Douglas MacArthur was born at an army post in Little Rock, Arkansas, on January 26, 1880. He was the son of Captain Arthur MacArthur and Mary Pinckney "Pinky" Hardy MacArthur.

In 1903 he graduated from the United States Military Academy at West Point, New York. He finished at the top of his class.

For the next half century, he pursued an illustrious military career. He served as an officer in France during World War I. For his heroic exploits there he was awarded a Distinguished Service Medal and two Purple Hearts.

He served as superintendent of West Point; military adviser to the Philippines; commander of the United States Army Forces in the Far East during World War II; and Supreme Commander Allied Powers, conducting the surrender of the Japanese and overseeing the occupation of Japan.

He undoubtedly would have liked to have been elected president of the United States. That goal eluded him in part because his controversial opinions and positions had made him a number of powerful enemies.

In his later years MacArthur lived quietly in New York and served as chairman of the board of Remington Rand. He made few public appearances.

Douglas MacArthur was born into a "bookish" home. He had little formal schooling. His mother "Pinky" tutored him using the many books in the family library.

His soldier father Arthur MacArthur was a self-educated man who had earned a law degree. He considered "reading (and talking) on all subjects the most delightful form of occupation," just as his son Douglas would when he was grown (Lee and Henschel, 9).

Arthur bought many books, trunks full, and had them sent to the base where he was serving at the time. Eventually, he built up a large private library of more than four thousand books, which Douglas inherited. The family library, of much importantance for young Douglas, was especially rich in American and British history and Chinese culture.

According to biographer William Manchester, Douglas' father and his father's library were important in providing Douglas with "a remarkable vocabulary, a mastery of Victorian prose, a love of neo-Augustan rhetoric, and a ready grasp of theory" (Manchester, 23).

During his teens MacArthur attended West Texas Military Academy. His time there proved to be significant in his intellectual development. In his *Reminiscences*, he wrote:

There came a desire to know, a seeking for the reason why, a search for the truth. Abstruse mathematics began to appear as a challenge to analysis, dull Latin and Greek seemed a gateway to the moving words of the leaders of the past. . . . Biblical lessons began to open the spiritual portals of a growing faith, literature to lay bare the souls of men. (MacArthur, 17)

Douglas' ability to read fast and his phenomenally good memory would serve him well throughout his life. Occasionally, however, it provided humor. In his *Reminiscences*, MacArthur tells the story of an event that took place at West Point when students were struggling with Einstein's theory of relativity.

The text was complex and, being unable to comprehend it, I committed the pages to memory. When I was called upon to recite, I solemnly reeled off almost word for word what the book said. Our instructor, Colonel Feiberger, looked at me somewhat quizzically and asked, "Do you understand this theory?" It was a bad moment for me, but I did not hesitate in replying, "No, sir." . . . And then the slow words of the professor, "Neither do I, Mister MacArthur. Section dismissed." I still do not understand the theory. (MacArthur, 27)

As a military leader, MacArthur had to read many official reports. But he also read a great deal of history, biography, anthropology, and American, British, and European fiction. He developed a lifelong habit of reading official and non-official materials before going to sleep at night, a habit cultivated by many famous, and many not-so-famous people.

Throughout his career, his fantastic memory enabled him to quote from the Bible and various classics when expounding upon a particular idea. In 1928, for example, he led the American contingent to the Olympic Games and reported to Calvin Coolidge on his leadership of the team. It was not a dry kind of communiqué typical of most officials. Instead MacArthur's stirring note reflected his knowledge of the classics.

In undertaking the difficult task, I recall the passage in Plutarch wherein Themistocles, being asked whether he would rather be Achilles or Homer, replied, "Which would you rather be, a conqueror in the Olympic Games or the crier who proclaims who are conquerors?" And indeed to portray adequately the vividness and brilliance of that great spectacle would be worthy even of the pen of Homer himself. (Lee and Henschel, 93)

On one occasion, before speaking against pacifism, he spent long evenings reading about the pacifist movement. He thought pacifism was wrong and wanted to understand it better before speaking about it. Such preparation was typical for MacArthur.

MacArthur married his second wife, Jean Marie Faircloth, in 1937. They spent their evenings reading or at the movies. (MacArthur loved movies as well as books.) Jean, a Southerner, encouraged his reading about Southern military heroes, apparently feeling such books would inspire him in his own military career. She frequently gave him biographies of Confederate generals. "These included Douglas S. Freeman's four-volume life of Lee; G.F.R. Henderson's two volumes on Stonewall Jackson; and J. A. Wyeth's *Nathan Bedford Forrest*" (Manchester, 177).

And MacArthur gladly read them. Being a speed reader, he could read three books in a day. Sitting in his favorite rocking chair he would also read many magazines and newspapers.

On various occasions book knowledge probably helped MacArthur in his battle plans. He had carefully studied *The Valor of Ignorance* written by John Lea in 1909. The book detailed previous campaigns in the Philippines. According to Willoughby and Chamberlain, MacArthur's knowledge of Lea's work helped him in "the long six-month struggle to hold Bataan and Corregidor, which saved the day until Allied defenses could be reorganized in Australia" (Willoughby and Chamberlain, 17).

Dostoevski's *Crime and Punishment* was perhaps MacArthur's favorite book. In the novel the police inspector Porfiry understood the conflicts and thought patterns of the mind of the murderer Raskolnikov. It was Porfiry's knowledge of Raskolnikov which eventually led to the undoing of the latter. Similarly, MacArthur understood the minds of his Japanese opponents better than other military commanders, and tried to make a "mental leap" to understanding what a Japanese general was planning (Manchester, 324).

While stationed in New Guinea during World War II, MacArthur lived in a bungalow previously occupied by a highly literate tenant. The shelves were packed with books. Unless preoccupied with battle reports, he would walk back and forth with a book open in his left hand. He read about Papuan aborigines, anthropology, and native lore. He also read the works of Zola, Shaw, Ibsen, and others. He used phrases from "this cultural smorgasbord" in communiqués he dictated each morning (Manchester, 324).

A lifelong student of the Bible, MacArthur was convinced that the Japanese would convert to Christianity and needed Bibles to assist in the process. He began a gigantic fund-raising drive, asked for support from Bible societies, and used military transport ships to carry millions of Bibles to Japan.

The effort to Christianize the country was not successful. The Japanese were not ripe for conversion. It provides, however, an illustration of MacArthur's belief in the power of the printed word. Probably the general never knew that many Japanese accepted the Bibles because the paper was an inexpensive substitute for black market cigarette paper which was much more expensive (See James, vol. 3, 290–291).

After being recalled from Japan because of serious policy disagreements with President Truman, MacArthur traveled the country making speeches. He often referred to or quoted various literary sources. As he had done throughout his career, he could aptly quote Napoleon, Lincoln, Plato, and the scriptures.

His understanding and use of language was unsurpassed. Appearing before congressional bodies after his recall to the United States, MacArthur never needed notes. He displayed a huge knowledge of history and culture. In answer to a single question he might cite the Caesars, medieval customs, the Magna Carta, Ireland's potato famines, and the French Revolution. His delivery was also dramatic and most effective. Senators were equally impressed by his talking and "acting" as well as by the content of his remarks.

His speech before the joint session of Congress in 1951 was especially memorable. He worked on it for a long time. He spoke mostly about Asia. His lifetime study of the Asiatic world paid off. He showed a phenomenal grasp of the history and culture of the Far East. The speech was a brilliant oratorical triumph. "None of the millions who saw him on television or heard him on the radio is likely to forget the tremendous emotional impact of his closing lines" (Lee and Henschel, 91).

MacArthur quoted a line from an old army ballad on several occasions.

> Old soldiers never die. They just fade away.

His speech was so effective, "legislators were sobbing their praise, struggling to touch his sleeve, all but prostrating themselves in his path" (Manchester, 661).

Unquestionably, MacArthur was a great reader. He remembered what he had read and used such knowledge brilliantly in his leadership.

IMPORTANT DATES IN DOUGLAS MacARTHUR'S LIFE

1880   Born in Little Rock, Arkansas.

1903   Graduated from West Point first in his class.

1905   Undertook a lengthy tour of the Far East with his parents.

1918   Fought in France. Decorated nine times for heroism.

1919   Became superintendent of West Point.

1925   Promoted to Major General, the youngest man to hold that rank at that time.

1936   Became Philippine Field Marshall.

1937   Married his second wife Jean Marie Faircloth.

1941   Given command of the United States Army Forces Far East.

1942   Bataan fell to superior Japanese forces. MacArthur proclaimed, "I shall return," and he became an American military hero. Awarded Congressional Medal of Honor.

1944   Made a five-star general.

1945   Designated Supreme Commander, Allied Powers (SCAP) by President Truman. Japanese surrendered to MacArthur on the battleship *Missouri*. Commanded the Allied occupation of Japan.

1951   Relieved of his command by President Truman after his public criticism of U.S. policies on limiting the war in Korea.

1952	Delivered keynote address at the Republican National Convention. Attempted unsuccessfully to deprive Dwight Eisenhower of the presidential nomination.
1961	MacArthurs made a sentimental tour of the Philippines.
1964	Died at Walter Reed Hospital. Entombed in Norfolk, Virginia.

SOURCES

Graybar, Lloyd J. "Douglas MacArthur," in *Great Lives from History: American Series*, vol. 3, Frank N. Magill, ed. Pasadena, Calif.: Salem Press, 1987.

James, D. Clayton. *The Years of MacArthur*, 3 vols. Boston: Houghton Mifflin, 1985.

Lee, Clark, and Richard Henschel. *MacArthur*. New York: Henry Holt and Co., 1952.

MacArthur, Douglas. *Reminiscences*. New York: McGraw-Hill, 1964.

Manchester, William. *American Caesar: Douglas MacArthur 1880–1964*. Boston: Little, Brown and Co., 1978.

Schaller, Michael. *Douglas MacArthur: The Far Eastern General*. New York: Oxford University Press, 1989.

Willoughby, Charles A., and John Chamberlain. *MacArthur: 1941–1951*. New York: McGraw-Hill, 1954.

MADONNA
(1958–)

Madonna is one of the world's top entertainers, talented, beautiful, controversial star of videos and movies. She is also considered one of the hardest working and most disciplined of performers. A shrewd businesswoman, Madonna is one of the richest women in show business.

Madonna Louise Veronica Ciccone was born in Bay City, Michigan, on August 16, 1958. She was brought up in a traditional family, headed by a father who was a strict disciplinarian. Although she loved him, she sometimes resented him as she resented the nuns in the Catholic grade schools who were also very strict. Although a rebel in school, Madonna got good grades in both grade school and in the public high school she attended, usually A's. Her father gave her a quarter for every A she received. Being paid for achievement "trained her to become competitive at an early age" (Bego, 18).

Madonna loved movies and pop music. Like many other young girls she wanted to be a movie star. She couldn't imagine, however, how someone from a "hick town" as she was could do so.

Madonna started taking ballet lessons when she was a teenager. With very high grades in high school and her dance training, she received a dance scholarship from the University of Michigan and enrolled in 1976. She didn't stay there long, however. She soon dropped out of the university and went to New York to pursue her dream of becoming a professional entertainer. Early years in New York were hard. She lived hand to mouth. "At one point," she said, "I was living in New York and eating out of garbage cans in the street" (Bego, 64).

Most would-be stars would have given up and gone home, but not Madonna. She persisted, making a living modeling, frequently nude, got a part in an underground movie, appeared with rock groups, danced, and in a year or so achieved some note as a performer in New York clubs.

She made her debut album *Madonna* in 1983. One song on the album "Holiday" became a smash hit.

From that time Madonna made numerous hit albums and appeared in a number of movies. Probably her most successful movie role was that of Eva Peron in the 1996 film version of Andrew Lloyd Webber's opera *Evita* for which she received the Golden Globe Award as best actress.

Since becoming famous and wealthy, Madonna has become one of the foremost advocates for people with AIDS. Of entertainers probably only Elizabeth Taylor has done more than Madonna to raise money for AIDS research and to fight discrimination against people with the dreaded disease.

As a teenager, Madonna spent hours reading magazines, such as *Seventeen* and *Glamour*. From the magazines she got ideas on clothes and how to show off her figure, which was unusually well developed for her age.

They gave her the sweater idea, a way to brighten up her school uniform by wearing hot pink, purple, and orange sweaters. She was never frightened of others laughing at her or jeering at her. (Thompson, 49)

In her studies Madonna excelled in poetry, French, and drama. In high school she helped found the drama club, the Rochester Adams High School Thespian Society. She became its star, playing the lead in student productions, including *Cinderella*, *The Wizard of Oz*, *Godspell*, and *My Fair Lady*. When she graduated, she got the school's Thespian Award.

The University of Michigan was noted for being a party school. While there Madonna partied as much as many other students, going frequently to local clubs with her friends.

Another side of Madonna, however, was also visible at the U. of M. She spent much of her time reading poetry, especially serious, philosophical works. She "devoured the dark poetry of Sylvia Plath and Anne Sexton" (Andersen, 51). Both Plath and Sexton were very popular at the time, especially with college students and other young people who were unhappy with all the rules and regulations imposed upon them by what they considered an unfair, old-fashioned society.

Reflections of some of the nonconventional and sombre ideas expressed by such writers can be seen in Madonna's own personal philosophy. Plath, for example, had written:

I couldn't stand the idea of a woman having to have a single pure life and a man being able to have a double life, one pure and one not.

Finally I decided that if it was so difficult to find a red-blooded intelligent man who was still pure by the time he was twenty-one I might as well forget about staying pure myself and marry somebody who wasn't pure either. Then when he started to make my life miserable I could make his miserable as well. (Bloom, 125)

In her personal appearances and videos, Madonna's attitudes towards women and sexuality are quite clear. She is noted as showing herself as at least an equal to the men she dances with and sometimes as a woman dominating them, never as a female victim.

Madonna's assertiveness is also apparent in her attitude towards Marilyn Monroe. She idolized Marilyn and sometimes appeared as Monroe in photos and in personal appearances. She found ways "to pay homage to the ill-fated sex goddess." Madonna, however, is much stronger than Marilyn, who committed suicide at the age of thirty-six. " 'I'm not Marilyn,' she has said again and again. 'I love my life, I'm in control, I'm not a victim' " (Andersen, 333).

Madonna met the actor Sean Penn in 1985. They became constant companions and in time wed. Although they eventually divorced, they were very close while their marriage lasted. One thing that impressed Madonna about Penn was his considerable knowledge of serious literature. She thought he was a real intellectual.

She delved deeply into a number of the writers with whom Penn was so familiar, and in conversations with her friends she showed she had really been studying their works. These included the great classic European writers Guy DeMaupassant, Honoré de Balzac, and Rainer Maria Rilke. She also studied modern American writers who wrote about the problems of youth and the disaffected: James Agee, Jack Kerouac, and J. D. Salinger.

In interviews Madonna frequently mentions books and authors whom she especially likes. She adored *The Sheltering Sky*, but hated the movie, "even taking its heroine's name as a temporary alias." She thought *Naked by the Window* and *Giovanni's Room* by James Baldwin "sufficiently compelling" to recommend them to an interviewer and to think of "optioning them for film projects" (Rettenmund, 25–26).

She once noted that "the author whose writing most reflects her sensibilities" was J. D. Salinger. An erotic book which she most enjoyed was Marguerite Duras' *The Lover*—the story of a teacher and his prepubescent conquest.

Other writers Madonna has mentioned as favorites include Lawrence Durrell, Louise Erdrich, F. Scott Fitzgerald, Ernest Hemingway, Henry James, D. H. Lawrence, Thomas Mann, Françoise Sagan, Anne Tyler, Kurt Vonnegut, Jr., and Alice Walker (see Rettenmund, 25–26).

As an actress, Madonna became noted for persistence in getting the roles she wanted and for preparing very carefully by reading and studying for those role. For example, in 1988 when Madonna was already a noted video star, she unexpectedly got a chance to star in a Broadway production of *Speed the Plow* written by the famous playwright David Mamet.

She had admired Mamet's work for years. She enjoyed *Glengarry Glen Ross*, and when she saw his film *House of Cards*, she decided he was a genius and knew that she "had to work with this man" (Thompson, 180).

Madonna carefully studied for the audition. It went well for Madonna, and she got the part even though numerous actors, some well known, had competed for the role.

There were six weeks of rehearsals, and Madonna's discipline paid off. Fellow actor Ron Silver, impressed with Madonna's hard work and serious attitude, said she was "the first one to know her lines—a professional" (Thompson, 181).

For years Madonna had dreamed of playing Eva Peron in the film version of Andrew Lloyd Webber's *Evita*. She had absolutely no assurance that she would ever get the part since a number of established movie stars also coveted the role. But she was convinced that she was the only person who could play Eva Peron the way the role should be played.

She studied assiduously for the role. She read volumes of literature about Eva Peron and about the Argentina of her time and, of course, studied the role for years. When the time came for her to read for the part, she was very nervous. But Webber and his colleagues were impressed, and she got the part. The rest is history. Many did not believe Madonna had the particular talent or vocal range to play Evita. The movie became a hit, and Madonna received excellent reviews for her acting and singing.

Although Madonna has often been controversial for her freewheeling, unconventional lifestyle and outspokenness, she also must be admired. She came from a poor background in a small town in the Midwest. Through hard work and persistence as well as talent, she has become one of the top performers of our time.

Reports on Madonna's reading interests indicate that they are quite varied, ranging from classic to modern writers. As might be expected for a controversial person like herself, a number of her favorite authors wrote controversial stories, often about the dispossessed. They include J. D. Salinger, Sylvia Plath, Louise Erdrich, Anne Sexton, and D. H. Lawrence.

IMPORTANT DATES IN MADONNA'S LIFE

1958   Born in Bay City, Michigan.

1976   Student at the University of Michigan.

1978   Arrived in New York. Worked for several years as a model and performer.

1979   Appeared in her first movie, an underground art film *A Certain Sacrifice*.

1983   Made *Madonna*, her debut album; since has had numerous hits.

1985   Married Sean Penn. Divorced, 1989.

1987   Made Broadway debut in *Speed the Plow*.

1992   Published the controversial, erotic book, *Sex*.

1996   Starred in film *Evita* for which she received the Golden Globe Award for best actress.

1999 Received three Grammy Awards for her recording *Ray of Light*: Best Dance Recording, Best Pop Album, and Best Short Form Music Video.

SOURCES

Andersen, Christopher. *Madonna Unauthorized*. New York: Simon & Schuster, 1991.

Bego, Mark. *Madonna: Blonde Ambition*. New York: Harmony, 1992.

Bloom, Harold, ed. *Modern Critical Views: Sylvia Plath*. New York: Chelsea House, 1989.

Rettenmund, Matthew. *Encyclopedia Madonnica*. New York: St. Martin's Press, 1995.

Robertson, Pamela. *Guilty Pleasures: Feminist Camp from Mae West to Madonna*. Durham, N.C.: Duke University Press, 1996.

Sexton, Adam, ed. *Desperately Seeking Madonna: In Search of the Meaning of the World's Most Famous Woman*. New York: Delta, 1993.

Thompson, Douglas. *Madonna Revealed*. New York: Leisure Books, 1992.

HORACE MANN
(1796–1859)

Horace Mann initiated the first comprehensive system of public education in the United States and also began the first state mental hospital in the nation. He believed in the value of reading for himself and advised others to read for their own self-improvement.

Horace Mann was born in Franklin, Massachusetts, on May 4, 1796, the fourth of five children. It was one of many American towns, probably the first, named after the great patriot Benjamin Franklin.

Horace's childhood was an unhappy one. His strongest memories of his early life were of working from dawn until dusk on the family farm. Even in the wintertime, when farm chores were done, there was no rest at all. Family members labored long hours at the tedious task of braiding straw for an industry that had sprung up in Franklin. Straw hats were made for ladies and were shipped for sales to Boston, New York, Providence, and elsewhere.

Horace was also frequently required to attend a church where the most gloomy Calvinist doctrines were preached. At the age of twelve he rejected those frightening beliefs and began to build up a more benevolent interpretation of Christianity by which he could live.

His education was sporadic. As a youngster, he never attended school for more than eight or ten weeks a year. In 1816, however, he carefully prepared for college, was admitted to Brown University, and in three years graduated with honors. He then studied law and was admitted to practice in 1825. Within a short time he was elected to the state legislature of Massachusetts.

Mann inspected prisons and jails, and was appalled by conditions in them, especially by the treatment of the mentally ill. As a result of his efforts, Massachusetts established the first state mental hospital in America.

After the creation of the state board of education, Mann gave up his political career and accepted the position of secretary of the board. He proved to be an excellent choice.

The Massachusetts school system had deteriorated badly due to lack of financial support and decentralized control. In his position as secretary of the board, Mann affected many improvements in public education. He did not have much power, but being a very persuasive leader, he was able to work a real revolution in education during his years as secretary.

He organized educational conferences, promoted the establishment of normal schools for the training of teachers, secured funds for salaries, new schools, and a minimum school year law. He also founded the *Common School Journal* and issued annual reports that had lasting influence on development of public schools throughout America.

In school Horace and the other children studied the *New England Primer*, which contained moral lessons as well as instruction in the alphabet. They were also required to memorize long sections of the *Westminster Assembly Shorter Catechism* and were frequently quizzed on their progress.

Mann was one of the brighter pupils. By the age of ten he was acquainted with the entire creed, and could answer questions about it with ease.

Ben Franklin decided to give a gift to Franklin, Massachusetts, apparently in appreciation for the citizens having named the town after him. According to one story, he first offered to donate a bell for the meeting house. Learning how serious the people were, however, he decided to give them a gift of books. He asked Reverend Richard Price of London to choose books to begin a library for the town. The collection consisted of 116 books, a fairly large number for the time. Many of the books were old histories and theologies of little interest to Mann and other children. Nonetheless, he plowed through their pages because he loved to read and there was little else available.

Mann's favorite work in the collection was a five-volume edition of *Gordon's Tacitus*. Although years later he deplored that fact that so many books glorified war, as a child, Horace was inspired by Tacitus, and made the stories his own.

He became a Roman of the Romans, conducting military campaigns against the weeds of the corn—making farming endurable because of the secret world of his imagination. (Tharp, 24)

One valuable lesson Horace learned from his parents was their love of learning and books. They revered learning and learned men and spoke of them "with enthusiasm and a kind of reverence" (Downs, 14).

The family taught Horace to take care of the few books they possessed as though they were sacred.

I never dog's-eared one in my life, nor profanely scribbled upon the title-pages, margin, or fly-leaf, and would as soon have stuck a pin through my flesh as through the pages of a book. (Downs, 14)

Mann's love of books was further fostered by Samuel Barrett, the itinerant alcoholic teacher who prepared him for Brown University. Barrett had a broad knowledge of the classics. Under him, Mann read Virgil, Cicero, the Bible, and other classical works.

The entrance examination at Brown consisted of reading accurately the classics, the Greek Testament, and writing Latin prose. He found the exam easy and passed it with flying colors.

In his professional publications, Mann wrote that many examples could be cited of ways in which noted people were influenced by reading.

Whoever has read modern biography, with a philosophic eye to the cause of the extraordinary characters it records, must have observed the frequent references that are made to some *book*, as turning the stream of life at some critical point in its course. In one of Dr. Franklin's letters, he says, that, when a boy, he met with a book entitled "Essays to do Good," which led to such a train of thinking, as had an influence on his conduct through life. (Filler, 62)

Mann also cited Sir Walter Scott as another example of the influence of reading. Scott had written repeatedly that his ability to write vividly about past times was due "to the books which he read when young" (Filler, 62).

A notorious character named Stephen Burroughs, however, according to Mann, began a life of ignominy after reading a particular book, *Guy, Earl of Warwick*: "Whoever looks deeper, sees that this ignominious life commenced when he was reading a pernicious book" (Filler, 62).

Mann recommended that good libraries be established throughout the land, and he noted the influence of libraries on the populace. He argued that towns in which good public libraries had been established had a population superior in intelligence to those which have no such libraries.

Mann's attitude towards books and libraries, although generally enlightened, was controversial by modern standards because he believed only "good" books, "serious" books should be made available. He saw little value, for example, in reading frivolous novels. He thought fiction and poetry were "inferior to scientific works" (Filler, xiv). He also deplored the fact that most books in libraries were written for adults and were not suitable for children. "With very few exceptions," he wrote, "the books were written for adults, for persons of some maturity of mind, and possessed already of a considerable fund of information" (Filler, 49).

He also was appalled that such a large proportion of books in libraries were histories of classical and modern periods containing information that he considered not suitable for the young. They so frequently glorified battles and massacres and "the destruction of human life." The books honored the men who had slaughtered the most people. Little mention was made of youth except as they are engaged in martial sports preparing them for "the grand tragedy of battle." Women were barely noted at all except when they graced "the triumphs of the conqueror" (Filler, 49).

Mann recommended that books be rewritten with children in mind, and that they be made widely available in libraries. He would have been pleased to have lived to see the phenomenal development of both public and school libraries that stock large collections of books suitable for the young.

After being appointed secretary of the new Massachusetts State Board of Education, Mann, knowing little about education, carefully studied the subject. His reading, as well as consultation with educational reformers, proved to him that schools were shabby, crowded, and small. Teachers were poorly paid and unprepared for their work. Talented teachers, such as Herman Melville and Henry David Thoreau, quit in disgust.

Appalled by the situation, he issued the first of his twelve annual reports on the state of education. The reports had great influence on the development of schools and libraries all over America.

Mann's love of books and libraries is apparent throughout his writings. He furthered his education by extensive reading, realized the value of reading, and recommended that people "read always."

Resolve to edge in a little reading every day, if it is but a single sentence. If you gain fifteen minutes a day, it will make itself felt at the end of the year. (Filler, 7)

IMPORTANT DATES IN HORACE MANN'S LIFE

1796   Born in Franklin, Massachusetts.

1819   Graduated from Brown University with honors.

1823   Admitted to the Massachusetts bar.

1827   Began serving in the Massachusetts House of Representatives.

1833   Elected to the Massachusetts Senate.

1837   Appointed secretary of the new Massachusetts State Board of Education. Issued the first of his twelve great annual reports on education.

1839   Established the first normal school for training teachers in the United States. Persuaded the Massachusetts legislature to establish a six-month minimum school year.

1848   Succeeded John Quincy Adams, who had just died, as Massachusetts representative in the United State House of Representatives where he strongly supported abolition of slavery.

1852   Appointed president of Antioch College.

1859   Died in Yellow Springs, Ohio.

SOURCES

Downs, Robert B. *Horace Mann: Champion of the Public Schools*. New York: Twayne Publishers, 1974.

Ellis, Robert P. "Horace Mann," in *Great Lives from History: American Series*, vol. 3, Frank N. Magill, ed. Pasadena, Calif.: Salem Press, 1987.

Filler, Louis, ed. *Horace Mann on the Crisis in Education.* Yellow Springs, Ohio: Antioch Press, 1965.

Messerli, Jonathan. *Horace Mann: A Biography.* New York: Knopf, 1972.

Tharp, Louise Hall. *Until Victory: Horace Mann and Mary Peabody.* Boston: Little, Brown and Co., 1953.

Williams, Edward I. F. *Horace Mann: Educational Statesman.* New York: Macmillan, 1937.

MARILYN MONROE
(1926–1962)

Marilyn Monroe is considered one of the greatest of all movie stars. Even though her career was relatively short, she became a lasting film icon. Graham McCann, in his biography of the star, noted that her influence on popular culture remains immense, "her image, her performance, her personality, her style, her secrets, her story" (McCann, 8).

The biography of Monroe in the *Encyclopedia of Hollywood* also contains the claim that her impact was enormous. Every studio in Hollywood tried to come up with their own version of the bosomy, blonde star. None, however, reached the heights of popularity achieved by Monroe. "Decades after her death she remains among Hollywood's most enduring and compelling screen personalities." (Siegel and Siegel, 289).

Marilyn Monroe had little education and always regretted she had not been encouraged to read as a child. To make up for that lack, she read a great deal after growing up.

Norma Jeane Mortenson (or Baker) was born in or near Los Angeles on June 1, 1926, to the then unmarried Gladys Mortenson who worked as a film cutter. Not long after Norma Jeane's birth, Gladys suffered a mental breakdown and was hospitalized. Little is known about her father, but Norma Jeane often dreamed that he resembled Clark Gable, one of her favorite movie actors.

Norma Jeane was brought up in a series of foster homes, perhaps as many as twelve, and she at one time resided in an orphanage. She attended a number of different public schools. Not being especially interested in academics, her school record was unimpressive.

At the age of sixteen, she married James Dougherty. It seems that one reason for the marriage was that Norma Jeane did not want to return to an orphanage or to another set of foster parents.

Already having the physical opulence that would make her famous, Norma Jeane worked as a photographer's model and appeared on the covers of several men's magazines. As a result, she received bids to appear in movies.

After taking the name Marilyn Monroe, she appeared briefly in several films. Her roles in *Asphalt Jungle* and *All About Eve* were minor, but she made a great hit with the public and received a huge amount of fan mail.

Within a short time she became one of Hollywood's biggest stars. She appeared in numerous films, often in sexy, dumb blonde roles. Desiring more serious material, she got kudos for her dramatic ability in such movies as *The Seven Year Itch, Some Like It Hot,* and *Bus Stop.*

Marilyn Monroe died an untimely death at the age of thirty-six of a drug overdose, probably suicide. Conspiracy rumors have persisted, however, and some believe that she may have been the victim of foul play.

Monroe became even more popular and more famous after her death. Years later she remains one of the most famous and most beloved movie stars of all time.

During her childhood, Norma Jeane was not encouraged to read, and consequently read very little, but she saw many, many movies and became fascinated with the film world of make believe. Before she was eight years old, she came to the attention of a rather off-beat woman named Grace McKee who worked in the production section of the movie industry and worshipped the movies. McKee became a mother figure for Norma Jeane. According to David Spoto, she became "the most important influence in Norma Jeane's life." "Without McKee," he wrote, "there might never have been a Marilyn Monroe" (Spoto, 34).

Childless herself, McKee lavished gifts and pretty clothes on the beautiful child. She also taught her how to dress, how to walk, and even how to smile and pout like Mary Pickford.

McKee frequently took Norma Jeane to the movies. They would often attend the early evening premieres. Like the other people in the crowd, they would wildly applaud the stars they adored. McKee constantly told Norma Jeane that she would become a great movie star. She would be as great or greater than Jean Harlow, who was McKee's idol.

Years later, Marilyn Monroe, attempting to improve herself, became an avid reader. She often read very serious, classic material, and people were surprised about her choices of writers. One time the director Joseph Mankiewicz found Monroe reading Rilke's *Letters to a Young Poet*. He asked her how she decided to read the work by the famous writer. Monroe responded:

I was never told what to read, and nobody ever gave me anything to read. You know—the way there are certain books that everybody reads while they're growing up? ... So what I do is—nights when I've got nothing else to do I go to the Pickwick bookstore on Hollywood Boulevard. And I just open books at random—or when I come to a page or a paragraph I like, I buy that book. So last night I bought this one. Is that wrong? (McCann, 44)

Mankiewicz told her it was not wrong, and that "there was no better way to select books for reading" (McCann, 44).

Marilyn also read when traveling. In hotel rooms at night before going to sleep, she would often read Proust, Thomas Wolfe, Freud, Dostoevski, and other famous writers. She took books by such authors to movie sets where she played dumb blondes. She built up a personal library filled with the classics.

She also studied Andreas Vesalius' *De Humani Corporis Fabrica,* a work about human bone structure. She marked many passages in the book, developed an encyclopedic knowledge of bone structure, and often instructed young friends on the topic.

Monroe was one of the first joggers in Hollywood, working to improve her physical fitness. She carefully studied *The Thinking Body* by Mabel Elsworth Todd, a book which "attempted to situate the body within the continuum of human psychology and physiology" (McCann, 44).

Marilyn also loved poetry. A friend, Norman Rosten, reported that she thought poetry went right to the heart of experience. He sent her a book of poetry, and she wrote him that she was touched by it and "spent all Sunday morning in bed" with the book (Summers, 152). Marilyn also attended the poetry reading sessions sponsored by Rosten. She enjoyed listening to others and reading herself (Summers, 152 and 153).

Walt Whitman had been a favorite of Marilyn's for a number of years. She loved his poems, which glorified common people, the type of people with whom she herself, being poor as a child, identified.

William Butler Yeats became another favorite. Rosten remembered her reading aloud a selection of Yeats with great feeling:

> For everything that's lovely is
> But a brief, dreamy, kind delight.
> O never give the heart outright . . .

When she had finished, Rosten noted:

[T]here was in the room almost a reverential hush no one dared interrupt. There seemed to be a tacit understanding not only of Yeats's wisdom but of the words' aptness for her who had just read them. (Spoto, 335)

Marilyn also wrote poetry. Some of her poems were serious, and others were just witty, funny little ditties.

Monroe's heavy reading was of concern to producers. They feared that if she came to be seen as an intellectual, it might hurt her popularity as a sex goddess.

Her reading has been the subject of derision by a number of writers and celebrities. McCann notes that the literature is filled with claims that Marilyn was simply a "dumb blonde" trying to impress people with her reading. He concluded, however, that "there is little evidence" to support such claims (McCann, 45).

Jack Paar, for example, a minor television and movie star, called her reading "pathetic." He claimed she only wanted to impress people by reading authors such as Proust. He argued she would have been better off to read simple materials such as *Little Women* and *Treasure Island* (McCann, 45).

It is reported that Frank Sinatra often shouted at her in public. "Shut up, Norma Jean. You're so stupid you don't know what you're talking about" (McCann, 50).

Even Marilyn's second husband, Joe DiMaggio, who apparently was deeply in love with her, did not understand her love of literature, a love he did not share. He was fascinated by television and comic books.

On one occasion Marilyn gave Joe a gold medal for his watch chain inscribed with a quotation from Saint Exupery's classic *The Little Prince*: "True love is visible not to the eyes, but to the heart, for eyes may be deceived." DiMaggio's response was, "What the hell does that mean?" (McCann, 46).

Such reactions were probably due, at least in part, to misogyny. Could a famous star, noted for her feminine voluptuousness, really be interested in improving her mind by reading serious literature? A number of people who knew Monroe personally argued that she was a very bright, witty woman whose reading was genuine and that she succeeded at least partially in educating herself.

Her third husband, Arthur Miller, noted that Marilyn did not always read a book through. He claimed, however, she had an uncanny ability to absorb the essence of an author's message.

Miller also recommended books to Marilyn. Monroe had long idolized Abraham Lincoln. Miller encouraged her to read Carl Sandburg's biography of that great president. She bought a copy of it, as well as a framed portrait of Lincoln, and kept them for the rest of her life.

Clifton Webb wrote that Marilyn was a very sweet and serious woman who read all the time. Eleanor Powell claimed that Marilyn was not at all like the "sex pots" she portrayed on the screen, but was an intelligent person and a fine actress. Before her last illness, Monroe was being considered for very serious dramatic parts, including Sadie Thompson in Somerset Maugham's *Rain*. Also, John Huston thought of casting her in Jean-Paul Sartre's screenplay *Freud*. Sartre, "a great cinefile," argued that she was one of the period's greatest actresses. Saul Bellow described her as "a very witty woman" (McCann, 50).

Monroe was proud of her attempts to improve her mind, to acquire culture and education. On one occasion she was asked if she realized that she was born under the same sign as Judy Garland, Rosalind Russell, and Rosemary Clooney. Chagrined, Monroe replied almost haughtily that she knew very little about those people, but that "she shared her sign with Emerson, Whitman, Bernard Shaw, and Queen Victoria" (Wagenknecht, 184).

Monroe was also able to wittily poke fun at herself when she appeared to be too serious. At a New York press conference, for example, she discussed her plans to make more serious movies, including her hope to play Grushenka in a film of Dostoevski's *The Brothers Karamazov*. When reporters ridiculed her, she disarmed them by responding, "Honey, I couldn't spell any of the names I told you" (Steinem, 174). On another occasion Monroe was asked if she spoke any foreign languages. She smiled and said she could hardly speak English!

Marilyn Monroe provides a good example of the importance of reading for young people. Even though one of the world's most famous celebrities, she felt incomplete because she had not developed her mind. She therefore undertook a serious program of reading at home, at the studio, and while traveling. She succeeded partially in her efforts to improve her understanding of herself and the world around her and would undoubtedly have made much more progress if she had not died at such an early age.

In her 1986 book, Gloria Steinem speculated on who Norma Jeane / Marilyn would have become had she lived into an era when women were beginning to be valued for their minds and hearts as well as "the bodies that house them." Noting the wide variety of interests Marilyn had developed, Steinem wrote:

A student, lawyer, teacher, artist, mother, grandmother, defender of animals, rancher, homemaker, sportswoman, rescuer of children—all these are futures we can imagine for Norma Jeane. . . . One also can imagine the whole woman who was both Norma Jeane and Marilyn becoming a serious actress and wise comedienne who would still be working in her sixties, with more productive years to come. (Steinem, 180)

IMPORTANT DATES IN MARILYN MONROE'S LIFE

1926   Born in Los Angeles.

1950   Appeared in *Asphalt Jungle* and *All About Eve*. Although the roles were small, she became phenomenally popular with fans.

1952–1953   Starred in *Niagara, How to Marry a Millionaire,* and *Gentlemen Prefer Blondes* proving she could do more than just look sexy and beautiful. She could sing, dance, and showed great comedic talent.

1954   Married Joe DiMaggio, the great baseball hero. The two were among the most adored personalities of the century. Their marriage was stormy, however, and lasted less than a year.

1956   Married America's leading playwright Arthur Miller. Gave a powerful dramatic performance as an aspiring entertainer in *Bus Stop*.

1956   Wishing to become a more serious actress, Monroe began attending sessions at New York's Actors Studio.

1959   *Some Like It Hot* in which she starred was released. It was one of the most popular movies of the decade, and her acting received very good reviews.

1962   Died in Los Angeles, possibly suicide.

SOURCES

Leaming, Barbara. *Marilyn Monroe.* New York: Crown Publishers, 1998.

McCann, Graham. *Marilyn Monroe.* New Brunswick, N.J.: Rutgers University Press, 1987.

Mailer, Norman. *Marilyn: A Biography.* New York: Grossett and Dunlap, 1973.

Maltin, Leonard. *Leonard Maltin's Movie Encyclopedia.* New York: 0Dutton, 1994.

Siegel, Scott, and Barbara Siegel. *The Encyclopedia of Hollywood.* New York: Facts on File, 1990.

Spoto, Donald. *Marilyn Monroe: The Biography.* New York: HarperCollins, 1993.

Steinem, Gloria. *Marilyn.* New York: Henry Holt and Co., 1986.

Summers, Anthony. *Goddess: The Secret Life of Marilyn Monroe.* New York: New American Library, 1985, 1986.

Wagenknecht, Edward. *Marilyn Monroe: A Composite View.* Philadelphia: Chilton Book Company, 1969.

MARTINA NAVRATILOVA
(1956–)

Martina Navratilova is considered one of the greatest women tennis players of all time, and one of the greatest of modern female athletes. In addition to her accomplishments in sports, as noted in the *Biographical Dictionary of American Sports*, Martina is one of the most friendly, cordial, and articulate of athletes, an inspiration, especially, "for all contemporary and future immigrants to the United States" (Porter, 382).

A native of Czechoslovakia, Martina defected to the United States in 1975. She became an American citizen in 1981.

Martina was born in Prague on October 18, 1956. Her stepfather was an economist, and the family was prosperous enough to take a vacation and go skiing every year. "Some people would even go to the ocean and we'd say, 'Gee, how did they afford that?'" (Navratilova with Vecsey, 60).

Her parents were very independent, refusing to join the Communist party. Martina said she probably picked up some of her attitudes of independence from them.

She began playing tennis in her native land, and proved to be exceptionally good. In 1973 she won the Czechoslovak National Championship. From then until her retirement from professional tennis she won a phenomenal number of tennis tournaments all over the world.

Martina has written her memoirs and successful mystery novels, which have a setting in the tennis world.

Rumors about her sexual preference have persisted for years. Finally, Martina announced that she was attracted to both men and women. Since then she has been one of the most effective spokespersons for the rights of gays and lesbians and has used her fame to fight discrimination against people with AIDS.

She has not regretted her decision to "come out" as a lesbian. The announcement has had a downside, however. She has not been offered the lucrative contracts for endorsing sports equipment that one would expect for such a famous athlete.

Martina was always an independent child. "I was so stubborn, so independent that I was more American than Czech, even as a little kid" (Navratilova with Vecsey, 60).

She contended that she might have been better off if she had been more like the well-known character in Czech literature, a bumbling soldier. His story is told in *The Good Soldier Svejk and His Fortunes in the War* by Jaroslav Hasek with illustrations by Joseph Lada. Svejk had learned to get along with authority since the country was almost always dominated by foreigners—Austrians, Germans, Russians. Svejk is a comic character with a big W. C. Fields nose. He seems stupid but is really clever in his own way. After being given orders to move to the front, he would wander about the countryside, visiting every bar he encountered, and then fall asleep in a bar.

They would be about to throw him in prison when he would give them one of his lopsided salutes and say, "Begging your pardon, sir," and then he would give this long explanation about how he was really trying to find the front, but it was dark out. Nobody could ever prove Svejk was lying or plotting, so he managed to stay out of jail. (Navratilova with Vecsey, 60–61)

During the centennial of Hasek's birth, apparently every bookstore in Prague had special editions of his Svejk book. National television had a special series about him.

One particular magazine had very important influences on Martina's attitudes. She and her sister had found a copy of the American magazine *Playboy* in their father's closet. There was very little pornography in Czechoslovakia at the time, so they were surprised to find the magazine. Martina was not really shocked by it, however. She just thought it rather silly. She also realized that Americans could read whatever they wanted, unlike Czechs who did not have access to such materials because of the restrictive laws of the Czech government.

They (the Americans) could read this kind of stuff. The socialist, puritan attitude never got through to me on any level. I'm against anything that's restrictive, people telling me what to do or what to think. (Navratilova with Vecsey, 61)

As an adult, Navratilova has read a variety of materials, including mystery stories, thrillers, fantasy, and numerous periodicals. She has enjoyed reading fiction, including the following which contain courageous characters who overcome many odds to lead full, independent lives, as Martina has done herself. These include *The Persian Boy* by Mary Renault; *The Foun-*

tainhead and *Atlas Shrugged* by Ayn Rand; *The Chronicles of Narnia* by C. S. Lewis; and *Brideshead Revisited* by Evelyn Waugh.

Martina also enjoys quality magazines and newspapers, such as *The New York Times, Vanity Fair, Wildlife Conservation, Time Magazine,* and *The New Yorker.* Another favorite of hers is *OUT,* which regularly publishes biographies of noted gays and lesbians.

Mysteries and thrillers by the following authors are also favorites: Ken Follett, Clive Cussler, and Anne Rice (November 4, 1996, letter from Nancy Falconer to John McCrossan).

In addition to enjoying reading, Martina has also enjoyed writing mystery novels. These include *The Total Zone* and *Breaking Point: A Novel of Suspense.* "It's fun writing fiction," she said, "because, number one, you can't get sued, and you can trash people and they know who they are" (Blue, 107). As might be expected her mysteries are set in the tennis world. Reviews of her work have been good.

It is revealing how influential the most unlikely kinds of reading can sometimes be. As noted above, Martina was not titillated when she saw *Playboy.* It simply made her realize that Americans had so much more freedom than Czechs, and the experience undoubtedly played an important role in her strong belief in freedom, her belief that people have a right to read what they please as well as a right to live their own lives as they want to.

IMPORTANT DATES IN MARTINA NAVRATILOVA'S LIFE

1956   Born in Prague, Czechoslovakia.

1973   Won Czechoslovak National Championship.

1975   Defected to the United States.

1978   Defeated Chris Evert. Ranked number one in the world by the Women's Tennis Association. In succeeding years broke many records and won a phenomenal number of tennis tournaments.

1981   Became United States citizen.

1983   Named Associated Press Female Athlete of the Year.

1985   Published *Martina* with George Vecsey.

1986   Won seventh Wimbledon championship.

1992   Campaigned against Colorado's discriminatory Amendment 2.

1993   Spoke before 500,000 at the Lesbian and Gay March on Washington.

1994   Honored at the Virginia Slims tournament in New York.

SOURCES

Blue, Adrienne. *Martina: The Lives and Times of Martina Navratilova.* New York: Birch Lane Press, 1995.

Falconer, Nancy (assistant to Martina Navratilova) letter to John McCrossan, November 4, 1996.

Navratilova, Martina, with George Vecsey. *Martina*. New York: Knopf, 1985.

Navratilova, Martina, and Liz Nickels. *Total Zone*. New York: Ballantine, 1995.

Nickels, Liz, and Martina Navratilova. *Breaking Point: A Novel of Suspense*. New York: Random House, 1996.

Porter, David L., ed. *Biographical Dictionary of American Sports: Outdoor Sports*. Westport, Conn.: Greenwood Press, 1988.

Zwerman, Gilda. *Martina Navratilova*. New York: Chelsea House Publishers, 1995.

GEORGIA O'KEEFFE
(1887–1986)

Georgia O'Keeffe, has been called "the foremost American exponent of representational expressionist painting" and along with Mary Cassatt is one of the most important women in the history of American art. She became a renowned painter at a time when most women artists were relegated to teaching art. This great artist was also a great reader, beginning in childhood and continuing throughout her life.

Georgia O'Keeffe was born on a farm in Sun Prairie, Wisconsin, on November 15, 1887, the daughter of Francis and Ida O'Keeffe. The family was both prosperous and intellectual where the children were taught the value of music, literature, and the life of the mind.

Her early education took place at a convent school where she pursued studies in painting and drawing. Later she studied at the Art Institute of Chicago, the Art Students League in New York and at Columbia University.

In 1917 Alfred Stieglitz, the man she would later marry, arranged her first solo show. That show marked the beginning of her long, very successful career as an artist. The show was phenomenally successful. The fact that the artist was a woman astounded the art world, since women artists were generally relegated to teaching.

Some of her early paintings reflected city views, such as New York City skyscrapers. Years later she began spending time in New Mexico, settling permanently there after her husband's death. That area's ancient Spanish architecture, mesas, and vegetation became a constant theme of her art. She is also noted for her many paintings of flowers in both abstract and realistic styles.

O'Keeffe became a legend in her own time, a cultural heroine not unlike a major film star. She received numerous awards and honors for her work, including honorary doctorates from a number of universities.

In O'Keeffe's childhood home, reading was part of the family ritual. Ida O'Keeffe read a variety of classic materials to her fascinated children who sat silently on the living room floor.

> When it grew dark, she would take the children in and read to them—travel stories and history—*The Life of Hannibal, Stanley's Adventures in Africa*, all *The Leatherstocking Tales*, the Bible, *Pilgrim's Progress, Arabian Nights*, and *The Life of Kit Carson*. It was Wild West stories of the cattlemen, buffalos and Indians that Georgia loved the best. (Pollitzer, 56)

Such adventurous tales undoubtedly helped shape Georgia's independent attitudes. According to Robinson, the "real-life adventurers and the fictious heroes were advocates for the romantic cult of the individual."

> The message conveyed by these triumphant heroes was that the individual has the power to act, to alter lives, to triumph over adversity, and to emerge victorious. The message was not lost on the listening children. (Robinson, 21)

Ida also read a great deal to herself. She thus showed the children "the great pleasure and exhilaration to be derived from music, literature, ideas, imagination, and the life of the mind" (Robinson, 21).

As a student and adult, O'Keeffe naturally studied books about art. She had, for example, read two books which would become important in her development. They were Kandinsky's landmark book *Concerning the Spiritual in Art* and Arthur Jerome Eddy's *Cubism*, which contained views of abstractions of natural forms.

> Kandinsky's insistence on the expression of "an inner necessity" and his analogies of color and music were later to become seeds for O'Keeffe's growing innovations in color and form." (Hoffman, 4)

During her early years of teaching, O'Keeffe subscribed to the radical journal *The Masses* and Stieglitz' magazine, *Camera Work*. These facts would seem to contradict "the prevalent assumption that O'Keeffe executed her first mature works in total ignorance of advanced European and American art" (Haskell, 2). Nonetheless, Haskell argues that "none of her contacts with the modernist theories being expounded in the early years of the century can account for the extraordinary group of charcoal drawings she executed that fall" (Haskell, 2).

In addition to professional reading, O'Keeffe's tastes in general literature reflected her independent type of mind. She favored works that presented strong women characters or women who were brutalized by men. Alfred Stieglitz, who was interested in feminism, encouraged such reading.

She read Ibsen, Dante, Nietzsche, and *Herland*, a feminist novel by Charlotte Perkins Gilman that challenged patriarchal society and "presented an idyllic, man-free society" (Robinson, 165).

She also tackled *Women as World Builders* by Floyd Dell and read Arthur's favorite Hardy novel *Jude the Obscure*. Arthur sent her a gift subscription to *The New Republic* and a copy of *Life and Youth*, a book of essays by Randolph Bourne. She also read Goethe's *Faust*, which Stieglitz had sent her. "I read it almost every day," she reported (Eisler, 132).

The great drama of the infernal bargain was Stieglitz's favorite work, so he claimed; its grip on Georgia surely had much to do with the donor. (Eisler, 132)

O'Keeffe especially liked D. H. Lawrence's books. She read most of his works including *Lady Chatterley's Lover,* and she read it a number of times.

In spite of his misogyny O'Keeffe thought he alone had expressed modern sexuality in words, particularly in *Lady Chatterley's Lover,* which was banned in the United States because of its heightened sexual content. Copies wrapped in plain brown paper were nonetheless passed clandestinely from reader to reader. (Hogrefe, 147)

She defended the book to her friend Ettie Stettheimer who thought its sex was too graphic. O'Keeffe recommended Stettheimer read it a second time to "truly come to appreciate the beauty of Lawrence" (Hogrefe, 147).

O'Keeffe also read Lawrence's *Women in Love* more than once. She did a number of paintings of the interior of the jack-in-the-pulpit flower which had interested her since her days in high school. A teacher had pulled back the jack to show the pupils what was inside. A similar scene occurrs in *Women in Love*, possibly influencing O'Keeffe's paintings, which Hogrefe describes as "passionate and sensual as they were cold and clinical" (Hogrefe, 154). Some believed the flower pictures represented female genitalia and condemned O'Keeffe for displaying such sexuality in her work. Others praised her, believing themselves to be witnessing the birth of a great new talent.

O'Keeffe also enjoyed discussing books and magazines with friends, including her close friend and confidante Anita Pollitzer. Beginning in 1914 when they lived in different parts of the country, O'Keeffe and Pollitzer wrote to each other frequently, sometimes daily. Their letters are filled with discussions of books and magazines as well as art and music, and Georgia, who sometimes felt isolated in small towns, was refreshed by Anita's packages of reading materials: "Books and magazines, dispatched by Anita from the Teachers College post office, were eagerly awaited and devoured by Georgia" (Giboire, xvi).

Knowing that O'Keeffe had a subscription to *The Masses*, Pollitzer wrote her indicating that she "was crazy" to see a copy of it. In response O'Keeffe sent her three copies. The two women also wrote to each other enthusiastically about the materials contained in Stieglitz' journal, *Camera Work*.

Their letters contain numerous references to general literature. In 1916, for example, Georgia wrote to Anita about the pleasure she had reading various dramatists, including Singe's *Riders to the Sea*, Murray's translation of *The Trojan Women*, and *Margot*, a story by a German named Suderman "a new man I had never heard of" (Giboire, 163). She also wrote Anita that she had enjoyed reading Ibsen's works, books by the Danish writer Selma Lagerloff, and Nietzsche.

> Have been reading Ibsen too—Funny the way we read the same things so often—read the Doll House last spring. Have been reading The Wild Duck and An Enemy of the People. They are great—you must read the Wild Duck particularly—Its tremendous—and I was reading Nietzsche too—about three weeks ago but someone borrowed my book for an afternoon and the afternoon isnt over yet—it has grown to be three weeks long. (Giboire, 248)

O'Keeffe's friendship with Anita deteriorated when O'Keeffe refused to allow her friend to publish the O'Keeffe biography she had encouraged her to write. Pollitzer had worked on the biography for fifteen years. When she submitted a draft to O'Keeffe in 1967, however, the latter threatened to sue if Pollitzer tried to publish it. O'Keeffe apparently objected to Pollitzer's optimism and rosy version of her life, which differed so much from O'Keeffe's own austere approach to her life and work.

The biography, *A Woman on Paper*, was eventually published in 1988. It was not intended to be a scholarly work, but one which would chronicle the early years of O'Keeffe's development as an artist by the woman who had been such a supportive friend for so long.

Frances Steloff, another close friend of O'Keeffe's, was the source of much of O'Keeffe's reading materials in the 1950s. Steloff owned the Gotham Book Mart in New York City. It was a popular gathering place for numerous literary people and included the best in modern literature by such authors as T. S. Eliot and James Joyce.

Georgia ordered many books from Steloff to be sent to her home in the Southwest. She bought books on housekeeping; Chinese art; and before journeying to Peru, she ordered a number of books on the Inca civilization. Steloff also sent O'Keeffe copies of books then banned in the United States, such as James Joyce's *Ulysses* and Lawrence's *Lady Chatterley's Lover*. To avoid detection by postal authorities, they were wrapped in plain brown paper.

O'Keeffe always enjoyed having friends read to her, just as her mother had done when she was a child. As a typical example, friend Maria Chabot read to O'Keeffe while they were camping. Among others she "read aloud from *Taras Bulba* and *Siddhartha*, Herman Hesse's story of the life of Buddha" (Hogrefe, 196).

In her eighties O'Keeffe found great energy in the spiritual life, an energy that would grow during her long life. She became especially attracted to Zen Buddhism and "talked excitedly" about it with friends. Robert M. Pirsig's *Zen and the Art of Motorcycle Maintenance* became a favorite book. She purchased copies of it and gave them to a number of people encouraging them to read it.

Georgia O'Keeffe read a great variety of materials throughout her long life. She especially favored books about strong, independent, unconventional people like herself. Undoubtedly, her extensive reading had an influence on her own life and work.

IMPORTANT DATES IN GEORGIA O'KEEFFE'S LIFE

1887	Born in Sun Prairie, Wisconsin.
1912–1917	Taught art in several different schools and colleges.
1917	O'Keeffe's phenomenally successful career began with the opening of her first solo show in New York sponsored by Alfred Stieglitz. Her bold original work, unlike any American art that preceded it, caught the attention of the world.
1924	Married Alfred Stieglitz, many years her senior, beginning a very unconventional marriage in which they spent much time apart.
1928	Began spending time in New Mexico where the vistas inspired many of her works of art.
1938	Received honorary doctorate from the College of William and Mary, the first of a number of honorary doctorates she would receive.
Mid-1940s	Purchased two homes in New Mexico.
1946	Alfred Stieglitz died.
1950s	Traveled extensively in Europe, Japan, and India. Incorporated Japanese techniques into some of her work.
1971	At eighty-four years of age, her eyesight began to fail. She continued to paint, however, until weeks before her death.
1970s and 1980s	Exhibitions of her work held in major art museums in New York, Paris, Chicago, San Francisco, and other cities.
1986	Died in New Mexico.

SOURCES

Eisler, Benita. *O'Keeffe and Stieglitz: An American Romance.* New York: Doubleday, 1991.

Giboire, Clive, ed. *Lovingly Georgia: The Complete Correspondence of Georgia O'Keeffe & Anita Pollitzer.* New York: Simon and Schuster, 1990.

Haskell, Barbara. "Georgia O'Keeffe Works on Paper: A Critical Essay," in *Georgia O'Keeffe: Works on Paper.* Santa Fe, N.M.: Museum of New Mexico Press, 1985.

Hoffman, Katherine. *An Enduring Spirit: The Art of Georgia O'Keeffe.* Metuchen, N.J.: Scarecrow Press, 1984.

Hogrefe, Jeffrey. *O'Keeffe: The Life of an American Legend.* New York: Bantam Books, 1992.

Pollitzer, Anita. *A Woman on Paper: Georgia O'Keeffe.* New York: Simon & Schuster, 1988.

Robinson, Roxana. *Georgia O'Keeffe: A Life.* New York: Harper & Row, 1990.

FRANCES PERKINS
(1882–1965)

Frances Perkins, appointed secretary of labor by President Franklin Roosevelt, was the first woman ever appointed to a United States president's cabinet. She thought Theodore Dreiser's *Sister Carrie* was the most important book written in America in a generation. As much of the rest of her reading, the novel focused on the struggles of working class people and greatly influenced her attitudes towards the poor.

Frances Perkins was born in Boston on April 10, 1882, and brought up in Worcester, Massachusetts, where her father ran a stationery business. Her family were comfortably upper middle class and staunchly Republican, as were all their friends and neighbors. Rebellious young Frances would sometimes shock them by claiming to be a Democrat. In adulthood she joined the Democratic party and had a long, successful association with leading Democrats: Al Smith, Governor of New York State, and President Franklin D. Roosevelt.

Perkins attended local schools and then enrolled in Mount Holyoke College for Women. That was at a time when few women attended college. She became class president, and received her bachelor's degree from Mount Holyoke in 1902. Perhaps the most important lesson she learned at Mount Holyoke was that there were many causes of poverty. People of her own class generally believed that people were poor because they were lazy or drunken.

One professor required her students to visit local factories, and Frances was horrified when she discovered the inhuman conditions under which many women and children, neither drunken nor lazy, had to work. She was inspired to do what she could to stop those abuses.

After finishing college, Frances taught school and worked for social reform groups for several years. Then feeling she needed more education, she enrolled at Columbia University where she received a master's degree in sociology and economics.

That same year she was appointed secretary of the New York Consumer's League. In succeeding years, she served on several other New York State commissions which worked towards improvement of conditions of workers, consumers, children, and immigrants. One of her major accomplishments during that period was successfully lobbying the New York State Legislature to restrict women's working conditions to fifty-four hours a week. That was long before the forty-hour week became standard for most workers.

In 1933 newly elected President Franklin D. Roosevelt appointed her secretary of labor. The first female cabinet member in U.S. history, she is given major credit for the enactment of such landmark social legislation as the Social Security Act and the Fair Labor Standards Act. In 1934 she published an influential book: *People at Work.*

After Roosevelt died in 1945, Perkins resigned from the cabinet. She accepted a professorship at Cornell University's School of Industrial and Labor Relations, lectured widely, and wrote a best seller entitled *The Roosevelt I Knew.*

Encouraged by her bookish father, young Fanny, as she was called in her youth, became a great reader. He often chose books for her himself from his ample library. She was taught basic household chores, but her father's books "attracted her far more than what went on in her mother's kitchen" (Severn, 12).

Fanny's heavy reading and family discussion of literature, art, and drama gave her quite an education. As a result she was very articulate in school. She found that her ability to express herself so well impressed her teachers and classmates and got her passing marks even when she had neglected her homework.

Fanny was a good student, but not superior. She got A's in English and speech, but in other subjects she did only moderately well and did not make the honors list.

College was a "mixed bag" for Frances. She felt that much of her education at Mount Holyoke was irrelevant. She thought college was preparation for continued learning in real life.

She did like studying English and German literature, and was active in the discussions of the literary society called The Sophocles Authors' Club. She also enjoyed performing in amateur theatricals, and was especially successful when she played a male role, Brutus, in a farce titled *The Lamentable Tragedy of Julius Caesar.*

Religion was always an important part of Perkins' life. At Mount Holyoke, "she led prayer meetings" (Severn, 16).

It was during her last year of college that Frances heard a speech by Mrs. Florence Kelley who had translated from the German a noted book by Engels, the English title being *The Condition of the Working Classes in England in 1844*. Kelley was also national secretary of the National Consumers' League, an organization working towards abolishing tenements, sweatshops, and child labor. Frances was amazed by what Kelley had to say, and years later she wrote that Kelley's speech "first opened my mind to the necessity for and the possibility of the work which became my vocation" (Martin, 52).

Theodore Roosevelt's inaugural address of 1905 was also significant in Perkins' development. Its powerful words helped persuade her that the pursuit of social justice would be her life's work.

During and after college, Frances read voraciously about the problems of poverty. One book that had a very strong effect on her was Jacob Riis's exposé of life in the slums.

She agonized over Jacob Riis's *How the Other Half Lives*, with its vignettes of poverty based on his experiences trudging through the streets and alleys of New York's Hell's Kitchen, Poverty Gap, the Mulberry Street Bend, Henry Street, and the Fourth Ward. (Mohr, 21–22)

The impact of that landmark book would remain with her the rest of her life.

In her own writing, Perkins emphasized the important role writers had played in movements to improve the lives of Americans. "Early in this century," she wrote in her book *People at Work*, "we in America became conscious of two things which linked us to the London which Charles Booth had showed—two things which had not been problems for our grandfathers."

One of these was a vast population—in our case largely foreign born—whose standards of living were not the old standards. The other was the existence of slums in which the people who worked herded together in order to be near their work under living conditions that had nothing to do with the American standard. (Perkins, *People at Work*, 40)

She also argued that short stories and novels had had a major impact on the attitudes of Americans alerting them to the plight of workers and other unfortunates. Those whose living conditions had become worse due to the impact of the industrial revolution. She noted that magazine readers were "lured" on by Myra Kelley and Josephine Daskam Bacon, who wrote about what living in the slums was like. And she argued there could be no more "gripping" piece than O. Henry's *Unfinished Story*, which recounted the life of Dulcie who worked long hours in a department store selling little trinkets and made only "six dollars a week" (Perkins, *People at Work*, 41).

In addition to *Sister Carrie*, Perkins was impressed with *Mrs. Wiggs of the Cabbage Patch*, a best seller, which told the story of a poor widow trying to bring up a large family with very little money. Upton Sinclair's novel *The Jungle* graphically portrayed conditions in the stockyards and packing houses of Chicago. His novel had such an impact that it resulted in the enactment of laws directed against impure food.

Perkins also emphasized the importance of libraries. She noted how crowded public library reading rooms were at all times and that many of their books were "worn to shreds." She strongly recommended that they be given considerably more money to provide needed books for their readers (Perkins, *People at Work*, 251).

Magazine and newspaper exposés also were influential. "The muckraking magazine writers like Will Irwin, Sam Merwin, Lincoln Steffens, Ray Baker," Perkins wrote, "startled the American people with documents of American life that showed deep suffering, social injustice, and indifference to it in large areas of our population" (Perkins, *The Roosevelt I Knew*, 16).

News stories alerted Americans to tragedies. Sympathy ran high for women factory workers in Troy, New York, who protested against the introduction of machines that would eliminate jobs.

New York had been roused; the *New York Journal* got out a special edition in support of the strikers; mass meetings were held. . . . Why should workers suffer because of machines! People began to wonder! (Perkins, *People at Work*, 45)

The tragedy of the Triangle shirt-waist factory fire in 1911 shocked and sickened Americans. The factory was located on the ninth and tenth floors of a loft building. Under the tables at which the girls and women worked were baskets into which scraps of material were dropped. Possibly a match or cigarette was accidentally dropped into the basket. No one could escape. The stairs were locked. Fatalities numbered 147, mostly females. Many of those killed had jumped from the windows "before the eyes of the helpless lookers-on." The tragedy, widely reported in the press, "was a torch that lit up the whole industrial scene," Perkins wrote. "The effect on the public," she wrote, "was electric." The general public began to understand the unsafe conditions under which "the wage earner lived and worked" (Perkins, *People at Work*, 50–51).

Studies exposed other hazards of factory work, including poisoning from lead and phosphorous, occupational disease, unsanitary conditions, and overcrowding. As a result, according to Perkins, the American public became not only concerned but also convinced that working conditions could be improved. In response to popular demand, "a Department of Labor was created to promote the 'good life' for the working people in terms of the Good Job" (Perkins, *People at Work*, 57).

It was the Department of Labor that Perkins would head years later when President Roosevelt appointed her secretary of labor in 1933. She served in that position until 1945.

Frances Perkins, a girl from a comfortable upper middle-class, well-to-do family, became a great force in vast improvements in the lives of millions of working people throughout the United States. She became aware of the problems of workers and slum dwellers through firsthand observation and by reading about them. Her belief in the power of the printed word was great, noting that writers who pointed out the problems of poor workers and slum dwellers had roused not only herself but many other Americans to problems and to eventual solutions.

IMPORTANT DATES IN FRANCES PERKINS' LIFE

1882   Born in Boston.

1902   Graduated from Mount Holyoke College.

1910   Received master's degree from Columbia University. Became executive secretary of the Consumers League of New York.

1913   Married Paul Caldwell Wilson. Successfully fought to keep her maiden name.

1918   Became first woman to serve on the New York State Industrial Board. Later appointed its chairman.

1928   Became industrial commissioner, State of New York.

1933   Received honorary doctorate from the University of Wisconsin.

1933–1945   Served as United States Secretary of Labor.

1934   Published *People at Work*.

1946   Published *The Roosevelt I Knew*.

1965   Died in New York.

SOURCES

Josephson, Matthew, and Hannah Josephson. *Al Smith: Hero of the Cities*. Boston: Houghton Mifflin Co., 1969.

Martin, George. *Madam Secretary: Frances Perkins*. Boston: Houghton Mifflin Co., 1976.

Mohr, Lillian Holmen. *Frances Perkins: "That Woman in FDR's Cabinet!"* Croton-on-Hudson: North River Press, 1979.

Perkins, Frances. *People at Work*. New York: John Day Co., 1934.

Perkins, Frances. *The Roosevelt I Knew*. New York: Viking Press, 1946.

Severn, Bill. *Frances Perkins: A Member of the Cabinet*. New York: Hawthorn Books, 1976.

JEANNETTE RANKIN
(1880–1973)

Jeannette Rankin was the first woman elected to the United States Congress. In 1916 she was elected to the House of Representatives from Montana.

Jeannette Rankin was born in Missoula, Montana, on June 11, 1880, the eldest of seven children. Her father was a builder/contractor, and her mother, before her marriage, had been a schoolteacher.

Jeannette attended local public schools and the University of Montana. She taught grade school for a short time. Then she traveled to Boston, Massachusetts, where she was shocked by the conditions in which people lived in the slums. Her experiences inspired her to serious study of sociology, economics, and public speaking, thus preparing herself for a major role in the causes in which she believed.

Rankin voted against the United States' entry into World War I. She was then labeled as unpatriotic and defeated in her bid for re-election in 1918.

During the intervening years, Rankin traveled throughout the nation advocating feminist causes, better conditions for workers, child labor laws, and world peace. She became one of the nation's leading peace advocates, helped form the Women's International League for Peace and Freedom, and campaigned against Reserve Officer Training Corps programs on college campuses.

At the age of sixty, Rankin was again elected to Congress. She cast the only vote in opposition to entering World War II. She realized she would not be re-elected, but, dedicated to peace, she believed the cause of peace was more important than her political career.

Rankin found school boring, and her grades were only average. She loved to read, however, to think about what she read, and to discuss ideas.

Her father always listened seriously to what Jeannette had to say. He let her tag after him and listen to his conversations with men who were leaders in Missoula. They talked about what was going on in the country and local politics. Her father seemed to take it for granted that young Jeannette could follow these talks. (Davidson, 11)

Being the oldest child, Jeannette often read to the younger ones. Her eyes often would fill with tears when she read stories in the Bible and other books.

She could also be frank about readings she did not like. On one occasion a teacher assigned her to read publicly Alfred Tennyson's "The Charge of the Light Brigade." "This is hideous. I can't read it," she responded (Giles, 30).

Unlike many of their neighbors', the Rankin family's life did not center around a church. The children, however, attended Sunday school and enjoyed hearing Bible stories there. Their great-uncle Bill Berry, who served as sheriff for many years, was an avowed atheist. He enjoyed debunking religion. He brought the children a book depicting Presbyterians throwing children into the fires of Hell because they had not been baptized. The children secretly pored over the book, knowing their parents would not approve of it.

Uncle Bill was also a storyteller, and the children loved hearing his tales of the gold rush, the early settlement of Montana, and especially stories about the Indians, "whose strange presence in their world was only dimly understood" (Josephson, 12).

Jeannette also learned a lot from stories told by Southern refugees of the Civil War who had settled in Montana.

She listened in wide-eyed wonder as the old Southerners gathered with her father in the ranchhouse parlor, spitting out tales of the war and life in the South as frequently as they spat streams of tobacco. They were rough and frank in their talk, and Jeannette was electrified by the atmosphere of it all, much to her mother's displeasure. (Giles, 24)

Rankin had read about the conditions of poverty in big cities, but she was still shocked by what she saw in the Boston slums. She was appalled by the conditions of the poor and less fortunate whose plights were ignored under laissez faire capitalism. It was not at all like Montana where she had seen few poor people. Returning to Montana, she spent endless hours reading about the conditions she had seen in the city.

She read more than ever, absorbing opinions and ideas about economics, politics and philosophy. She seldom sat down without a book or magazine in her hands, reading mostly about causes, ideas, news, politics and current affairs. (Giles, 33–34)

Rankin's experience was similar to that of Jane Addams who fifteen years earlier had seen how wretched life was in London's East End. Reading things by and about Jane Addams inspired Rankin.

Jane Addams, who had been toiling at Hull House in Chicago for nearly two decades, had the most notable and productive influence on Jeannette, advocating female involvement in social problems to encourage an upswing in the quality of life in America. (Giles, 36)

According to Josephson:

Learning now what the founder of Hull House was trying to do to mitigate those conditions, Jeannette began reading avidly the current literature of protest: the muckraking magazines, the works of Jacob Riis, Jack London, Henry George, and particularly anything she could lay hands on by or about Miss Addams. (Josephson, 22–23)

Rankin's experiences at the New York School of Philanthropy, forerunner of the Columbia University School of Social Work, were significant in her development. In addition to study and reading, she was required to go out into the community observing the problems of various groups of underprivileged people.

Fortunately for Rankin, the school was the center of an intellectual revolution in social and economic thought called progressivism. Some of the nation's leading progressives were on the faculty. These included Florence Kelley of the National Consumer's League; Booker T. Washington, the black leader and educator; Louis D. Brandeis, one of America's leading lawyers and economic intellectuals; and Edward T. Devine, editor of *Survey* magazine.

Progressivism was not socialism. It was a movement calling for preservation of democracy, but a democracy in which the powers of the constitution would be enforced. Monopolies would be broken; voting rights would be granted to all; fair wages would be paid to workers.

At that time, "middle-class American women were discouraged from reading anything more suggestive than the Sears and Roebuck catalogue" (Giles, 37). At the School of Philanthropy, Rankin "was being primed with books on human misery and the economics of civilization" (Giles, 37). Herbert Spencer's concept of Social Darwinism was studied. His philosophy of survival of the fittest was rejected as a theory proffered by the rich in order to protect their wealth at the expense of the rest of the population.

The school's curriculum was tough. Rankin studied such topics as social reform, labor disputes, racial progress, and criminal sociology. She was intrigued by Simon N. Patten's *New Basis of Civilization*. In it he argued that poverty could be eliminated by a more efficient society in which goods and services were more widely distributed.

Rankin's sister Mary was worried about the fact that Jeannette's studies seemed to encourage socialism. Jeannette wrote her, emphasizing that there was nothing wrong in studying social problems. She referred to "Saint Simon N. Patten" whose ideas were popular at the school. She noted that Patten placed the blame for social ills on outmoded ideas about economics and the many modern writers who admired the theories of "old writers such as Adam Smith, Mill and Malthus and tried to fit them to present conditions or to fit conditions to false theories" (Giles, 38).

These studies prepared Rankin to be a leader in the woman's right to vote movement. What she learned also gave her information and inspiration in her fight for world peace.

For the rest of her life Rankin continued to study movements in which she was interested. For example, she was strongly influenced by her study of Thoreau and Gandhi. Both had espoused the theory of civil disobedience. Gandhi had refined those ideas to his theory called Satyagraha, "a philosophy that enabled a whole people to change society by acting in defiance of unjust laws without violence" (Josephson, 173). "Jeannette was coming to the conclusion that these men had found the only way in which wars between nations could be avoided" (Josephson, 173–174).

Rankin made her first trip to India in 1946 and returned there six more times in succeeding years. She was always welcomed there by the leaders of their passive resistance movement. Unfortunately, she never met Gandhi. She met his son, however, during a trip to South Africa. Under his father's direction he had taken part in a passive resistance movement in Praetoria and the Transvaal.

Her admiration for Gandhi was unbounded. She wrote:

Gandhi . . . was the greatest philosopher of our time. He had two things he taught people: truth and non-violence. If his philosophy doesn't hold, we are lost. (Giles, 192)

Rankin continued to be a popular speaker for many years. She rallied people to the causes in which she believed. In 1972 she became the first person to be named to the National Organization for Women's Susan B. Anthony Hall of Fame, an award for the world's outstanding feminist. Then in her nineties, she expressed her ideas on women's roles strongly and succinctly. Most of the women in attendance at the National Organization for Women (NOW) ceremony were young. They greatly admired Rankin and considered her a living legend, linking them to the battles won by the early suffragists.

Rankin's speech looked to the future.

Women must devote all their energies today in gaining enough political offices to influence the direction of government. . . . We are here together to work together for the elimination of war. . . . My dream has always been that women would take this responsibility. (Davidson, 91)

Rankin rose from a small town in the West to become one of the world's leaders in the quest for women's rights and pacifism as well as fair working conditions and wages. Her study of great thinkers contributed significantly to her ideas and to her ability to provide leadership for the causes in which she so strongly believed.

IMPORTANT DATES IN JEANNETTE RANKIN'S LIFE

1880	Born in Missoula, Montana.
1902–1904	Graduated from the University of Montana. Taught grade school, then worked as a dressmaker. Visited Boston slums where she was shocked by the grinding poverty of so many workers.
1908	Attended New York School of Philanthropy. Later attended the University of Washington.
1910	Began active work on campaigns for women's suffrage. In succeeding years traveled widely promoting suffrage.
1916	Elected to the United States House of Representatives, the first woman elected to the United States Congress. She voted against the United States entry into World War I, the only member to do so. Later defeated in her bid for re-election.
1941	Returned to Congress. Voted against entering World War II, the only member of Congress to so vote. Public outcry against her vote ended her chances of being re-elected.
1946–1967	Visited India, the Mideast, Africa, Asia, Mexico, and South America observing lives of the people. Became an absolute pacifist in favor of total disarmament. Gave widely reported speech against the Vietnam War.
1970	Attended U.S. House of Representatives celebration of her ninetieth birthday.
1972	Gave magnificent speech at ceremony at which the National Organization for Women named her the first member of the Susan B. Anthony Hall of Fame.
1973	Died in Carmel, California. Her ashes were scattered over the sea.

SOURCES

Davidson, Sue. *A Heart in Politics: Jeannette Rankin and Patsy T. Mink.* Seattle, Wash.: Seal Press, 1994.

Fireside, Bryna J. *Is There a Woman in the House . . . or Senate?* Morton Grove, Ill.: Albert Whitman & Co., 1994.

Giles, Kevin S. *Flight of the Dove: The Story of Jeannette Rankin.* Beaverton, Ore.: Touchstone Press, 1980.

Josephson, Hannah. *Jeannette Rankin: First Lady in Congress: A Biography.* Indianapolis: Bobbs-Merrill Co., 1974.

Read, Phyllis, and Bernard L. Witlieb. *The Book of Women's Firsts: Breakthrough Achievements of Almost 1,000 American Women.* New York: Random House, 1992.

RONALD REAGAN
(1911–)

"I'm a sucker for hero worship" Ronald Reagan wrote. He especially liked books in which the hero succeeded while living by "standards of morality and fair play" (Cannon, 18). Some of his favorite writers are Mark Twain, Sinclair Lewis, Pearl Buck, Damon Runyon, H. G. Wells, and other classic American and British authors. On a lighter side, he especially likes Westerns, stories of the heroes of the old American West.

Ronald Reagan was born on February 11, 1911, in Tampico, Illinois, in a bedroom of a five-room flat above the store where his father worked. He attended local public schools and graduated from Eureka college.

He worked as a radio sports announcer for several years and made his film debut in 1937 in a movie entitled *Love Is in the Air*. He generally appeared in forgettable "B" movies, but he received critical acclaim for his performances in *Knute Rockne* and *King's Row*.

Reagan entered politics in middle age when he was elected governor of California. He twice ran unsuccessfully for the Republican nomination for president of the United States. Then in 1979 he received the nomination and went on to win the election becoming the fortieth president. He was re-elected for a second term four years later.

Reagan believed he learned to read before entering school "through a kind of osmosis." His mother always came into the bedroom and read stories to Ronald, or "Dutch," as he was sometimes called, and his brother: "As she read, she followed each line on the page with her finger and we watched. I think I just picked it up that way" (Ronald Reagan, 25).

By the time he was five years old, he was reading newspapers. In his autobiography, he described the way in which his father learned of his son's reading ability. His father found him on the living room floor with a newspaper spread out in front of him. When asked what he was doing, Dutch responded, "Reading the paper," and he proceeded to read something for his dad. "The next thing I knew, he was flying out the front door and from the porch inviting all our neighbors to come over and hear his five-year-old son read" (Ronald Reagan, 25). He continued reading newspapers throughout his youth and mature years.

Ronald seemed to be a prodigy to his mother who would have him read for the neighbors. His reading performances brought him great approval from those who heard him. Such activity probably built up his self-confidence, which he would use when he later became a performer and a politician.

Even though he hated the glasses he had to wear because of his near-sightedness, the glasses were also a blessing because they made "his two favorite pastimes—reading and the movies—much more pleasurable" (Edwards, 52).

When he was ten, Reagan became a member of the local public library. He checked out an average of two books a week, usually preferring boys' adventure stories, stories about heroes, and nature stories, often reading until late at night.

He read most of the Rover Boys books. He also enjoyed Edgar Rice Burroughs' Tarzan series, and Burt L. Standish's Frank Merriwell series, *Frank Merriwell's Bravery, Frank Merriwell's Foes,* and *Frank Merriwell's Sports Afield.* Those books "ranked as favorites, for they were checked out twice each" (Edwards, 53).

He also read everything he could about the wildlife and birds in the Rock River Valley. He particularly enjoyed a book about the great white wolves of the north entitled *Northern Lights.* He read it over and over imagining himself being with the wolves in the wild.

Reagan's mother gave him a book containing Robert W. Service's "The Shooting of Dan McGrew." He read it many, many times both as a youth and as an adult, and memorized it. Years later if he had trouble sleeping he would recite it silently until he bored himself "into slumber" (Ronald Reagan, 31).

During his early years in Hollywood, many of his compatriots thought Reagan, with his rather "juvenile sense of humor" and big glasses, was quite silly. Therefore, they were surprised at the knowledge he had about complicated facts. They didn't realize that when he was alone he read "voraciously" on such topics as politics, government, and history. He read such leading newspapers as the *Washington Post, The Wall Street Journal,* and *Christian Science Monitor,* "and even printouts . . . of the daily *Congressional Record*" (Edwards, 230).

In a 1942 interview with Reagan at the height of his popularity as a movie star, he mentioned favorite books, quite a varied list of works. They included Sinclair Lewis' *Babbitt;* Mark Twain's *The Adventures of Tom Sawyer; Turnabout* by Thorne Smith; and works by Pearl Buck, H. G. Wells, Damon Runyon, and Eric Maria Remarque.

After entering politics, Reagan continued his habit of reading widely in newspapers, Republican newsletters, and such magazines as the *Reader's Digest*, and the very conservative *Human Events*. In his many political talks he would often use stories torn out of a newspaper or periodical to illustrate a point he wanted to make about his conservative political philosophy.

Generally such stories were on target. Sometimes, however, he made huge gaffes, such as when he, on a number of occasions, quoted a report about a Chicago "welfare queen" who lived in luxury and drove expensive cars. It turned out there was no such person. The story was made up.

On another occasion he said "the finest oil geologists in the world" had told him that U.S. reserves of oil exceeded Saudi Arabia's. Columnist Mark Shields joked that the comment belied Reagan's belief that there is more oil under Yankee Stadium than there is in the Middle East (Cannon, 260).

Citing a report in a conservative periodical, Reagan stated that it cost the Department of Health, Education and Welfare three dollars to deliver one dollar's worth of goods. The report was false, the actual cost was 12 cents (Cannon, 260).

In 1948, years before running for political office, Reagan spent time in England filming *The Hasty Heart*. Anne Edwards states that his time there had "a strong influence on him." He began, on his first trip abroad, to see a world beyond the United States. He became interested in British politics and history, and read whatever he could to understand them better. He also loved to go down to the bar in the Savoy Hotel and discuss such weighty topics (Edwards, 365).

Not surprisingly, one book that Reagan especially liked during the early 1960s was Barry Goldwater's *The Conscience of a Conservative*. Discussing his decision to campaign for Goldwater in the 1964 presidential race, Reagan wrote: "*The Conscience of a Conservative* contained a lot of the same points I'd been making in my speeches, and I strongly believed the country needed him" (Ronald Reagan, 138–139). In later years many considered Reagan a major disciple of Goldwater. He preached his ideas when he ran for political office and attempted to put those ideas into law once elected.

While serving as president, Reagan's daily routine at the White House started with a light breakfast and reading of *The New York Times* and *The Washington Post*. As president, he also would read many official documents during the day. After a long day of work he would "go to bed with a novel or another book." He also might read some magazine about horses and riding, one of his favorite avocations (Ronald Reagan, 250).

Reagan avidly read Western novels even sometimes when ill. Maureen Reagan tells the story of her father's reading a Louis L'Amour Western during his hospital recuperation from a 1985 operation for the removal of a malignant growth from his colon (the growth was caught in time and the malignant cells removed):

Dad had been reading a Louis L'Amour novel which he had by his bedside. When it came time for the First Lady and Dr. Hutton to leave for the evening, Nancy insisted that Dad turn out the light and get some sleep. He did, and they all said their good-nights. But as the doctor closed the door behind them, he noticed from the crack under the door that the President had turned his light back on. He wanted to read a while longer. . . . Not even a little thing like colon surgery could keep Dad from his Westerns. (Maureen Reagan, 344)

Maureen also reports Reagan's enjoyment in reciting "The Shooting of Dan McGrew." When she was a small child, she would beg him to recite it, and he would "really ham it up," acting out all the incidents in the poem (Maureen Reagan, 40).

The comic strip "Doonesbury" was another favorite of Reagan's, even though it often made fun of him. During the 1980 campaign, the strip did an extended satire on Reagan's brain. Even then, he not only did not avoid it, but read it, apparently with enjoyment, before heading out on the campaign trail (Cannon, 28).

Reagan had always read books, magazines, and newspapers for education and entertainment. His reading had a lasting effect on him. At the age of sixty-six he noted:

All in all, as I look back I realize that my reading left an abiding belief in the triumph of good over evil. There were heroes who lived by standards of morality and fair play. (Cannon, 19)

IMPORTANT DATES IN RONALD REAGAN'S LIFE

1911	Born in Tampico, Illinois.
1937	Made his debut as a movie actor.
1940	Established his reputation as an actor when he played George Gipp, the famous Notre Dame football star, in the film *Knute Rockne*.
1942	Entered the United States Army. Poor eyesight disqualified him for combat duty. Made army training films in California.
1947	Elected president of the Screen Actors Guild.
1947	Appeared as a friendly witness before the House Un-American Activities Committee, which was investigating alleged communist infiltration of the film industry. Claimed he never named names of suspected communists.
1954–1962	Employed as spokesperson for General Electric Company. In his speeches he extolled the virtues of free enterprise and warned against the evils of big government.
1966	Elected governor of California.
1980	Elected as president of the United States. Elected to a second term four years later.

SOURCES

Cannon, Lou. *Reagan*. New York: G. P. Putnam's Sons, 1982.

Edwards, Anne. *Early Reagan*. New York: William Morrow and Co., 1987.

Griswold, Jerry. "Young Reagan's Reading," *The New York Times Book Review*, August 30, 1981.

Reagan, Maureen. *First Father, First Daughter: A Memoir*. Boston: Little, Brown and Co., 1989.

Reagan, Ronald. *An American Life*. New York: Simon and Schuster, 1990.

Wills, Garry. *Reagan's America: Innocents at Home*. Garden City, N.Y.: Doubleday, 1987.

ELEANOR ROOSEVELT
(1884–1962)

Eleanor Roosevelt, an inveterate reader, described reading as "the oldest and most interesting recreation there is" (Black, 307). She read a wide variety of books, especially history, biography, fiction, and poetry. She also read newspapers every day in order to keep up with current events.

Anna Eleanor Roosevelt was born on October 11, 1884, in New York City. Her family was not wealthy, but they were an old patrician American clan. Eleanor was not a pretty child. In fact, she was sometimes called an "ugly duckling." It would only be years later that Eleanor would discover that homely features "were not such a handicap after all." She came to realize that "intellectual achievement and social responsibility were what really mattered" (Hareven, 8).

Eleanor's mother and father both died when she was a child, and she was brought up by her maternal grandmother. She was educated in private schools in the United States and England. During her teens she exhibited a strong interest in and concern for the poor, establishing "a lifetime pattern of involvement in two worlds: the patrician world of her family and the netherworld of the disadvantaged" (Bussey, 1951).

At the age of twenty-one she married Franklin D. Roosevelt, a distant cousin. FDR became one of the most successful politicians in American history, being elected governor of New York and then president of the United States for four consecutive terms.

Eleanor Roosevelt became the most publicly active first lady in American history. During her husband's political career and after his death, she traveled the nation meeting with many groups and giving numerous speeches. She also wrote voluminously, publishing newspaper and magazine columns and authoring several best-selling books.

In 1945, after Franklin's death, President Harry Truman appointed Mrs. Roosevelt to be the first American delegate to the United Nations. As chair of the UN Commission on Human Rights, she successfully steered the commission's Declaration of Human Rights to ratification by the UN. During John F. Kennedy's presidency, she chaired the Kennedy Commission on the Status of Women. The Commission's report gave wide publicity to the inequalities faced by American women, and it is considered one of the major documents that led to the modern women's movement.

Eleanor's mother, father, and French teacher played important parts in developing the small child's interest in books and reading. Her mother, Anna Hall Roosevelt, often read to her, and Eleanor in turn read to her mother. Eleanor, who wrote poetry, would also recite her poems for her mother.

Her father often recommended things Eleanor should read. When she was eight years old, for example, she could recite a good part of Longfellow's *Hiawatha* because it was a favorite poem of his.

Mlle. LeClerq, who taught Eleanor French, required that she memorize many Bible verses in French. Eleanor thought it was a waste of time. Only later did she realize that such learning by heart had been very useful in that it helped develop her memory.

After Eleanor was orphaned and moved to her grandparents home, she was frequently left alone. Occasionally her aunt and uncle would play with her and read poetry, but the only playmate of her own age lived five miles away. Reading became a favorite and beloved pastime. As Lash noted:

There were long summer days when she would lie on the grass or climb a cherry tree with a book, sometimes forgetting to appear at meals. On rainy days the attic was her favorite spot. She often awakened at dawn and just as often violated her grandmother's injunction that she was not to read in bed before breakfast. The library was full of her grandfather's heavy theological works, but there were also Dickens, Scott, and Thackeray. (Lash, *Eleanor and Franklin*, 67)

Sometimes there was also a forbidden modern novel, which Eleanor would steal from her aunts, "purely because I heard it whispered that the contents were not for young eyes" (Lash, *Eleanor and Franklin*, 67).

Young lonely Eleanor would often "cry and cry" over books in which main characters suffered being orphaned, just as she had suffered. These included Florence Montgomery's *Misunderstood*; du Maurier's *Peter Ibbetson*, and Hector Mallet's *Sans Famille*.

In later years Eleanor Roosevelt noted some of her favorite childhood books. They included Dickens' *Old Curiosity Shop, Tale of Two Cities, Oliver Twist,* and *Dombey and Sons*; Longfellow's poems; Kipling's *Light That Failed*; Walter Scott's *The Talisman*; Mark Twain's *The Prince and the Pauper*; Dinah M. Craik's *The Little Lame Prince*; and Ouida's *Dog of Flanders* and

Nuremberg Stove. She also had enjoyed George Eliot's *The Mill on the Floss, Romola,* and *Silas Marner.* (Lash, *Eleanor and Franklin,* 68).

Eleanor Roosevelt loved imaginative literature—fiction and poetry. She claimed fiction to be the most interesting type of literature for those who like to study people. She argued that in fiction "the author can really tell the truth without hurting any one and without humiliating himself too much" (Roosevelt, *This Is My Story,* 358). "He can tell what he has learned through observation and experience of the inner workings of the souls of men" (Roosevelt, *This Is My Story,* 358).

Eleanor Roosevelt also loved reading, listening to, and reciting poetry in gatherings of family and friends. She especially liked traditional poetry. In fact her taste in poetry "was far from avant garde." Favorite authors included such poets as Emily Dickinson, Archibald MacLeish, and Carl Sandburg, "writers whose rhythms were compelling and whose meanings were clear" (Lash, *Eleanor: The Years Alone,* 186).

Mrs. Roosevelt also sometimes read poetry in public. For example, she served as narrator of a recording of Serge Prokofieff's musical fairy tale *Peter and the Wolf.* Her performance elicited mixed reviews. *Time* magazine, often critical of both Franklin and Eleanor Roosevelt, lambasted her recording, referring specifically to her high voice as wild and shrill. Other critics, however, noted that she was not a professional performer but gave a credible reading. One said she sounded like a grandmother reading a little story to her grandchildren (Lash, *Eleanor: The Years Alone,* 186).

On her many trips, Eleanor Roosevelt spent time reading. She was in great demand as a lecturer even in her later years, and often spent one or two weeks a month traveling throughout the United States and abroad. When in her seventies she wrote:

I do not grow weary of travel and I do not tire easily—not so easily as some younger people I know. . . . I generally find pleasure in travel because it gives me an opportunity to catch up on my reading. In fact, I do most of my reading for pleasure on airplanes since at home there seldom seems to be time to pick up the many books that interest me. Incidentally, if I have a complaint about the kind of life I lead, that is it—I simply cannot find time to read as much as I wish. (Roosevelt, *On My Own,* 19)

Eleanor Roosevelt also frequently recommended books to family members and the public. In letters to her daughter Anna she often suggested books Anna might read. The following is typical: "Do read Ernest Hemingway's book [*For Whom the Bell Tolls,* a novel of the Spanish Civil War], horrible but so well written & a great book I think" (Asbell, 128).

She also recommended books to her husband Franklin. She noted that he always read a great deal and was a very fast reader.

He had an amazing ability to skim through any kind of book and get everything out of it. When I gave him *Gone with the Wind* to read, he handed it back to me in a very short time. He couldn't possibly have read it so quickly, I was sure, and I told him so —but I couldn't catch him out on a single point. (Roosevelt, *This I Remember*, 117)

In her publications, Mrs. Roosevelt recommended reading books and discussing them with friends. She also urged parents to read aloud to their children, deploring the fact that so many young people do not read very much. She speculated that one reason might be that they have not learned to read very fast and to understand what they are reading.

Being highly respected and loved by so many people, Mrs. Roosevelt often received letters begging her for help in all kinds of problems, personal and public. Her comments on one such letter illustrate how much she cared about teaching people to read.

She had received a "pathetic" letter from a man who was seventy-four years old. He begged her to do all she could to see that adult education classes in his community were not discontinued because it had meant so much to him to learn to read. "I am not the only one. My next door neighbor is 81 and he learned to read last winter, and it has just made life over for us" (Black, 306).

Commenting on his letter, she wrote:

We have come a long way. We have done a great deal, but we still have a lot that can be done to improve our educational system, and we still have a tremendous amount to do with our libraries. We have got to make our libraries the center of a new life in the mind, because people are hungry to use their minds. (Black, 306)

She commented further on the value of libraries and books.

I feel that the care of libraries and the use of books, and the knowledge of books, is a tremendously vital thing, and we who deal with books and who love books have a great opportunity to bring about something in this country which is more vital here than anywhere else, because we have the chance to make a democracy that will be a real democracy. (Black, 307)

IMPORTANT DATES IN ELEANOR ROOSEVELT'S LIFE

1884	Born in New York City.
1894	Both parents died and she went to live with her maternal grandmother.
1899	Studied in England under Madame Marie Souvestre who had a great influence on the young Eleanor encouraging her creativity and independence of mind.
1905	Married distant cousin Franklin D. Roosevelt.
1921	Franklin contracted polio. Eleanor struggled to help him keep alive his dream of a political career.
1928	Campaigned for FDR's successful bid for New York State governor.
1932	Traveled throughout the United States campaigning for her husband's successful bid to become president of the United States.

1933–1945 The White House years. She became the most active first lady in history, working indefatigably on behalf of the less fortunate: farmers, laborers, minorities.

1945 After Franklin's death, appointed by President Truman as first American delegate to the newly formed United Nations where she served until 1952. Chaired the Commission on Human Rights, which drafted the UN Declaration of Human Rights.

1961 Reappointed a delegate to the United Nations by President Kennedy.

1962 Died in New York City.

1963 The Commission on the Status of Women, which Mrs. Roosevelt had chaired, published its report which, along with Betty Friedan's *The Feminine Mystique*, did much to spur development of the modern feminist movement.

SOURCES

Asbell, Bernard, ed. *Mother and Daughter: The Letters of Eleanor and Anna Roosevelt.* New York: Coward, McCann & Geohegan, 1982.

Black, Allida M., ed. *What I Hope to Leave Behind: The Essential Essays of Eleanor Roosevelt.* New York: Carlson Publishing, 1995.

Bussey, Charles J. "Eleanor Roosevelt," in *Great Lives from History: American Series,* vol. 4, Frank N. Magill, ed. Pasadena, Calif.: Salem Press, 1987.

Hareven, Tamara K. *Eleanor Roosevelt: An American Conscience.* Chicago: Quadrangle Books, 1968.

Lash, Joseph P. *Eleanor and Franklin: The Story of Their Relationship, Based on Eleanor Roosevelt's Private Papers.* New York: W. W. Norton & Co., 1971.

Lash, Joseph P. *Eleanor: The Years Alone.* New York: W. W. Norton & Co., 1972.

Roosevelt, Eleanor. *On My Own.* New York: Harper & Brothers, 1958.

Roosevelt, Eleanor. *This I Remember.* New York: Harper & Brothers, 1949.

Roosevelt, Eleanor. *This Is My Story.* New York: Garden City Publishing Co., 1939.

BEVERLY SILLS
(1929–)

Coloratura soprano Beverly Sills, named Belle Silverman at birth, was one of the greatest opera singers of the twentieth century. She is unique in a number of ways. First of all, she showed that an American-born and American-trained singer can reach the pinnacle of the opera world. Great opera stars generally came from abroad, and even Americans who scale operatic heights receive much of their training in Europe. Sills thrilled audiences singing in the high range required in coloratura roles. For generations most coloraturas simply stood and sang the right notes. In addition to singing beautifully, Sills added drama to her roles, as noted by music historian Winthrop Sargeant. "Miss Sills has given them new dimension, making them into dramas, as well as coloratura vehicles" (Sargeant, 78).

Sills is also unique in that she became an outstanding administrator of world-famous performing arts companies. She has been more successful in that type of work than any other singer. Sills was also noted for reading extensively about the operas in which she performed. Such study helped her add depth to her performances.

Belle Silverman was born in Brooklyn, New York, on May 25, 1929. When she was seven, her name was changed to Beverly Sills. It was decided that the new name would look better on a theater marquee. Her father, Morris Silverman, was an insurance salesman from Rumania, and her mother, Shirley Bahn Silverman, from the Ukraine, loved music and nourished Beverly's operatic ambitions.

When Belle was born, she came out of the womb with a bubble in her mouth. She was nicknamed Bubbles, and family and close friends called her by that name.

Belle began performing when she was very young. She first performed on the radio at the age of three.

Sills' operatic career began at the age of eighteen when she made her debut with the Philadelphia Civic Opera. From then until she retired as a singer, she performed in great opera houses throughout the world.

Young Bubbles had a very high I.Q. and loved reading. She did not read children's books, such as *Winnie the Pooh*, however, until she was an adult. Her father thought she should read adult books. One she enjoyed when she was ten was *Gone with the Wind*.

I got very excited when Rhett Butler put his hand on Scarlett O'Hara's bosom.... I remember thinking: *Oh, my this is the kind of book Sidney and Stanley* [Sills' brothers] *hide under their beds*. (Sills and Linderman, 17)

Both Sills' maternal grandfather and her father were devotees of newspapers. Early every Sunday Grandpa Bahn arrived with bagels, cream cheese, butter, and a variety of newspapers. Each child got one paper. Stanley got the *Herald Tribune*, Sidney got the *Daily News*, and Bubbles got the *Daily Mirror*. "We'd all eat breakfast, read the papers, and wait for Mama and Papa to wake up" (Sills and Linderman, 6).

When in school Bubbles' father would drive her to DuBrow's cafeteria before school started. He would have four newspapers in hand, and they would have breakfast and read them.

We'd then sit and read the papers, and Papa would ask me questions about some of the day's news stories. It was a wonderful way to learn what was going on in the world. I felt very close to my father. He'd leave me in Dubrow's at around seven-twenty, and I'd sit there reading the papers until it was time to go to school. (Sills and Linderman, 26)

The news was very bad at that time. World War II had started. The papers reported what Hitler was doing to the Jews in Germany. Bubbles and her father knew how important it was that America win the war.

Bubbles saw her first opera when she was eight. Her mother took her to the Metropolitan to see Lily Pons in Delibes' *Lakme*. In succeeding months she saw a number of additional operas. She became interested in the stories and characters and asked her mother to buy her a book of opera tales. For Christmas Bubbles got a large yellow volume entitled *Operas Every Child Should Know*. "It was a Bible for me; there is no other book that I have reread as often" (Sills, *Bubbles: An Encore*, 23).

When she began touring with opera companies, Sills did a great deal of general reading of a variety of authors. These included Oscar Wilde, Ernest Hemingway, and many others. Reading became an expensive hobby for her as she traveled from town to town: "I used to buy a hardcover book in one city, read it all day on the bus, sell it in the next city to a used book store,

and with the money buy another new book" (Sills, *Bubbles: An Encore,*
45–46).

At about the same time, in addition to reading serious literature while
traveling, Sills also read books on bridge. Her brother had taught her to
play, and she read up on the subject in order to perfect her skill.

Sills is noted for the extensive amount of study and reading she did
when preparing for a particular operatic role. Such research gave her additional insight into the particular parts she sang and her ability to bring dramatic impact to her performances.

In preparing to sing a particular role, Sills memorized not only her own
part but also the roles of the other singers in the opera. The only exception
was the last scene of *Lucia di Lammermoor*. She did not memorize those lines
because her character, Lucia, does not sing a note in that scene.

She also read the stories on which operas were based. On one occasion
director Desire Defrere brought Sills a copy of Anatole France's classic story
Thais and emphasized that when portraying a figure in the literature, she
should read about that figure first. Sills wrote:

I have always followed that advice, going back to the original Lucia, the original
Traviata, the original Manon. I have found it the ideal way of gaining insight into a
character that is perhaps not so obvious in the treatment given it by the composer.
(Sills, *Bubbles: An Encore,* 44)

One example of how reading helped Sills in her career is provided by her
experience with *Lucia di Lammermoor*. Early in her career she had sung the
mad scene in the opera wearing what most sopranos did: a very light-
weight nightgown. Then she read *The Bride of Lammermoor,* the novel by
Walter Scott on which the opera was based. She discovered that Scotland's
castles are cold and drafty. So the next time she sang the role, she wore a
warm, heavy garment.

In preparation for playing Queen Elizabeth in Donizetti's *Roberto
Devereux,* Sills did extensive research. *Devereux* is the tragic story of the ill-
fated love affair between Elizabeth and Essex.

A reporter who called on her in her New York apartment before the opening of *Roberto Devereux* found her studying up on Queen Elizabeth from an assortment of
about thirty books, some of them biographies of Elizabeth, others historical studies
of her times. "I've just about got that woman cold," she said happily, and added, "I
don't want to be an exhibitionist coloratura who merely sings notes. I'm interested
in the *character*." (Sargeant, 85)

After retiring from singing, Sills became a noted administrator of performing arts venues. As an administrator, Sills pioneered in offering opera
in English. For operas sung in Italian, French, or German, she introduced
"supertitles." The electronic "supertitles" were flashed above the stage giv-

ing the English translation at the same time an opera star was singing in a foreign language, thereby bringing a whole new generation of Americans to opera.

She served as general director of the New York City Opera, then as manager of the Metropolitan Opera. In 1994 she became chairwoman of the board of New York's Lincoln Center, the largest performing arts center in the world. She was "the first performing artist" to hold such an important administrative position (Blumenthal, 236).

Beverly Sills is a great role model for American young people, not only those who aspire to a musical career but also to those who have other ambitions. A girl from an obscure Brooklyn family, trained in the United States, Sills became a superstar in a field largely reserved for those who were born and/or trained in Europe.

Sills read a great deal from her childhood on, thus improving her general education. Her extensive study of the operas in which she appeared was remarkable, gave her insight into the characters she portrayed, and added to her ability to portray them convincingly.

IMPORTANT DATES IN BEVERLY SILLS' LIFE

1929   Born in Brooklyn, New York.

1936   Took the name Beverly Sills, a name which would look better on theater marquees.

1947   Made her operatic debut as Frasquita in *Carmen* with the Philadelphia Civic Opera.

1953   Debut, San Francisco Opera.

1955   Debut at the New York City Opera.

1958   Performed in *The Ballad of Baby Doe*. Received rave reviews both for her singing and for her acting ability.

1960s   Received acclaim as a prima donna for her performances in a variety of roles, classic and modern in a number of opera houses.

1975   Debut at Metropolitan Opera, New York.

1979   Became general director, New York City Opera.

1991   Became managing director, Metropolitan Opera.

1994   Became Chairwoman, Lincoln Center, New York.

SOURCES

Blumenthal, Ralph. "Beverly Sills, at 66, Stars in Her Grandest Role," in *The New York Times Biographical Service*, February, 1996, pp. 236–238.

Kerby, Mona. *Beverly Sills: America's Own Opera Star*. New York: Viking Kestrel, 1989.

Kushner, David Z. "Beverly Sills," in *Great Lives from History: American Women Series*, Vol. 5, Frank N. Magill, ed. Pasadena, Calif.: Salem Press, 1995.

Sargeant, Winthrop. *Divas*. New York: Coward, McCann & Geohegan, 1973.

Sills, Beverly. *Bubbles: A Self-Portrait*. Indianapolis: Bobbs-Merrill, 1976.

Sills, Beverly. *Bubbles: An Encore*. New York: Grosset & Dunlap, 1981.

Sills, Beverly, and Lawrence Linderman. *Beverly: An Autobiography*. Toronto: Bantam Books, 1987.

STEVEN SPIELBERG
(1947–)

Steven Spielberg's movies have earned more money than those of any other producer/director. According to the *Guinness Book of World Records*, his *Jurassic Park* made over $913 million worldwide up to June, 1997. *The Lost World* earned more than $100 million in five and a half days—faster than any other movie (*The Guinness Book of World Records*, 200).

Spielberg is also one of the best movie makers in history. Five of the films he directed were included among the top 100 movies of all time as voted on by 1,500 experts chosen by the American Film Institute—more than any other director. Alfred Hitchcock and Billy Wilder had four each. Spielberg's *Schindler's List* was the only contemporary film among the top ten on the list (" 'Citizen Kane' tops all-time 100 movie list," 2b).

Steven Spielberg was born on December 18, 1947, in Cincinnati, Ohio. He was the first child of Arnold and Leah Spielberg. The family moved to Phoenix, Arizona, when he was still a child. At the age of five or six he saw his first movie, Cecil B. DeMille's *The Greatest Show on Earth*. From then on his main interest was going to movies, and in high school, making his own films.

While still in his teens, he made a forty-minute World War II movie entitled *Escape to Nowhere*. It won first prize in a statewide contest for amateur film makers (McBride, 12).

During his college years Spielberg went to movies constantly. He also would bluff his way into movie studios to observe famous directors.

His short film, *Amblin'*, won several awards. It also brought him to the attention of Universal's television unit, which awarded him a seven-year contract. In following years he directed a number of episodes of popular television shows, including *Marcus Welby, M.D.* and *Columbo*.

He also made movies for television of which *Duel*, starring Dennis Weaver, was the most popular. His first huge hit, *Jaws*, earned critical praise and became an enormous box-office success. From then on almost every Spielberg picture received much critical praise and earned a great deal of money.

Although winning many awards for his movies, Spielberg was "snubbed" by the Academy of Motion Picture Arts and Sciences for a number of years. Finally, however, in 1994 *Schindler's List* was nominated for eleven Academy Awards and received seven, including those for best director and best picture.

Steven's father wanted his son to learn to love literature. He gave him a copy of Hawthorne's classic, *The Scarlet Letter*. Steven did not like it at all. So he drew stick figures of a bowler knocking down pins and when he flipped the pages, the pins came falling down. He facetiously called it his "first film adapted from another medium" (Sanello, 17).

At an early age, Spielberg developed a passion for science fiction—books, magazines, and films. Otherwise he disliked reading, being a very slow reader, possibly due to dyslexia. Ironically, some of his best films are based on books, not only science fiction works, but on realistic works, such as *The Color Purple* and *Schindler's List*.

In adulthood he described his attitude towards reading as follows.

I was not a reader, and I'm still not a reader. . . . I'm a very slow reader. And because I'm so slow, it makes me feel guilty that it might take me three hours to read a 110-page screenplay that I even wrote the story for. So I don't read a lot. I have not read for pleasure in many years. (Sanello, 18)

He also, however, argued that it was a shame he did not have the same kind of passion for reading he had for movies.

In grade school, however, he read a great deal of science fiction. Steven also wrote fantastic stories that he would read to his class. Many of the students' stories were boring, but Steven's were fun to listen to, and the students looked forward to his storytelling.

When he went to scout camp, Steven read amazing stories while other boys were engaged in such activities as putting up tents. He provided entertainment for the other boys by telling them stories that were both entertaining and frightening for the other boys. He was not very popular with the other boys except when telling his mesmerizing tales.

Spielberg biographer Joseph McBride argues that the image of Spielberg telling stories around the campfire is "archetypal."

Spielberg's TV series *Amazing Stories* started each week with a montage showing the development of storytelling through the ages, beginning with a caveman spinning stories around a campfire. (McBride, 79)

A number of Spielberg's movies reflect his consuming interest in science fiction/horror stories. These include *Jurassic Park, Close Encounters of the Third Kind, Raiders of the Lost Ark, E.T. The Extra-Terrestrial, Jurassic Park,* and *Jaws.*

The idea for his 1975 film, *Jaws,* came to Spielberg after reading Peter Benchley's novel, which he picked up in a studio office. He was captivated by the story about a great white shark that terrifies a town.

After reading the book, Spielberg recalled wanting "to do *Jaws* for hostile reasons. I read it and felt I had been attacked. It terrified me, and I wanted to strike back." (Ferber, 52)

The Color Purple (1985) is another one of Spielberg's best movies based on a book, Alice Walker's novel of the same title. Kathleen Kennedy gave Spielberg a copy of the book and encouraged him to read it. He had told her about how he had been discriminated against, and she thought *The Color Purple* might make a good emotional match.

"You know, it's a black story," she told him. "But that shouldn't bother you because you're Jewish and essentially you share similarities in your upbringing and your heritage." (McBride, 367)

He read it and said he loved it. The 1985 film about American blacks received excellent reviews and became one of Spielberg's greatest movies. It was nominated for eleven Academy Awards. Astonishingly, however, Spielberg himself was not nominated as best director. Some speculated that the Academy's snub of Spielberg was due to jealousy.

Empire of the Sun (1987) was based on J. G. Ballard's book. Spielberg admitted that from the moment he read the autobiographical novel, he wanted to make the picture. He was fascinated by the story of a boy's loss of innocence during World War II. In a number of ways, "the character of Jim reflected Spielberg himself, who had had to contend with the traumas of an unjust world while growing up" (Ferber, 98).

Schindler's List, based on Thomas Keneally's book, is the gripping story depicting the horrors of the Holocaust, specifically about a German industrialist who risked his safety to employ Jews in his factory and thus save them from death. It was Spielberg's first film dealing with his Jewish heritage. Unlike Woody Allen, whose films often deal with Jewish characters, Spielberg had never felt comfortable with his Jewishness. He wanted to be a part of the majority, and his movies were made to interest suburbanites. In fact, he has been called "the poet of suburbia" (McBride, 19).

When visiting Poland to make *Schindler's List,* however, Spielberg remembered all the stories his grandparents had told him about Jewish history. His "Jewish life came pouring back" to him, and he frequently cried (McBride, 414).

At the time of making *Schindler's List* he became very proud of his Jewish roots. His mother had always wanted him to make a movie about Jews, and finally he did. He announced that *Schindler's List* was for her.

Spielberg's *Jurassic Park* was released in 1993, the same year as *Schindler's List*. It was based on Michael Crichton's best seller, and it focused on dinosaurs, another childhood obsession. It became a box-office champion.

In addition to movies based on stories written by others, Spielberg has used his fertile imagination to develop ideas and write scripts for other successful films. For example, he spent about two years writing the script for a movie containing subjects that had fascinated him since childhood: alien and space life. The film was *Close Encounters of the Third Kind*, released in 1977.

He came up with the idea for *E.T. The Extra Terrestrial* while filming *Raiders of the Lost Ark* in Tunisia. The story concerns a lonely child who discovers a friend in an alien. He thought about his own experiences as a ten year old.

It was a tale of friendship between a lonely earthbound child and a 900–year-old alien who has been left behind, a story that Spielberg believed represented how he felt as a child: lost, lonely, alienated. Spielberg said, "[The film was] a personal movie for me, and closer to my heart than any movie I've ever made before." (Ferber, 76)

For someone who is not a great reader, Spielberg has undoubtedly stimulated reading among countless people. After release of his films based on books, both book stores and libraries see large increases in the demand for the books on which the films are based.

IMPORTANT DATES IN STEVEN SPIELBERG'S LIFE

1947   Born in Cincinnati, Ohio.

1961   His film *Escape to Nowhere* won first prize in a statewide contest for amateur filmmakers.

1969   Received a seven-year contract to direct television shows for Universal.

1974   Made his first feature film, *The Sugarland Express*. Hired to direct the film version of Peter Benchley's best-selling novel *Jaws*. It became the highest-grossing film in history.

1977   His *Close Encounters of the Third Kind* is released.

1982   *E.T.* released to great critical and box-office success.

1985   *The Color Purple* was released.

1993   Two of his most successful films released: *Jurassic Park* and *Schindler's List* for which he received Academy Awards for Best Picture and Best Director. Since then, a number of his films, including *Amistad* and *Saving Private Ryan* have won a number of prestigious awards.

SOURCES

Brode, Douglas. *The Films of Steven Spielberg*. New York: Citadel Press, 1995.

" 'Citizen Kane' tops all-time 100 movie list," *St. Petersburg Times*, June 17, 1998.

Ferber, Elizabeth. *Steven Spielberg*. Philadelphia: Chelsea House Publishers, 1997.

The Guinness Book of World Records. Stamford, Conn.: Guinness Media, 1997.

Hargrove, Jim. *Steven Spielberg: Amazing Filmmaker*. Chicago: Childrens Press, 1988.

McBride, Joseph. *Steven Spielberg: A Biography*. New York: Simon & Schuster, 1997.

Sanello, Frank. *Spielberg: The Man, the Movies, the Mythology*. Dallas: Taylor Publishing, 1996.

Taylor, Philip M. *Steven Spielberg: The Man, His Movies, and Their Meaning*. New York: Continuum, 1992.

ELIZABETH CADY STANTON
(1815–1902)

Elizabeth Cady Stanton's crucial role in the women's movement was long overshadowed by that of Susan B. Anthony. The reason was largely because she, unlike Anthony, was involved in issues other than a woman's right to vote, and many feminists feared that her activities on other issues would harm the drive for woman's suffrage.

Cady Stanton was significant among feminists of her time for her "radicalism and brilliance."

She was an abolitionist when few dared to be, a skeptic at a time when religious devotion was mandatory for women, a champion of votes for women three-quarters of a century too soon, and doubtful about marriage when it was most sacrosanct. (O'Neill, 1052)

The revival of feminism in the 1960s, however, created a new, greatly enhanced appreciation of what Cady Stanton did. Her work led to much progress on a variety of issues on which she concentrated. Many now believe her work overshadowed most feminists of her time, including Susan B. Anthony. In fact Anthony herself acknowledged that she was the junior partner in her relationship with Cady Stanton and that Cady Stanton was the real founder of the organized women's rights movement in the United States.

Elizabeth Cady was one of six children born into an upper class family on November 12, 1815, in Johnstown, New York, the daughter of Daniel and Margaret Cady.

Little Elizabeth Cady developed a habit of reading whatever she could get her hands on. As she grew, her reading of earlier feminists gave her ideas she used to attack the theories of male superiority in her many speeches and writings.

Elizabeth was brought up in a very strict family. "The Cady children feared, rather than loved, their parents, who were kind and somewhat indulgent but limited by the strict Puritan ethic so common in that day" (Oakley, 16). Consequently, Elizabeth's childhood was not a very happy one, often forbidden to do things she liked to do. One day she asked her Scotch nurse, a stern Presbyterian, "I was wondering why it was that everything we like to do is a sin, and that everything we dislike is commanded by God or someone on earth" (Elizabeth Cady Stanton, 10).

Various incidents in her early life convinced Elizabeth that women were treated most unfairly. Her father told her on more than one occasion that even though she was very bright, he wished she were a boy. She was dismayed to discover that a woman's property, property she had paid for, was automatically transferred to her husband when she married.

She wanted to attend Union College but had to attend Troy Female Seminary because she was a girl. Fortunately, she discovered that that seminary, founded by Emma Willard, was unlike other schools for girls, which were typically finishing schools. It provided a good academic education. Elizabeth excelled there and perfected her writing skills, which she would later use to effect as a successful author.

She disapproved of women having to vow to obey their husbands. Therefore, when she married the prominent abolitionist Henry Brewster Stanton in 1840, she insisted that that promise not be in the wedding ceremony. She also kept her maiden name Cady while adding Stanton, always known as Elizabeth Cady Stanton.

Cady Stanton traveled to London with her husband Henry to attend the World Anti-Slavery Convention to which he was a delegate. Elizabeth was shocked and angered when she discovered that women had to sit in the balcony and could not speak at the convention. She proposed to Lucretia Mott, the Philadelphia Quaker preacher, that they hold a women's rights convention as soon as they return to the United States, and Mott agreed.

For a number of years following their return, however, Cady Stanton was busy caring for her husband and seven children. Nevertheless, she never lost her dream of such a meeting and in 1848 Cady Stanton and Mott organized the first women's rights convention. The meeting launched the women's rights movement in the United States.

Cady Stanton modeled the major document for the convention after the Declaration of Independence. It called for many reforms, including the admission of women to institutions of higher education, the right to enter professions, and an end to a double standard of sexual morality. Resolutions based on these arguments gained unanimous approval at the convention.

Cady Stanton was elected the first president of the National Woman Suffrage Association. She spent her time lobbying for suffrage and did extensive lecturing on family life and child rearing.

For the rest of her life Cady Stanton remained a phenomenally important leader in reform movements. She served as president of various reform groups, and spoke and wrote widely on reform topics.

Elizabeth Cady Stanton noted that she could not recall exactly when she learned the alphabet. She had pleasant memories, however, of a spinster teacher, Maria Yost, "who patiently taught three generations of children the rudiments of the English language." She also introduced them to old-fashioned schoolbooks such as *Murray's Spelling Book*, which included pictures of Old Father Time and the farmer stoning the boys in his apple tree. "The interesting Readers children now have were unknown sixty years ago. We did not reach the temple of knowledge by the flowery paths of ease in which our descendants now walk" (Elizabeth Cady Stanton, 9).

When she was not yet eleven, Elizabeth's only brother, "a man of great promise" and the pride of his father's heart had just graduated from Union College. Unfortunately, he returned home to die. Viewing the body in its casket, Elizabeth's father was devastated. Elizabeth was also devastated when her father said he wished she were a boy.

Elizabeth thought she could make up for the loss by excelling in her studies. From that time on she spent many hours reading the books in her father's library.

She begged a neighbor, the Reverend Simon Hosack, to teach her Greek. She excelled in her studies, won two prizes in Greek, including a Greek testament, and was sure her father would appreciate her success.

She ran all the way home to show her prize to Judge Cady and eagerly awaited his praise. Her father was indeed proud of her, but once more she heard the bitter phrase, "My daughter, it's a pity you were not a boy." (Oakley, 18)

The Rev. Hosack was so proud of Elizabeth that he promised to will her his Greek lexicon, his testament and grammar, and four volumes of Scott's commentaries.

Elizabeth felt that every book she read taught the divinely ordained headship of man. She never gave in to that idea.

Still intent on winning her father's praise, Elizabeth spent many hours in his law office. She listened to his conversations with clients and law students and read law books. She discovered how unfair many laws were to women. One law was especially galling. She discovered that when a father died, he usually left his property to his son, and the mother then became dependent on him. "If the relationship between the mother and son (or daughter-in-law) were not smooth, the result could be tragic for the older woman" (Oakley, 18).

She also found that a wife might make money herself by sewing or raising chickens in order to buy food. Her husband, however, had every right to take such money and spend it on anything he wished, including whiskey.

Young Elizabeth threatened to cut such laws out of the law books. Her father explained to her that it would do no good. He told her that when she grew up, she could go to Albany and get the legislators to change the laws so they were fair to women. Elizabeth determined to do so. She decided that somehow she would reform unjust laws.

Henry and Edward Bayard were two of the young law students who got their training in Judge Cady's office. They selected books and reading for the Cady girls: "Fresh from college, they made our lessons in Latin, Greek, and mathematics so easy that we studied with real pleasure and had more leisure for play" (Elizabeth Cady Stanton, 27).

Edward, who was ten years older than Elizabeth and married her elder sister, Tryphena, loved children and soon became her confidant. Henry, however, was a great tease. He would read Elizabeth the most outrageously anti-female laws and then "laugh gaily at her dismay" (Lutz, 9).

Henry also read passages from the Bible indicating that women should be subject to men. He read *The Taming of the Shrew*, the Shakespeare play which so forcefully portrayed the "superiority" of the male sex. All the arguments, however, that "pointed to the divine headship of man" only strengthened Elizabeth's conviction. She would never consent to the idea that men were superior to women (Lutz, 9).

Elizabeth Cady enjoyed the progressive curriculum at Emma Willard's Troy Female Seminary except for a time when she had a very serious crisis. She, along with classmates, attended a number of revival meetings conducted by Charles G. Finney, a noted evangelist. She responded to his strong Calvinism with its emphasis on hell and damnation and fell into a serious depression so intense she thought she might be losing her mind.

Her family came to her aid, however, taking her to Niagara Falls for a vacation. She recuperated by resting, reading, and discussing ideas with her brother-in-law Edward Bayard. He questioned the Cady family's conservatism and introduced Elizabeth to liberal writers.

Elizabeth found the work of the Scottish philosopher George Combe particularly helpful. Combe "abjured religion to focus on producing mental health through physical exercise, mental discipline, and the rational integration of body and mind, and he had a wide readership among American intellectuals and reformers" (Banner, 13–14). Combe's work not only assisted Elizabeth in her current crisis "but also in the formulation of her mature feminist philosophy" (Banner, 14).

Refreshed after her reading and resting at Niagara Falls, Elizabeth returned in a healthy frame of mind. She had "taken her first steps toward religious liberalism"(Banner, 14).

While at the Troy Seminary Elizabeth made the acquaintance of Scottish pupil Henrietta Dewar. Henrietta was a devotee of Sir Walter Scott, and she would read and recite his novels and poetry "with a fine Scotch burr." Stanton wrote that Miss Dewar "made literature live for me" (Stanton and Blatch, vol.1, 40).

Edward Bayard often visited the Troy Seminary and discussed history, philosophy, poetry, law, and other topics with the girls. They read together many novels "without number."

The long winter evenings thus passed pleasantly, Mr. Bayard alternately talking and reading aloud Scott, Bulwer, James, Cooper, and Dickens, whose works were just then coming out in numbers from week to week, always leaving us in suspense at the most critical point of the story." (Stanton and Blatch, vol. 1, 51)

No year was considered complete without a visit to Gerrit Smith in Peterboro, New York. Although wealthy, Smith lived simply and contributed huge sums to reform causes. His mansion was one of the stations on the "underground railroad." He had been a staunch Calvinist, but the church did not condemn slavery as a sin and its "attitude toward slavery had made him question traditional beliefs." He therefore urged a practical Christianity (Lutz, 15).

Every morning the family gathered and Smith would read from the Bible and say a short prayer. Elizabeth often read the framed text above his door "God is Love," and for the first time she realized religion could be a comfort.

While there she became involved in frequent antislavery and women's rights discussions with the Smith family and friends and had access to many books. She also read the abolitionist paper *Liberator* whenever she could. Through reading and discussion, abolitionist leaders became heroes to her—Frederick Douglass, born a slave; the publisher of the *Liberator*, William Lloyd Garrison; James G. Birney, the southerner who freed his slaves; George Thompson, the English abolitionist; and Lucretia Mott, the Quaker, "who spoke at antislavery meetings where women were supposed to keep silent" (Lutz, 14).

As she matured, Cady Stanton read widely in the work of feminists and other liberal writers, including Mary Wollstonecraft and Margaret Fuller.

Wollstonecraft and Fuller provided her with the ammunition to attack prevailing notions of male superiority and to advance the strikingly modern argument that whatever differences existed between men and women were cultural and not innate. (Banner, 71–72)

Although Cady Stanton was dismayed that women could not speak at the London World Antislavery Convention, she was fortunate to meet Lucretia Mott and other prominent women there. They carried on lengthy discussions of the rights of women, including the ideas of feminist authors and their objections to traditional interpretations of the Bible placing women subject to men.

Cady Stanton had thought much about the liberal works she had read and "now to hear Lucretia Mott freely discussing what she had scarcely dared think was such joy that the wonders of the British Museum paled in comparison" (Lutz, 30).

In addition to feminist theorists Cady Stanton was strongly influenced by writers who stressed individual responsibility. Ralph Waldo Emerson, who emphasized the importance of self-knowledge through contemplation, was one of her favorite authors. She also praised John Stuart Mill's *On the Subjection of Women* "as the best treatise yet written on women's oppression, which Mill traced not to law or society, but primarily to individual relationships between men and women" (Banner, 75).

Cady Stanton was undoubtedly the most influential writer of her time on women's issues. Her writings on suffrage and on a variety of other women's issues "were so extensive that it would be appropriate to consider her the chief theorist or intellectual of the late nineteenth century women's rights movement" (Smith, 2148).

She wrote numerous pamphlets and magazine and newspaper articles and letters on abolition and women's right to vote. She also wrote and spoke extensively on marriage and divorce and property rights for women.

She also published *The Woman's Bible*. It was a revised version of biblical scripture, which questioned the treatment of women.

[The purpose of *The Woman's Bible* was] to make women question the theological doctrines, so derogatory to them, which had been evolved by the clergy in past ages and were still being preached from the pulpit. That women could go to church and listen docilely to sermons on texts which declared they were inferior beings and the cause of man's downfall were incomprehensible to her. (Lutz, 295)

She was dismayed and deeply hurt when she found that Susan B. Anthony and other women's leaders ignored or denounced *The Woman's Bible*. They feared her "radical" ideas would cause the public to assume the woman's suffrage movement was irreligious.

Cady Stanton co-authored three volumes of the monumental *History of Woman Suffrage*, and towards the end of her life she published her autobiography, *Eighty Years and More*. Her writings are still carefully studied by students and others interested in the development of the rights of women and other reformist issues.

In her last years, having some leisure, Stanton "filled her days with reading" (Griffith, 216). She read poetry and many novels as well as nonfiction works. Among the imaginative writers she favored were Charles Dickens, George Eliot, Mark Twain, Charlotte Brontë, William Thackeray, Alfred Tennyson, and Leo Tolstoy.

She noted humorously that Mark Twain's fun was only equaled by his morals. She was critical of Tolstoy's *Anna Karenina*. She disapproved of the fact that the women in the novel were all quite unhappy. She believed their depression was due to their looking to men, rather than to themselves, for happiness.

She also had some leisure to read many philosophical and historical works. These included James Boswell's *Life of Johnson*; Herbert Spencer's *Education*; Matthew Arnold's *Essays in Criticism*; and Andrew White's *A History of the Warfare of Science with Theology*. Among the biographies she read were those of George Eliot, William Lloyd Garrison, Alfred Tennyson, and George Washington.

Cady Stanton's vast knowledge of literature was helpful to her in her many speeches and writings. She frequently quoted or referred to the many philosophers, novelists, and poets she had read. Longfellow was a favorite poet, and on occasion she quoted from his work. For example, when speaking on the joys of old age, she recited one of his poems she liked best: *Morituri Salutamus*.

> Ah! Nothing is too late
> Till the tired heart shall cease to palpitate,
> Cato learned Greek at eighty; Sophocles
> Wrote his grand Oedipus, and Simonides
> Bore off the prize of verse from his compeers
> When each had numbered more than four score years,
>
> For age is opportunity no less
> Than youth itself, though in another dress.

As she grew older, Cady Stanton began to lose her sight. It was a terrible privation. Although she could write without glasses, she could not even read her own writing. Undaunted, and in good health otherwise, she hired a reader and typist to assist her.

This attitude was typical of Cady Stanton.

Such optimism and resourcefulness were characteristic. Stanton accepted the reality of her circumstances and emphasized the positive elements. "I never encourage sad moods." (Griffith, 216)

IMPORTANT DATES IN ELIZABETH CADY STANTON'S LIFE

1815	Born in Johnstown, New York.
1830–1833	Attended Troy Female Seminary, conducted by Emma Willard.
1840	Married Henry Brewster Stanton. At her request, the traditional promise to obey her husband was omitted. She took the name of Stanton but also kept her maiden name Cady. Attended world antislavery convention in London. Her husband was a delegate. Met Lucretia Mott there.

1848	Cady Stanton and Lucretia Mott called the first Women's Rights Convention in Seneca Falls, New York.
1851	Met Susan B. Anthony, beginning their lifelong friendship.
1863	Organized the Women's Loyal League with the goal of winning the Civil War and freeing the slaves.
1869	Elected president of the National Woman Suffrage Association. Held the office for twenty-one years. Began lecture tours for the Lyceum Bureau and became one of their most popular speakers.
1881–1886	Co-authored the *History of Woman Suffrage.*
1885	On her seventieth birthday, she was honored by a nationwide celebration.
1887	Began work on *The Woman's Bible*, published in 1895.
1898	Published her reminiscences, *Eighty Years and More.*
1902	Died in New York City.

SOURCES

Banner, Lois W. *Elizabeth Cady Stanton: A Radical for Woman's Rights.* Boston: Little, Brown, and Co., 1980.

Griffith, Elizabeth. *In Her Own Right: The Life of Elizabeth Cady Stanton.* New York: Oxford University Press, 1984.

Lutz, Alma. *Created Equal: A Biography of Elizabeth Cady Stanton, 1815–1902.* New York: Octagon Books, 1974. (Reprint of 1940 work.)

Oakley, Mary Ann B. *Elizabeth Cady Stanton.* Old Westbury, N.Y.: Feminist Press, 1972.

O'Neill, William L. "Elizabeth Cady Stanton," in *Encyclopedia of American Biography*, 2nd ed. John A. Garraty and Jerome L. Sternstein, eds. New York: HarperCollins, 1996.

Smith, Harold L. "Elizabeth Cady Stanton," in *Great Lives from History*, Vol. 5, Frank N. Magill, ed. Pasadena, Calif.: Salem Press, 1987.

Stanton, Elizabeth Cady. *Eighty Years and More: Reminiscences 1815–1897.* Boston: Northeastern University Press, 1993 publication of 1898 work.

Stanton, Theodore, and Harriot Stanton Blatch, eds. *Elizabeth Cady Stanton*, 2 vols. New York: Arno & The New York Times, 1969 reprint of 1922 edition.

HARRIET BEECHER STOWE
(1811–1896)

Harriet Beecher Stowe's book, *Uncle Tom's Cabin*, which vividly described the horrors of slavery, is one of the most influential books ever published. It sold at least 300,000 copies in its first year. It was the first book by an American to sell as many copies as those written by popular British writers Charles Dickens, Jane Austen, the Brontë sisters, and Sir Walter Scott. As a result, she became the most famous American woman of her time.

Harriet had read great imaginative literature from her childhood on. Had she not done so, she might never have achieved such success as a writer. Books which influenced her own writing the most were those written by Sir Walter Scott.

Harriet Beecher Stowe was born on July 14, 1811, in Litchfield, Connecticut, the seventh of nine children. Her father was Lyman Beecher, a strict Calvinist minister, and her mother was Roxana Foote Beecher. Roxana Beecher died when Harriet was only four.

Harriet attended local schools, and when her father Lyman and sister Catharine went to Cincinnati in 1832, she accompanied them. Lyman became president of Lane Theological Seminary. Catharine established a school for women at which Harriet taught. While there she saw firsthand the evils of slavery in Ohio and especially in nearby Kentucky, and she became an ardent abolitionist.

In 1836 Harriet married Calvin Stowe, a professor at Lane, and they had five children in eight years. She supplemented their small income by writing short stories. In 1850 they returned to New England where she began writing a long story of slavery based on what she had observed in Ohio and Kentucky.

The story was published in book form in 1852 under the title *Uncle Tom's Cabin, or Life Among the Lowly*. Abolitionists loved it, but many Southerners condemned it. It was dangerous to possess a copy in the South.

Several years later Stowe published another antislavery novel, *Dred: A Tale of the Great Dismal Swamp*. It also was very successful although not achieving the same phenomenal acclaim as *Uncle Tom's Cabin*.

Stowe's fame spread throughout the world. She traveled widely on lecture tours throughout America and made several triumphant visits to Europe. In England she was feted by such luminaries as Dickens, Thackeray, and William Gladstone.

Stowe was present when the Emancipation Proclamation was adopted by the United State Senate. When the document was approved, senators and visitors rose in a body to pay homage to the woman who had mobilized such support for the adoption of that history-making proclamation.

During her remaining years Stowe wrote many short stories, articles, and a number of popular novels about New England life. Although well received, none of those works achieved the lasting critical approval of her antislavery works.

Harriet Beecher resented that she was usually excluded from all the interesting games and adventures her brothers participated in because she was a girl. Lyman Beecher recognized her talents but thought it was too bad she was a girl.

Nonetheless, he saw to it that she had a good education and gave her access to the books in his study located in a garret at the top of the house. She recalled the happy times she spent there as a child.

High above all the noise of the house, this room had to me the air of a refuge and a sanctuary. Its walls were set round from floor to ceiling with the friendly, quiet faces of books.... Here I loved to retreat and niche myself down in a quiet corner with my favorite books around me. (Charles Edward Stowe, 9)

According to Hedrick, Harriet "turned to books for solace and reward; in both a figurative and literal sense, they did finally enable her to climb higher than her brothers" (Hedrick, 19).

Although many of the books in her father's study were heavy theological tomes which Harriet did not understand, she found others which fired her imagination. She read the Bible hour after hour for both inspiration and pleasure. She especially delighted in the romantic poetry of the Song of Solomon, read it over and over, and memorized it.

She found a copy of *The Arabian Nights* at the bottom of a barrel of old sermons. She was fascinated by the stories, read them over and over, and learned them by heart. The beloved stories in *The Arabian Nights* took her to foreign lands. When the boys were out in rough play or on fishing expeditions, Harriet would curl up in a corner and happily read the fascinating, enchanted tales.

Another work which delighted Harriet was Cotton Mather's *Magnalia Christi Americana*. Her father had brought a new edition of the work home, and Harriet devoured it. Although the dramatic stories contained materials about witchcraft and the strange doings of Indians, one could be entertained by them because they had a high moral purpose. Harriet found them as fascinating as *The Arabian Knights*. She was also inspired by them, just as Nathaniel Hawthorne had been.

Harriet also read many novels which Lyman Beecher considered "trash." He warned her that such reading might interfere with her spiritual development, but Harriet would not give up her books.

She read many British writers, including Shakespeare, Milton, Dickens, Lord Byron, and Sir Walter Scott. She was thrilled with Byron's romantic poetry. She read his *The Corsair*, and was "astonished and electrified" by it (Jakoubek, 28).

News of Byron's death in 1824, left young Harriet despondent.

Upon hearing the news of his passing, she climbed a hill behind the house in Litchfield and "lay down among the daisies looking up into the blue sky, and thought of that great eternity into which Byron had entered, and wondered how it might be with his soul." (Jakoubek, 28)

Although Lyman Beecher disliked most novels, he examined Walter Scott's works and said he approved of them. "I have always disapproved of novels as trash," he said, "but in these is real genius and real culture" (Wagenknecht, 144).

Scott, who authored such popular novels as *Ivanhoe*, *The Bride of Lammermoor*, *The Talisman*, and *Rob Roy*, "became a Beecher family institution." Harriet's sister Catharine wrote ballads "after his style, and with her friend Louisa Wait at the piano" the house was filled with Scottish songs (Hedrick, 20).

While they sat around the kitchen table the Beechers would discuss Scott and see who could relate the most incidents from his novels. Scott's *Ivanhoe* was a special favorite. They read it seven times over, and memorized much of it.

After her mother died when she was a small child, Harriet paid long visits to her maternal grandmother and aunts. They were Episcopalian and somewhat more liberal than Harriet's puritanical father. They introduced her to literature she had not found at home. Grandmother Foote read to her from the Bible "and talked about Bible characters as if they were real people" (Wagenknecht, 135). She also read from the works of Samuel Johnson and other noted writers. Aunt Mary Foote read poetry to Harriet, and she read it beautifully.

As an adult, Stowe was convinced of the importance of reading for herself and others. She had books all over the house, not only in the library. She wanted them conveniently located so she could read whenever the spirit so moved her. She often became thoroughly engrossed in reading. For example, when on the streetcar she often read favorite books, and sometimes forgot to get off at her stop and traveled to the end of the line.

Stowe was also interested in what other people read. When visiting friends or acquaintances, she would often inspect the books on their shelves. She had little regard for those who did not cherish books.

Stowe encouraged her children's reading. She would gather her children and her servants about her most evenings and read to them for several hours. The most favorite author was, of course, Walter Scott. She read through most of his historical novels.

She also had a special bookcase containing Scott's works, and when she visited Scotland, she made a point of touring places mentioned in his stories.

Throughout her adult years Stowe also participated in literary parties and picnics. She was known for gathering friends about and reading aloud important novels of the time.

Charles Dickens was one writer who had an influence on Stowe. Being an admirer of hers, Dickens said he could see some of his work reflected in her writing. Although she criticized Dickens for having so much tippling in his novels, she admired him because he wrote so movingly about common men and women, those who were oppressed, neglected, and forgotten.

Dickens's more democratic spirit validated the concerns of nineteenth-century women's culture and of the literary realism that Stowe and other women writers would develop from it. Unlike Byron and Bulwar, who scorned "the common sympathies, wants, and sufferings of every day human nature," Dickens "shows us that our coarse, common world, can be made a very agreeable and interesting place." (Hedrick, 156)

Undoubtedly, however, the writer who exerted the most influence on Stowe was Walter Scott. In reading Scott to herself and to others, she learned how to write a novel that would move readers to joy and sorrow.

Scott was worth more to her as a literary influence than all other writers put together. We should suspect that she had reread his novels before writing *Uncle Tom's Cabin* even if we did not know the fact, for the book recalls him not only in its specific techniques of story-telling but even more in its grasp and vision of the life of a people. . . . And this is quite as true of *Dred*, which is *Old Mortality* transferred to a Southern setting. (Wagenknecht, 144)

Abraham Lincoln may have been exaggerating somewhat when he referred to Harriet Beecher Stowe as the woman who started the Civil War. Nonetheless, her great book *Uncle Tom's Cabin* exerted a powerful influence on turning Americans, and civilized people all over the world, against the institution of slavery. Her extensive reading contributed towards her ability to write materials that would convince millions of people of the evils of slavery.

IMPORTANT DATES IN HARRIET BEECHER STOWE'S LIFE

1811   Born in Litchfield, Connecticut.

1832   Went to Cincinnati, Ohio, with her father and sister. Taught there in the school established by her sister Catharine.

1834   Published her first story in the *Western Monthly.*

1836   Married Professor Calvin E. Stowe.

1852   Published *Uncle Tom's Cabin,* a tale of slavery based on her observations in Ohio and Kentucky.

1856   Published *Dred: A Tale of the Great Dismal Swamp*, another antislavery novel.

1860s to   Published numerous articles on a variety of topics and a number of
mid-1880s   light, popular novels.

1896   Died in Hartford, Connecticut.

SOURCES

Cross, Barbara M., ed. *The Autobiography of Lyman Beecher*, 2 vols. Cambridge, Mass.: Belknap Press of Harvard University Press, 1961.

Cross, Barbara M. "Stowe, Harriet Beecher," in *Notable American Women, 1607–1950: A Biographical Dictionary*, Edward T. James, Janet W. James, and Paul S. Boyer, eds. Cambridge, Mass.: The Belknap Press of Harvard University Press, 1971.

Crozier, Alice C. *The Novels of Harriet Beecher Stowe*. New York: Oxford University Press, 1969.

Hedrick, Joan D. *Harriet Beecher Stowe: A Life*. New York: Oxford University Press, 1994.

Jakoubek, Robert E. *Harriet Beecher Stowe*. New York: Chelsea House Publishers, 1989.

Stowe, Charles Edward. *Life of Harriet Beecher Stowe Compiled from Her Letters and Journals.* Boston: Houghton, Mifflin and Co., 1889.

Wagenknecht, Edward. *Harriet Beecher Stowe: The Known and the Unknown*. New York: Oxford University Press, 1965.

HARRY S TRUMAN
(1884–1972)

Harry Truman was one of the best read presidents America has ever had. He probably read more, and on a greater variety of topics, than any modern president. This fact is especially significant since Truman had no college education and had always had poor eyesight.

Truman became a book lover when he was a little boy and continued to read voraciously throughout his life. He especially enjoyed and learned from history and biography, and he also liked poetry. He claimed his reading was an important factor in his success and that everyone should read good books to prepare for life.

While interviewing the retired president for his book, *Plain Speaking*, Merle Miller asked him whether he could remember a time when he had not read. Truman responded: "No, I can't, not unless I was sick, and even then if I could manage it, I'd prop up a book and read on the sickbed" (Miller, 53).

Harry Truman was born into a Missouri farm family on May 8, 1884. His early life was spent on farms and in the small city of Independence where his family moved in 1890.

Childhood was very pleasant for middle-class children such as Harry. It was a time when the pace of life was much slower than it became in later times. Years later, Truman wrote fondly of the time his family spent on his grandparents' farm.

We had the whole 440 acres to play over and 160 acres across the road for the same purpose. Some of my happiest recollections are the years on the Young farm when I was between the ages of three and six. (Harry Truman, *Memoirs*, vol. 1, 113)

The children apparently had an equally grand time when the family moved into a big house in Independence. They made friends quickly with all the neighborhood children, and "all the boys and girls for blocks around congregated at our house" (Harry Truman, *Memoirs*, vol. 1, 115).

Harry graduated from high school in 1901. He had expected to go to college but was unable to do so because of family financial problems. He applied to Annapolis and West Point but was turned down because of his eyesight.

Therefore, at seventeen years of age he went to work. As many young men without a college education he worked in a number of unsatisfying jobs.

In 1917 Truman went to war and saw action in France. He claimed that his wartime experience changed him enormously and that much of his education took place during his time in the service where he successfully commanded a group of quite unruly men. His daughter Margaret noted:

As many another man was to find in the years to come, they discovered that no one pushed Harry Truman around. . . . As a student of military history, my father had a clear-eyed perception of how an army was supposed to operate. (Margaret Truman, *Harry S. Truman*, 59–60)

Truman returned to civilian life on May 6, 1919, when he was thirty-five years old. One month later he married Elizabeth (Bess) Wallace.

Truman and a friend, Eddie Jacobson, went into business together running a haberdashery store in Kansas City. The store was at first quite successful, but it fell victim to the recession of 1920 and 1921, when business failures tripled overnight. Unlike many whose businesses failed, Truman refused to declare bankruptcy. He spent the next fifteen years paying off the $12,000 debt.

Finally, at the age of thirty-eight, Harry Truman found a career which would bring him fulfillment. He had for many years dreamed of entering politics. In 1922 with the help of the local Democratic organization, he was elected to a county judgeship.

During the next dozen years he pursued a successful career in local politics. Then in 1934 he was elected to the United States Senate where he served until 1944 when he was elected vice-president under President Franklin D. Roosevelt.

When Roosevelt died in 1945, Truman became president and thus joined the company of heroes whom he had so long admired in all the histories and biographies he had read. He was elected to a full term in that office in 1948 narrowly defeating the Republican candidate Thomas E. Dewey. He could have run for another full term in 1952, but chose not to do so.

On leaving office, Truman returned to Independence. He had become a popular folk hero, noted for his honesty and "plain speaking." During the first two weeks of retirement he received 70,000 letters, almost all of them favorable.

Like other former presidents, Truman received offers of a number of jobs in which he would have to do very little but would collect a huge salary. He turned down all such offers:

Oh, yes. I could have been a millionaire and then some I guess. But they weren't interested in hiring me. They were hiring an ex-President. They wanted to cash in on that, and they offered me, oh, a lot of six-figure salaries to do nothing much at all. . . . I wouldn't let them do it, though. I'd rather die in the poorhouse. (Miller, 430)

Instead of making a lot of money for doing "nothing much at all," Truman concentrated on putting his presidential papers in order and writing his memoirs.

Harry's mother taught him to read before he was five years old, but she was disturbed to find that he had difficulty reading the newspaper. The oculist she took him to found that he had very poor eyesight and needed glasses. The glasses helped him see much better but were a great handicap in playing rough and tumble sports since the doctor had strictly warned him about the danger of breaking his glasses and injuring his eyes. On occasion, however, he still joined in sports serving as umpire in baseball games.

The great advantage of the glasses, however, was that they opened up the world of books to him. That's when his passion for reading began, and he would spend many hours absorbed in his books.

Harry's favorite childhood books were the four-volume set of biographies by Charles Francis Horne—*Great Men and Famous Women*. According to Margaret Truman, those books made him "fall in love with history." She wrote that he frequently said that "reading biographies is the best way to learn history." He believed in the "great man" theory of history. In other words that "men make history," and "history does not make the man" (Margaret Truman, *Harry S. Truman*, 52).

Another favorite book of Harry's was the Bible, which he had read through "cover to cover" at least twice by the time he was twelve. He became such an expert on the scriptures that he was often asked to settle religious disputes among the various branches of his family who were divided among Baptists, Presbyterians, and Methodists.

The Independence Public Library was one of Harry's favorite haunts. "My time was spent in reading, and by the time I was thirteen or fourteen years old I had read all the books in the Independence Public Library" (Harry Truman, *Memoirs*, vol. 1, 116).

When grown up, Truman always continued his habit of reading. He often read two or three books at a time, "always making notes in the margins, especially in history books. . . . Frequently . . . very often he knew much more than the writer, the historian. . . . His favorite word was 'bunk,' and I guess it still is" (Miller, 111).

In addition to history and biography, Truman was a devotee of poetry. He explained his fondness for certain poems as follows:

Reporters just tell what has happened, and they don't do too good a job of it a lot of the time, but poets, some of them, they write about what's going to happen. . . . Tennyson knew there were going to be airplanes, and there was going to be bombing, . . . and someday . . . a parliament of man. (Miller, 429)

Truman was especially fond of Tennyson. He read everything he had ever written. He especially liked *Locksley Hall*. Ever since he graduated from high school, he carried copies in his wallet. When one copy wore out, he would copy it again and put it back in his wallet.

The prophetic lines from *Locksley Hall* which foretell horrible wars and eventual development of a universal parliament, such as the United Nations, are quoted in Miller's book. The poem contains these hopeful lines:

> Till the war-drum throbb'd no longer, and the battle-flags were furl'd
> In the Parliament of Man, the Federation of the world.
> There the common sense of most shall hold a fretful realm in awe,
> And the kindly earth shall slumber, lapt in universal law. (Miller, 428–29)

Truman believed everyone, including political leaders, should be readers. He argued that historical background gained from reading would make them much more effective than if they did not have such background.

On various occasions Truman recommended books to others. When operating his haberdashery store, the store became a "hangout" for a lot of old army buddies. Even though he was only in his mid-thirties, the men apparently considered Harry a wise older brother or father figure, and often asked him for advice on all kinds of problems. His advice often included suggestions of particular books to read.

One young man who asked for such advice was Albert A. Ridge who later became a judge. At the time Ridge was working as a clerk in the county courthouse, and he asked Harry about law school.

Truman told Ridge a man could do anything he set his mind to, and he encouraged Ridge to go to night school to study law, but he indicated that knowing just the law wasn't enough. He encouraged Ridge to "study about the nature of man and about the culture and heritage of Western civilization in general" (Miller, 111).

He also gave Ridge a list of books he should read. The list included many historical, philosophical and literary classics: Plutarch's *Lives*; Plato's *Republic*; Caesar's *Commentaries*; Gibbon's *Decline and Fall of the Roman Empire* (which Harry had read through several times); Benjamin Franklin's *Autobiography*; *Missouri's Struggle for Statehood*; and the Bible, (preferably the King James Version, which Truman considered the best). He also advised Ridge to read Robert Burns, Byron, and Shakespeare. He recommended all of

Shakespeare, but especially *Hamlet, King Lear,* and *Othello.* He also strongly recommended the Sonnets.

Another example of Truman's giving such advice occurred when Governor Orville Freeman of Minnesota wrote him asking for a list of books which might help him make the difficult decisions a governor must make. Freeman indicated that he knew Truman's reading had been exhaustive and asked for some biographies and historical novels or histories "which you felt pointed up particularly the decision-making process" (Ferrell, *Off the Record,* 355). Truman sent Freeman a detailed letter noting a number of books he had read which gave him help in his work.

Among other works, the list included Carl Sandburg's books on Abraham Lincoln; Marquis James' books about Andrew Jackson; Claude Bowers' books on Jefferson, especially his *Jefferson and Hamilton;* the memoirs of General Grant; Abbott's *Makers of History;* and Gibbons' *Roman Empire;* He noted that in addition to reading the Bible many times, he had read Plutarch's *Lives,* which details the activities of the great Romans.

Truman noted he had read everything he could find about men who made history.

It has been a life-time program for me, and if you start out even on this incomplete list, you will find it a lengthy study but well worthwhile. It will keep you out of mischief too. (Ferrell, *Off the Record,* 355–56)

Truman considered it essential for a president to leave a written record. He was saddened that so few presidents "told their own stories." He noted that no one, not even those closest to a president, know "all the reasons why he does certain things and why he comes to certain conclusions" (Harry Truman, *Memoirs,* vol. 1, ix).

He especially deplored that Americans do not know much about what really went on in Abraham Lincoln's mind because his son Robert destroyed so many of the papers of that great president. Truman determined to leave a record of his own life and during his retirement wrote two volumes of memoirs.

As for myself, I should like to record, before it is too late, as much of the story of my occupancy of the White House as I am able to tell. The events as I saw them and as I put them down here, I hope may prove helpful in informing some people and in setting others straight on the facts. (Harry Truman, *Memoirs,* vol. 1, ix)

Truman's memoirs are written in a first-person, easy-to-read, almost chatty style. One can just imagine him sitting down and talking with friends not only about affairs of state but also about his personal activities and innermost thoughts.

In addition to writing memoirs, another major project of Truman's retirement years was organization of his presidential library in Independence.

He wanted it arranged so that everyone, including young people, could understand the work of a president. Each of the rooms was designed to contain exhibits relating to one of the major functions of a president.

According to Margaret Truman:

The library, which was dedicated in 1957, is one of the great joys of Dad's old age. He worked on the planning of every detail, down to the art work on the walls. He even persuaded Thomas Hart Benton, the great Missouri painter, to contribute a striking mural. (Margaret Truman, *Harry S. Truman*, 562)

The well-read Harry Truman, wearing his thick glasses, was often ridiculed and vilified by his political enemies and by the press while he was in office. But history has been kind to him. In the years since he left office, one historian after another, and some organizations of historians, have declared that he was one of the best presidents in United States history.

Unquestionably his vast reading had much to do with his success as leader of the most powerful nation in the world. He strongly believed that reading good books prepared people for leadership.

IMPORTANT DATES IN HARRY S TRUMAN'S LIFE

1884	Born in Lamar, Missouri.
1901	Graduated from high school.
1917	Began service in the army in France during World War I.
1919	Married Bess Wallace.
1919–1921	Ran a haberdashery store and studied law.
1926–1934	Served as a presiding judge in Jackson County, Missouri.
1935–1944	Served as Democratic senator from Missouri.
1944–1945	Served as vice-president of the United States under President Franklin D. Roosevelt. In April, 1945, when President Roosevelt died, Truman succeeded him as president.
1945–1952	Served as president.
1957	Dedicated the Truman Library in Independence, Missouri.
1972	Died in Kansas City, Missouri.

SOURCES

Ferrell, Robert H., ed. *The Autobiography of Harry S. Truman*. Boulder: Colorado Associated University Press, 1980.

Ferrell, Robert H., ed. *Off the Record: The Private Papers of Harry S. Truman*. New York: Harper and Row, 1980.

Miller, Merle. *Plain Speaking: An Oral Biography of Harry S. Truman*. New York: Berkley Publishing Corp., 1973.

Truman, Harry S. *Memoirs*. vol. 1, *Year of Decisions*. Garden City, N. Y.: Doubleday, 1955.

Truman, Harry S. *Memoirs*, vol. 2, *Years of Trial and Hope*. Garden City, N.Y.: Doubleday, 1956.

Truman, Margaret. *Harry S. Truman*. New York: William Morrow & Co., 1973.

Truman, Margaret, ed. *Where the Buck Stops: The Personal and Private Writings of Harry S. Truman*. New York: Warner Books, 1989.

GENE TUNNEY
(1898–1978)

Gene Tunney, one of the greatest boxers of all time, was also a great reader. He especially loved the classics. He did not fit the stereotype of boxers being all brawn and no brain. Asked why he read the classics so much, he responded that they helped him win fights.

Tunney's story is a real Horatio Alger rags-to-riches tale. As a young man he worked for several years for low pay as a clerk in New York City. Less than ten years later he had become light heavyweight champion of the United States. A few years after that he knocked out the "unbeatable" Jack Dempsey and became heavyweight champion of the world.

Gene Tunney was born of Irish Catholic parents on May 25, 1898, in New York City. He graduated from St. Veronica's parochial school and La Salle Academy. Then he went to work as an accountant with the Ocean Steamship Company until the outbreak of World War I in 1917.

He did not have a great deal of boxing experience before entering the marine corps during World War I. Nonetheless, while in the marines he won the light heavyweight championship of the American Expeditionary Force in France.

After returning to the United States, he won numerous fights until a 1926 match with the champion Jack Dempsey. Dempsey was widely expected to win, but Tunney beat him.

A year later Tunney and Dempsey fought again in the famous "long count" fight. It seemed that Dempsey was winning as Tunney went down. The referee started counting and motioned Dempsey to his corner. But Dempsey remained standing defiantly over his foe until the count of four was reached. The referee started counting all over again, and Tunney gained his feet at the count of nine and won the fight.

Tunney retired from the ring in 1928 and married the heiress Mary Josephine (Polly) Lauder. They had four children, including United States Senator John V. Tunney.

He continued to be very active after leaving professional boxing. He served on the boards of numerous banks and other corporations. He was a director of the Boy Scouts of America, and he formed the Young Voters Exchange, which brought many first-time voters to the polls in 1940. During World War II, Tunney, always a physical fitness advocate, directed athletic and physical fitness programs for the United States Navy.

Tunney had always loved literature. Many thought his love of reading was fake. Noted writer and commentator Paul Gallico disagreed with that view:

Probably no athlete ever has had to take the public beating that fell to Tunney on his way to realizing his ambitions. He was caught groping for light, serenity, and education and ridiculed for it. . . . We kidded him nearly to oblivion about Shakspere [*sic*] and books because we thought it was a phony pose. But that wasn't the part that was phony. That was real. (Gallico, 86)

Gene Tunney started reading classics when he was in grade school. He enjoyed reading many of the adventure stories that boys like, such as James Fenimore Cooper's *Leatherstocking Tales* and *The Spy*; and other historical novels by Winston Churchill, Victor Hugo, and Alexandre Dumas.

During his teen-age years he especially liked adventure stories. Jack London was a special favorite. He particularly loved London's *The Sea Wolf* and *Call of the Wild*. Years later Tunney met Jack London's daughter in Moscow. She told him her father had modeled the hero in his novel *The Abysmal Brute* after him, prophesying that Tunney would become a champion fighter. Tunney considered that a great compliment since he thought the character in the book was a really admirable person (Tunney, "Me and Shakespeare," 29). Gene's older cousin, John, impressed that the boy was winning amateur bouts, came to look him over. John, who had "the customary Irish regard for fisticuffs," was surprised to see Gene reading Cooper's *The Spy*.

"You're reading that book?" he demanded.
"Yes," I replied. "I like to read."
He shook his head in wonder. "A fighter reading books," he said. "That's mighty strange."
He showed no signs of disapproval—only wonder.
"Just the same, kid, I like your looks." (Tunney, "Me and Shakespeare," 29)

That was perhaps Tunney's first experience of the attitude so many people took when they found he loved classics. They thought it was funny a great boxer liked to read! Tunney just thought it was natural. He liked it, and he learned from it.

Tunney heard about a story called *The Game*, and he decided he must read it because it was about boxing. He got a copy at the public library, and it made a strong impression on him. He read it "avidly, tensely, with the impressionable earnestness of youth" (Tunney, "Me and Shakespeare," 29).

The story was about a young boxer who was killed in a bout. It affected Tunney so much that he stopped boxing until he went into the marines.

While at St. Veronica's school Tunney showed an interest in drama. He acted in a number of plays "and could recite the speeches of Portia, Antonio, and Shylock," from *The Merchant of Venice* (Heimer, 8).

His real interest in and love of Shakespeare did not begin, however, until he was serving in the marines in France. Another serviceman owed Tunney a favor, and asked what he could do. Tunney, surprised and not knowing what to ask, requested the other give him one of the copies of Shakespeare he had. The other man gave him *The Winter's Tale*, one of Shakespeare's most difficult plays.

I waded stubbornly through it, although I could make little sense of it. No wonder, it was my luck to begin with just about the toughest of Shakespeare. *The Winter's Tale* can be thorny going even for an accomplished student, let alone a young prize fighter turned Marine. I read the play again and again—I always was obstinate—in fact, I read it five times before I understood it. (Tunney, "Me and Shakespeare," 103)

After that Tunney read "simplicities," *Macbeth, Othello, The Merchant of Venice*—"real push-overs."

I trained on them. Getting into shape for savage Army bouts and winning the championship of the A.E.F. I trained on the reveries of Hamlet and the sighs of Juliet. (Tunney, "Me and Shakespeare," 103)

Tunney became "addicted" to reading, and reading became a part of his routine when getting ready for fights. Each day in training he followed the same routine. Up at dawn for hours of road work. Then he would have a big breakfast at nine A.M. At three in the afternoon, bag punching, rope skipping, and sparring with a partner. Tunney spent the six hours between breakfast and his three o'clock routine reading. Since he was in training most of the year, he did a great deal of reading.

Before each major fight he would select a particular book, and he would read it slowly at a leisurely pace, and concentrate on it. Literature provided the best means for him to relax and keep from worrying. For example, before he fought Levinsky for the light heavyweight championship of the United States, he read *Les Miserables*.

Though I had read it twice before, I was then for the first time making the acquaintance of the philosophy of *Les Miserables*, reading again those pages of deep-hearted Victor Hugo prose. (Tunney, "Me and Shakespeare," 104)

Before his first fight with Jack Dempsey, Tunney read *The Way of All Flesh*. It was a long, leisurely book about life over three generations, about the lives of English clergy which "took one eons away from the fight racket."

In the book, I was in another world. I rate *The Way of All Flesh* as a No. 1 asset in my training for Dempsey—it did the job of getting the fight off my mind, ridding me of worry, overcoming fear. The literary opus was one of the reasons why I went into the ring cool of head and steady of nerve—and won the championship. (Tunney, "Me and Shakespeare," 106)

He read Somerset Maugham's *Of Human Bondage* before fighting Dempsey the second time, and it had the same effect. It calmed him, helped prepare him to win again.

Tunney's reputation for reading Shakespeare and other serious literature spread far and wide. Often kidded about it, he was also respected. A professor at Yale, William Lyon Phelps, asked him to lecture to Yale students on Shakespeare on April twenty-third, the day traditionally assigned as Shakespeare's birthday. Tunney chose one of the more difficult works to talk about, Shakespeare's *Troilus and Cressida*. Several hundred students came to hear him, and he was made a member of Pundita, an honor society for scholars and wits.

Tunney liked a number of modern American and British writers. He enjoyed their books, and he enjoyed meeting them. Ernest Hemingway was a favorite. He met and got to know Hemingway, and said that when Hemingway was good as in *Farewell to Arms*, no writer could be better.

He became a friend of Thornton Wilder and George Bernard Shaw with whom he carried on a long correspondence. Tunney had been asked to play the lead in a movie version of one of Shaw's lesser known works about a fighter. Tunney had read the book, and was not too impressed with it. He said publicly the characters were shallow and the story had little action.

His comments were quickly picked up by the newspapers. When Shaw heard about Tunney's comments, he said he agreed with him. It was not one of his better works.

In addition to being a dedicated reader, Tunney was a good writer. He wrote his book, *A Man Must Fight*, without using a ghost writer, as most celebrities do. The book received good reviews.

Tunney published many articles in major magazines, including *Saturday Evening Post*, *Reader's Digest*, and *Atlantic Monthly*. His articles dealt with boxing, physical fitness, and the psychology of fighting.

Tunney had a lifelong interest in education and recommended that young people take their education very seriously. One time veteran newsman Jim Kilgallen asked him about that. Tunney replied that if he were young again, he would not become a prize fighter. "Education," he said, "is the most valuable capital an ambitious youth can have nowadays" (Heimer, 258).

One of Tunney's most revealing statements on the relationship between his boxing and reading was made after he finished his professional career. He continued to enjoy reading all kinds of materials and said: "I've discovered that while I needed reading as an accompaniment to boxing, I do not need boxing as an accompaniment to reading" (Tunney, "Me and Shakespeare," 112).

IMPORTANT DATES IN GENE TUNNEY'S LIFE

1898   Born in New York City.

1915   Graduated from La Salle Academy. Took a job as a clerk for the Ocean Steamship Company.

1918   Won light heavyweight championship of the American Expeditionary Force in France.

1922   Became light-heavyweight champion of the United States.

1926   Defeated Jack Dempsey and became heavyweight champion.

1927   Fought Dempsey again and retained heavyweight champion crown.

1928   Retired from the ring as undefeated world champion. Married heiress Mary Josephine (Polly) Lauder.

1932   Published *A Man Must Fight*.

1938   Elected chairman of the board of the American Distilling Co. Served on boards of a number of additional corporations and financial institutions.

1955   Elected to Boxing Hall of Fame.

1978   Died in Greenwich, Connecticut.

1987   Named the fifth greatest heavyweight of all time by *The Ring*.

SOURCES

Gallico, Paul. *Farewell to Sport*. New York: Knopf, 1938.
"Gene Tunney, Who Beat Dempsey Twice for Ring Title, Is Dead at 80," in *The New York Times Biographical Service*, November, 1978.
Heimer, Mel. *The Long Count*. New York: Atheneum, 1969.
Porter, David L., ed. *Biographical Dictionary of American Sports: Basketball and Other Indoor Sports*. Westport, Conn.: Greenwood Press, 1989.
Tunney, Gene. *A Man Must Fight*. Boston: Houghton Mifflin Co., 1932.
Tunney, Gene. "Me and Shakespeare," *Saturday Evening Post*, May 24, 1941.

MARK TWAIN
(1835–1910)

According to a standard textbook for American high school literature classes, Mark Twain is "the most celebrated humorist in American history."

His ability to make us laugh has contributed to the singular popularity of his books, not just in Twain's own time but in following generations. Since humor is by nature very difficult to translate from language to language, it is even more surprising to find that Twain's appeal has traveled throughout the world. (*Elements of Literature*, 450)

A great writer, Twain was also a great reader. He was often seen carrying books around with him wherever he went. If books are not good company "where will I find it?" he wrote (Sanborn, 85).

Samuel Langhorne Clemens, was born on November 30, 1835, in the small town of Florida, Missouri. In 1839 the family moved to Hannibal, Missouri, on the banks of the Mississippi River. In adulthood he adopted the pen name "Mark Twain," a term which he heard frequently when he worked as a river boat pilot. It meant two fathoms of safe water.

Sam had little formal schooling. He had to go to work in 1847 after his father died, and thus obtained much of his education by reading.

In succeeding years Sam held a number of different kinds of jobs. He worked as a printer, a typesetter, a newspaper reporter, a gold and silver prospector, and a river boat pilot.

He also wrote and published a number of humorous sketches about frontier life during that period. He achieved national fame as a writer when he published "The Celebrated Jumping Frog of Calaveras County." He became a spokesman for the vanishing American frontier.

In 1866 he moved to New York City and then to Hartford, Connecticut. His most productive years occurred after moving East. Although he wrote on a variety of topics, Twain is most noted for his ability to write realistically and humorously about life on the frontier. His three classics are *The Adventures of Tom Sawyer, Life on the Mississippi,* and *The Adventures of Huckleberry Finn.*

Twain also became famous as a lecturer, sought after for his humorous, homespun style. In 1895 his lecturing helped save him from ruin. The financial success of *Huckleberry Finn* and *The Personal Memoirs of U. S. Grant* which Twain published convinced him that he was a business genius. Unfortunately, he invested in a typesetting machine and lost considerable money on the venture. Rather than declaring bankruptcy, he undertook a successful round-the-world lecture tour which provided funds to pay off many of his debts.

Twain received many honors for his writing. These included honorary doctorates from Yale University, the University of Missouri, and Oxford University.

Sam Clemens' boyhood in the Mississippi River town of Hannibal, Missouri, was fairly typical of that of most poor boys brought up in the small town Midwest. He had many chores to perform but also enjoyed numerous adventures with his friends; hiking, camping, fishing, and playing pretend games, such as Robin Hood and his merry men. They called a grove of oaks and elms Sherwood Forest, and they kept bows and arrows, wood swords, and other implements which they used "to enact scenes from Robin Hood" (Sanborn, 37).

In reading he favored fabulous stories, tales of chivalry, enchantment, and adventure, the same types of stories which he would write one day and which would make him so famous. He also read some of the books he got at the Sunday school library, but most of them were not to his taste. They were too pious and pallid.

In addition to being a great reader, Sam was also a great storyteller. When asked what he had done during the day, he would give an account of his adventures "with many embellishments and considerable humor" (Sanborn, 33).

Sam's father owned the only copy of *The Arabian Nights' Entertainments* in town. Sam read it over and over and knew most of the tales by heart. He often told "Aladdin and the Wonderful Lamp," and "Ali Baba and the Forty Thieves" to his playmates. Sam also enjoyed *Ivanhoe, Robinson Crusoe, Gulliver's Travels,* and *Don Quixote* as well as the Robin Hood tales.

Sam also read Robert Bird's *Nick of the Woods,* a novel about life in the Kentucky wilderness as well as other books he called "wildcat literature." These included works credited to Davy Crockett; T. B. Thorpe's tall tale, *The Big Bear of Arkansas;* and Seba Smith's "Major Jack Downing" letters.

Mark Twain had a lifelong love of the story of Joan of Arc, the courageous young woman who liberated France. His fascination with Saint Joan started this way. One blustery day in the fall of 1850, while he was walking along the street, a paper blew across his path. He picked it up, read it, and found it was about something he had never heard of. It concerned "the imprisonment and persecution of Joan of Arc." He wanted to know more about the story which seemed like a novel, so he asked his brother and his mother about her. They both assured Sam that she had been a real person. He then began reading everything he could find about the Maid of Orleans. He also began reading medieval history and literature. That became a lifelong passion.

Years later he wrote the romanticized novel *Personal Recollections of Joan of Arc* under a pseudonym. He wanted the book to be judged on its own merits, not as a work by Mark Twain. While critics generally cited *Huckleberry Finn* as Twain's greatest novel, he himself was on record saying that he felt *Joan* was his best book.

A noted Twain scholar argued that *Joan of Arc* is a much better book than some suppose. Nonetheless, Twain "loved and revered Joan herself too much to evaluate anything he might write about her dispassionately" (Wagenknecht, 60–61).

While moving from one place to another Sam always carried his love of books and reading with him. When he was eighteen, he went to New York to work as a printer, and he discovered the largest library he had ever seen. It was a working man's library and could be used free of charge by printers. He spent many evenings there reading Shakespeare, Cervantes, Sir Walter Scott, and Fielding. He also was interested in essays, and read those by Bacon, Johnson, and Lamb. He tried reading Jane Austen, but did not like her work. He stated one time that a good library would be one without Jane Austen.

I often want to criticize Jane Austen, but her books madden me so that I can't conceal my frenzy from the reader; and therefore I have to stop every time I begin. (Bellamy, 44)

Sam sent humorous letters back to Hannibal describing the strange and fabulous things he saw in the big city of New York, and they were published in *The Hannibal Journal*. That was the beginning of his long career of writing funny stories. The editor wrote the following introduction.

The free and easy impudence of the writer of the following . . . will be appreciated by those who recognize him. (Sanborn, 84)

Several years later Sam settled in Keokuk, Iowa, where his brother offered him a job working on the city directory. While there, he honed his speaking skills and made a great hit giving a speech at a printer's banquet.

He convulsed the audience with his humor and received long and loud applause. For the rest of his life, he was noted as a great lecturer, interspersing serious comments with funny stories which kept audiences' rapt attention.

He also continued his passion for books. A friend said he often saw Sam carrying a book by Dickens or Poe, or some book on English history or exploration. Without question, his heavy reading increased his verbal and writing abilities and gave him considerable material for his writing and speaking.

Mark Twain was not known to plagiarize, but like all writers, he was influenced by reading. He knew the Southern and Southwestern humorists well, many of whom are relatively unknown today. They found humor in the problems and the oddities of frontier life, and their funny sketches were published widely in newspapers throughout the country. Twain "made free use of all this frontier humor in his own work" (Bellamy, 45).

One of the great classic writers who influenced Twain was Cervantes. Shades of *Don Quixote* can be seen in Twain's works, including the characters of Tom Sawyer and Huckleberry Finn.

His alter ego "Mr. Brown," moreover, was an imaginary companion who expressed "earthy, skeptical, and irreverent thoughts" which the writer noted in a number of his works. This traditional literary device "was possibly suggested to Sam by Sancho Panza in *Don Quixote*" (Sanborn, 277).

Explorations of the Valley of the Upper Amazon by William Herndon also had considerable influence on Twain. In his early twenties, he was fascinated by what Herdon said about the coca trade. He decided to go to Brazil and make his fortune.

Although he did not make the trip to the Amazon and become a coca tycoon, he became a river boat pilot and adopted the name Mark Twain. His experience on the river gave him considerable information which he used in some of his greatest writing, including *Tom Sawyer, Huckleberry Finn,* and *Life on the Mississippi*.

In his mature years Twain read as much as ever, including history, biography, and travel books. He also favored robust, romantic poetry, including Byron, Wordsworth, Kipling and Shelley. He enjoyed the poems of the Midwestern writer James Whitcomb Riley which had a strong nostalgic appeal for him. The *Rubaiyat* of Omar Khayyam was another of his greatest favorites.

His very favorite poet was Robert Browning. He read his work assiduously, and studied the poems very hard before reading them to his friends.

At his home in Hartford he held "Browning evenings" at intervals during 1886 and 1887. His hearers found his readings from Browning exquisite. (Bellamy, 46)

The influence of Mark Twain has been enormous. His writing, has captured the imagination of countless millions of people, especially those books drawn from his own experiences. Undoubtedly, many people who might not read heavy tomes by "more serious" writers find Twain's humor infectious. And even his most humorous works contain lessons about the relationships between people. A passionate reader, Twain's reading undoubtedly contributed to his success as an author and lecturer.

IMPORTANT DATES IN MARK TWAIN'S LIFE

1835   Born in Florida, Missouri.

1839   Family moved to Hannibal, Missouri, on the Mississippi River where he grew up.

1847   Began work as a printer. In succeeding years worked as a typesetter and newspaper writer.

1857   Became a riverboat pilot on the Mississippi River.

1865   Published "The Celebrated Jumping Frog of Calaveras County," his first great success which brought him national fame.

1876   Published *The Adventures of Tom Sawyer*.

1883   Published *Life on the Mississippi*.

1885   Published *The Adventures of Huckleberry Finn*, his most important novel.

1895   Undertook around-the-world lecture tour to clear his many debts.

1896   Published *Personal Recollection of Joan of Arc*.

1906   Published *What Is Man?* one of his most pessimistic works.

1910   Died in Redding, Connecticut.

SOURCES

Brooks, Van Wyck. *The Ordeal of Mark Twain*. New York: E. P. Dutton, 1920.

Bellamy, Gladys Carmen. *Mark Twain as a Literary Artist*. Norman: University of Oklahoma Press, 1950.

Elements of Literature: Fifth Course: Literature of the United States with Literature of the Americas. Austin, Texas: Holt, Rinehart and Winston, 1997.

Neider, Charles, ed. *The Autobiography of Mark Twain Including Chapters Now Published for the First Time*. New York: Harper and Brothers, 1959.

Sanborn, Margaret. *Mark Twain: The Bachelor Years: A Biography*. New York: Doubleday, 1990.

Wagenknecht, Edward. *Mark Twain: The Man and His Work*, 3d ed. Norman: University of Oklahoma Press, 1967.

JOHN WANAMAKER
(1838–1922)

John Wanamaker, founder of America's largest and most innovative retail store, believed in the importance of books for society. To promote reading, he opened the nation's largest bookstore and sold books at lower prices than other booksellers.

Wanamaker was born in Philadelphia on July 11, 1838, the eldest of seven children. Every morning he was up at four o'clock and worked until late in the evening helping his father who was a brickmaker.

As a teenager, he began working as a men's clothing salesman, and in 1861 he and a brother-in-law invested their savings in a clothing store in Philadelphia. Within ten years, Wanamaker's was the largest retail store in the United States. He continued to expand and opened the Wanamaker's store in New York, one of the largest department stores in that city.

Wanamaker was the first merchant to buy full-page newspaper ads for which he wrote much of the copy. His store was the first to be lit completely by incandescent lamps. He also guaranteed money back if for any reason an article did not please the customer, a revolutionary idea for the time. By 1878, the ground floor of his store in Philadelphia covered three acres and was the largest retail selling space in the world. Wanamaker sold nearly everything, for a time even airplanes and automobiles.

Wanamaker was a paternalistic employer. He set up a mutual benefit society for them; training classes for clerks; and established other educational and welfare services. He was probably the first in his type of business to designate all Saturdays in July and August as full holidays with full pay.

In addition to his business, Wanamaker was very active in religious work. He organized the Bethany Sunday School for adults and children in Philadelphia. It became one of the largest such schools in America, and he served as president of the Philadelphia Y.M.C.A. (Young Men's Christian Association). Although a devoted Christian himself, Wanamaker was not narrowly sectarian. He respected all religions, believing that there are many roads to God, and every person must take his own.

Active in politics, he was appointed postmaster general of the United States and served in that office from 1889–1893. Passage of the rural free delivery act in 1893 was a major achievement during his tenure as postmaster general.

Wanamaker's passion for reading started when he was a boy and persisted throughout his life. He commented:

People who saw me when a boy often thought I had a tumor or some extraordinary growth where my pockets were—they were so stuffed out with books or bits of paper I had put there to study in my spare moments. (Appel, 15)

The first book John read as a child, apart from the Bible, was *Robinson Crusoe*. It remained in his family for many years. When a successful businessman, *Robinson Crusoe* was one of the books he most often gave to boys (Appel, 16).

Other books he read as a boy were *Pilgrim's Progress* and Benjamin Franklin's works. He also had a well-worn dictionary.

He started reading the Bible as a child and continued to read it throughout his life. When he was eleven years old, he bought a small red leather Bible from his Sunday school teacher. It cost him $2.75 which he paid for in small installments from his own hard-earned money. "Looking back over my life," he recounted, "that little red Bible was the foundation on which my life has been built, and it has made possible all that has counted most in my life" (Conwell, 13). He also noted

As a boy, so far as I know I was not religiously inclined. But the Bible told me there was a God and how the world was created and that the attributes of God were justice, mercy, love and truth, and that injustice, selfishness, cunning, jealousies, dishonesties and falsehoods of human nature have never brought permanent success to individuals or nations. (Appel, 17)

In 1871 Wanamaker bought and became publisher of the *Sunday School Times* in order to save it from ceasing publication because of financial difficulties. To save money in printing the *Times*, he opened his own printing house.

He also printed all the flyers and pamphlets produced for his retail stores, of which there were a great many. According to Gibbons, he was the first merchant in America, and probably even in the world, to have his own printing plant (Gibbons, vol. 1, 192).

He became a leading publisher of magazines: *Everybody's Journal*, *The Farm Journal*, *The Ladies' Journal*, and *Book News Monthly*. Although these publications promoted Wanamaker's retail business, they also contained general articles and news. *Everybody's Journal* was an illustrated, popular general magazine sold at a reasonable price, one of the first ten-cent magazines. It attained a large circulation of 100,000 by 1900. The *Farm Journal*, which first appeared in 1877, within a few years sold over one million copies.

The *Ladies' Journal* was published in order to attract women customers. It contained signed articles, poems, and features devoted to "fashions, business, society, and home interests." Wanamaker's *Book News Monthly* was probably the first publication devoted to book reviews.

Wanamaker's belief in the importance of books was unique among merchants of his time. By 1877 his bookstore was the largest in America.

Frequently he classed reading matter with the mails, the telegraph, and transportation facilities as public necessities. He contended that by virtue of their wares publishers had an obligation to the public greater than that of most business men. (Gibbons, vol. 1, 204)

Believing that books were essential in the development of society, he fought to keep book prices down. In addition to low prices for all customers, discounts were given to regular customers, to other booksellers, to college professors, and to clergymen.

Wanamaker believed American books were not only overpriced but also of poor quality. He considered both the physical condition and the content of books being sold in America inferior to those being sold elsewhere, especially in England.

The English newsstands contained an assortment of publications "fit for a civilized people." He protested against the high prices being charged for books in America and argued that the low types of books being peddled in America make "a library of ignorance vulgarly bound" (Gibbons, v. 1, 203–204).

One case was particularly appalling to him. The *Memoirs* of General Ulysses S. Grant were published in May, 1886. The book was issued by Charles L. Webster and Company, the firm in which Mark Twain had an interest. It became an immediate best seller, and was considered an excellent personal account of the Civil War.

Wanamaker was greatly disturbed, however, that copies would be made available only by subscription through agents at a relatively high price. Therefore, he secured a large supply of the books, and sold them in his own store at a lower price than that being charged by the agents.

Wanamaker was a good writer frequently composing his own advertising copy. Like Benjamin Franklin, he also became a popular author of brief philosophical maxims, often writing them on the backs of envelopes while traveling by train between Philadelphia and New York. According to Joseph H. Appel, he wrote five thousand such pieces, four thousand of which appeared in his advertisements. His brief, wise sayings were reminiscent of Benjamin Franklin's *Poor Richard's Almanack*. For example:

Happy is the man who chooses his life's work carefully and stands by it faithfully to the end.
Nobility is elective and not hereditary.
We have no one to fear except ourselves.
No man can dream character unto himself—he must hammer and forge himself into a man.
Mankind is one family.
Neither nations nor individuals have an unchallengeable right to walk over each other.
No day seems long enough to those who love their work.

Wanamaker remained active in his work into his eighties. He was in good health until almost the very end of his life. Knowing that he loved to read and write, he was asked to write his autobiography. He replied that his life could be summarized in just a few words: thinking, trying, toiling, and trusting in God.

IMPORTANT DATES IN JOHN WANAMAKER'S LIFE

1838	Born in Philadelphia.
1861	Opened clothing store of Wanamaker and Brown in Philadelphia.
1869	Following death of partner Brown reorganized firm as John Wanamaker and Company.
1870–1883	President of Philadelphia Y.M.C.A.
1876	Transformed huge Pennsylvania Railroad depot into his new department store.
1889–1893	Served as Postmaster General of the United States.
1896	Opened large Wanamaker store in New York City.
1922	Died in Philadelphia.

SOURCES

Appel, Joseph H. *The Business Biography of John Wanamaker: Founder and Builder.* New York: Macmillan, 1930.

Conwell, Russell H. *The Romantic Rise of a Great American.* New York: Harper & Brothers, 1924.

Gibbons, Herbert Adams. *John Wanamaker.* 2 vols. New York: Harper and Brothers, 1926.

Ingham, John, ed. *Biographical Dictionary of American Business Leaders.* Westport, Conn.: Grenwood Press, 1983.

Mahoney, Tom, and Leonard Sloane. *The Great Merchants: America's Foremost Retail Institutions and the People Who Made Them Great.* New York: Harper & Row, 1966.

GEORGE WASHINGTON
(1732–1799)

Unlike most American political leaders of his time, George Washington, the Father of Our Country, was not a great reader. He read relatively little. A few works he did read, however, had a powerful effect on him.

Little is known about George Washington's early life. Such stories as the cherry tree incident and his inability to tell lies, although inspiring, had no basis in fact. They simply arose from the imagination of his early biographer Parson Weems.

It is known, however, that Washington was born on a family estate in Virginia in February, 1732. He was a shy and reserved boy.

His home life was far from happy. His mother, Mary Ball Washington, was a "majestic" and "powerful" woman, but "all her power was centered on herself."

Whatever George attempted that was not in her immediate service, she attempted to stop. (Flexner, *George Washington*, 19)

George's father died when he was eleven. Unlike his half-brothers, George was not sent to fine schools in England which his father had planned for him, perhaps because of family financial difficulties. He never attended university, and never learned French, the international language of diplomacy in his time. He was one of the very few American presidents whose formal education was so limited.

According to the inheritance laws of the time, his older brother Lawrence received the bulk of his father's estate. George determined that he would make his own fortune.

When still a youth, George realized the family needed money, and he took a job surveying. He proved to be very proficient in that work.

George loved his half-brother, Lawrence, very much. He considered him his best friend and was devastated when Lawrence died from a wasting disease.

George inherited Mount Vernon. He managed the estate well, it prospered, and it always served as a welcome refuge to him from the pressures of politics.

During the French and Indian War, George Washington served as an aide to the British general Edward Braddock. He commanded the Virginia militia defending the frontier from French and Indian attacks.

In 1775 he was named commander of the continental forces. He led his colonial troops in many battles against the British until Cornwallis surrendered in 1781.

Washington presided over the Federal Constitutional Convention, and was unanimously elected the first president in which office he served for two terms. He wearied of political life, however, refused to serve a third term, and returned to his life as a farmer at Mount Vernon.

No one knows for sure how George Washington learned to read. According to one story, he was taught his letters by a convict employed by his father. The tale may be apocryphal but it could be true. Many such people came to America from England, and some of the better educated probably worked as tutors.

According to biographer Marcus Cunliffe, "all we can assume is that George got some education between the ages of seven and eleven" (Cunliffe, 30).

Notebooks he kept as an adolescent show that, among other things, he had learned some Latin and mathematics and had read a little English literature. He also copied out a poem called "True Happiness," which bespoke of the pleasures of a happy home, something George did not have.

One work which had a great impact on young George was *Rules of Civility and Decent Behavior in Company and Conversation*. Compiled by sixteenth-century Jesuits for instruction of young French noblemen, the rules consisted of more than one hundred maxims for the proper conduct of a young gentleman.

The *Rules* dealt with such practical matters as being respectful and courteous to those in your presence; table manners; clothes; ways to act with superiors, equals, and inferiors; even not scratching oneself, singing, or cleansing one's teeth in the presence of others.

Years later Washington coined maxims of his own and they "are much closer to the *Rules of Civility* than to the Sunday school forgeries" which Parson Weems attributed to the youthful Washington.

Telling the truth is nowhere urged, but courteous dissimulation is. As for acting "against the moral rules," that is only forbidden in the presence of inferiors. Nothing is said about obedience to the Deity or getting into heaven: ethical behavior has its own reward . . . as it makes you well thought of in society. (Flexner, *George Washington*, 22)

Copying the rules became a labor of love for young George. He did not have the advantage of the excellent education his brother Lawrence had received in England. Ferling speculates that George "may have been lured to read the *Rules* when he compared his own rustic manners to Lawrence's urbane demeanor" (Ferling, 6).

The *Rules* which Washington learned so well as a young man were of benefit to his future career since they were "aimed at that profound courtesy to one's fellow men that grows from careful attention to the effects of one's own acts on the feelings of others" (Flexner, *George Washington*, 22–23).

Washington was very moved by the blank verse play *Cato* by Addison. It is the story of the noble Roman statesman who fell on his sword rather than surrender to the tyranny of Julius Caesar's conquering armies.

George Washington loved this play. He quoted from it in his correspondence; he ordered it to be performed in 1778 at Valley Forge; he even used a line from it in his Farewell Address. Historians disagree about the extent to which Washington deliberately emulated the play's hero. But there is little doubt that Roman stoicism, mediated through a British stage play written in 1713, exerted an indelible influence on America's first president. (Nash, 17)

Although not a great reader, Washington was a prolific writer. The many pieces he left have given scholars ample materials to study his life and work.

His personal file of documents—diaries, financial accounts, letters written and received [contained in] about 75,000 folios—is at the Library of Congress. (Flexner, *George Washington*, 353)

Washington was never really a scholar, and even in his later years he rarely read books unless they served some practical purpose, such as giving information on farming methods. Nonetheless, he had great respect for books. He wrote: "I conceive a knowledge of books is the basis upon which other knowledge is to be built" (Whitney and Whitney, 4).

One expects that those who love reading and read a great deal would be influenced by their reading. Washington provides an example of the type of person who has read relatively little but is strongly influenced by just a few works.

IMPORTANT DATES IN GEORGE WASHINGTON'S LIFE

1732	Born in Westmoreland County, Virginia.
1747	Took up surveying.
1752	Received first military appointment as a major in colonial forces.
1754	Defended Fort Necessity against attack by the French in the French and Indian War.
1759	Married Martha Custis, a wealthy widow.
1774	Delegate to the First Continental Congress.
1775–1783	Led the Continental Army to victory over the British.
1787	Chosen president of the Constitutional Convention.
1789–1797	First president of the United States.
1797	Retired from the presidency to live at Mount Vernon.
1799	Died at Mount Vernon, Virginia.

SOURCES

Alden, John R. *George Washington: A Biography*. Baton Rouge: Louisiana State University Press, 1984.

Clark, Harrison. *All Cloudless Glory: The Life of George Washington from Youth to Yorktown*. Washington, D.C.: Regnery Publishing, 1995.

Cunliffe, Marcus. *George Washington: Man and Monument*. Boston: Little, Brown and Co., 1958.

Ferling, John E. *The First of Men: A Life of George Washington*. Knoxville: University of Tennessee Press, 1988.

Flexner, James Thomas. *George Washington: The Forge of Experience (1732–1775)*. Boston: Little, Brown and Co., 1965.

Flexner, James Thomas. *Washington: The Indispensable Man*. Boston: Little, Brown and Co., 1965–1972.

Nash, George H. *Books and the Founding Fathers: A Lecture to Commemorate the Year of the Reader, Delivered on November 1, 1987*. Washington, D.C.: Library of Congress, 1989.

Whitney, David C., and Robin Vaughn Whitney. *The American Presidents*, 8th ed. Pleasantville, N.Y.: Reader's Digest Assn., 1996.

EMMA WILLARD
(1787–1870)

Emma Hart Willard founded what was, in effect, the first women's college in America, the Troy Female Seminary in Troy, New York. Unlike women's schools which taught drawing, dancing, and other activities considered suitable for young ladies, Troy emphasized strong academic subjects, just like men's colleges, which women were not allowed to attend. Many noted women, including numerous influential school teachers were trained there.

Emma Hart was born into a simple but intellectual home, the daughter of Samuel Hart and his second wife Lydia Hinsdale Hart. She was the ninth of ten children. She attended local schools. Eager to learn, she became a voracious reader and also taught herself geometry at the age of thirteen.

When still in her teens, she began teaching the young children in the district school. She was an inspired teacher, made her subjects interesting, allowed recreation periods, and gave much praise to her students.

Her reputation for teaching grew, and she accepted a position as head of a female academy in Middlebury, Vermont. She met and married Dr. John Willard there. Some years later she founded and directed the Troy Female Seminary.

At the school girls and young women pursued a tough curriculum similar to that at the best men's colleges. In addition to reading, writing, spelling, and grammar, the curriculum included geography, algebra, natural philosophy, geology, and botany. Subjects emphasized in finishing schools, such as drawing, dancing, and painting, were also taught.

When she retired, Willard turned the school over to her daughter-in-law, Sarah Lucretia Hudson Willard, and her son, John Hart Willard. The school was later named the Willard School after Emma Willard.

As a small child Willard learned to love both oral storytelling and reading. Samuel Hart was a good storyteller. He told the children fascinating tales about American heroes. One, for example, was about Isaac Lee, a local hero who was reputed to have Herculean strength. He reputedly could toss barrels of cider into a cart as other men tossed pumpkins. In another story he was an excellent athlete in a number of sports. It was reported that on one occasion he even tossed a bull.

Stories about the American Revolution were especially popular with the family.

Emma sat on [her father's] knee wide-eyed, eager, and absorbed, fired with an intense patriotism which she carried with her all through her life. He told of the British burning New London, of his part in defending the coast towns, of Uncle Orrin Lee as a drummer boy, of Uncle Samuel Lee who nearly starved in a prison ship, of spies, of Washington, of the daring, impulsive young Lafayette, of Paul Jones and the Bon Homme Richard. (Lutz, *Emma Willard: Daughter of Democracy*, 13)

Willard's father was also instrumental in Emma's becoming a great reader. She wrote; "My father, happily for his children . . . used to teach us of evenings and read aloud to us; and in this way I became interested in books and a voracious reader" (Hoffman, 18–19).

She was exposed to all the great literature of her time. Books were very expensive in those days, and every one in the family library was treasured by them. Emma noted that she was fortunate the family library had few novels, therefore she had to read all kinds of instructive nonfiction before she became addicted to fiction.

At their fireside the Harts read history, philosophy, travel, and literature together. The parents read aloud works by all the great writers: Gibbon, Addison, Steele, Pope, Watts, John Milton, Geoffrey Chaucer, and Shakespeare. One of the children would also sometimes read to the family, stopping to ask questions about what they had read.

The village library was also an important source of books for Emma. It supplied her with such works as "Plutach's lives, Rollins' Ancient History, Gibbon's Rome, many books of travels, and the most celebrated of the British poets and essayists" (Hoffman, 19).

When she was about nineteen Emma went to Hartford to further her education by attending a day school. While there she lived with her cousin Dr. Sylvester Wells and his wife Eunice. Wells respected Emma's keen mind and conversational ability. She especially enjoyed discussing French philosophers and their emphasis on reason.

While living with her husband Dr. John Willard in Middlebury, Vermont, Emma was fortunate that his nephew John lived with the couple while he attended Middlebury College. Young John shared his class notes and books with Emma. Many of the books such as Paley's *Moral Philosophy* and

Locke's *Essay Concerning Human Understanding*, were never taught in women's colleges.

Emma studied religiously and asked John to examine her on what she had learned. In that way she taught herself the equivalent of what the men learned at Middlebury.

Her eyes were thus opened to how deficient women's education was. She realized that girls were taught very little. Books published for women at the time taught them that they were inferior to men and reminded them of the biblical injunction that men should dominate women. Her own ability to learn what was taught in the men's colleges convinced her that females were entirely able to master serious academic subjects.

This close contact with the course of study in a college opened her eyes to what women were being deprived of....She had not realized how girls were taught mere smatterings while their brothers had every educational advantage. She had proved for herself that women were able to pursue higher studies. (Lutz, *Emma Willard: Pioneer Educator,* 19)

At Willard's Troy Female Seminary, serious literature was emphasized throughout the curriculum. Religious instruction was nonsectarian Christian. When studying history, students also studied geography and literature of the same period. For example, along with ancient history, the pupils also studied ancient geography and such works as the *Iliad.*

Shakespeare received much attention. His plays served as textbooks for oral reading. A teacher would choose a play for her class to study and assign a character to each student.

[W]hen the reading had been practiced in class until it was perfectly done, the play was read before the whole school to the delight of readers and audience. The youthful Portias, Shylocks, and Bassanios lived in an enchanting make-believe world for weeks, a wonderful bit of romance in the clocklike routine of the school. (Lutz, *Emma Willard: Pioneer Educator,* 92)

Willard especially enjoyed romantic literature. Sir Walter Scott was her favorite author, and she spent many, many hours reading the *Waverly Novels, Marmion,* and *The Lady of the Lake.*

In the evening Willard often read Scott's works to the students. His *The Lay of the Last Minstrel* was a work she read most frequently.

On one occasion someone remarked that Scott was not a great author. Willard, outraged, responded:

As well might you say that a gun fired on the Alleghanies, that was heard upon the shores of the Atlantic and Pacific, was not a great gun, as to say that Scott, whose poems are read wherever the English language is spoken, and are translated into the languages of Europe, is not a great poet. (Lutz, *Emma Willard: Pioneer Educator,* 96)

Willard loved and had memorized the works of many poets. When she visited London, her favorite cathedral was Westminster Abbey. Even though less grand than other English and European churches, she was fascinated with it because it contained the poet's corner. She addressed a number of the statues with the particular poet's verses.

Willard also wrote a great deal of poetry herself. Some poems celebrated special occasions, some were sent to graduates of her school, and she also wrote hymns.

A favorite hymn sung at the end of examinations was written by Mrs. Willard. It recognized that the Creator was responsible for the students' ability to learn.

> O Thou, the First, the Last, the Best!
>   To Thee the grateful song we raise,
> Convinced that all our works should be
>   Begun and ended with Thy Praise . . .

When her father died in 1813, she wrote a poem emphasizing his most notable trait, his dedication to freedom.

> He held, it was a right which free-born man
> Possessed, to freely think, and freely speak;
> Nor deemed it good inquiry to repress
> And with authorities to silence reason;
> Nor e'er would he, dishonest to himself,
> Permit his reason thus to be subdued.

Willard's best known hymn is *Ocean Hymn,* otherwise known as *Rocked in the Cradle of the Deep.* She wrote it when on an ocean voyage. It became a very popular song which inspired countless people with its call for trust in God's protection.

Willard authored many important textbooks and articles. Her books and other publications were very popular and were used in many schools. Her writing greatly extended her influence as an educator and brought attention to her school.

Among her many works were the very popular *History of the United States; A System of Universal History in Perspective; A Plan for Improving Female Education;* and a book of poems, *The Fulfillment of a Promise.*

She also published an innovative work entitled *A Treatise on the Motive Powers Which Produce the Circulation of the Blood.* It gained her broad recognition, and she became one of the first women admitted to the American Association for the Advancement of Science.

Willard's educational innovations and many books and articles on education of women and other topics "proved the right of women to intellectual equality" (Rudolph, 613).

As noted in the *Dictionary of American Biography*, Emma Willard "was the first woman publicly to take her stand for the higher education of women and the first to make definite experiments to prove that women were capable of comprehending higher subjects. Her Troy Female Seminary was looked upon as a model both in the United States and in Europe" (*Dictionary of American Biography*, 232).

She read and studied assiduously on a very wide variety of topics. This activity helped prepare her to successfully pursue her truly historic role in development of education for women.

IMPORTANT DATES IN EMMA WILLARD'S LIFE

1787   Born in Berlin, Connecticut.

1807   Became head of the Female Academy in Middlebury, Vermont.

1809   Married Dr. John Willard.

1814   Because of family financial difficulties, opened the Middlebury Female Seminary.

1821   Opened the Troy Female Seminary in Troy, New York. It was in effect the first women's college with a strong academic curriculum.

1838   Retired from the Troy Female Seminary.

1843   Began campaigning with the leading educator Henry Barnard for more public schools, better buildings, and equal opportunities for women as teachers.

1854   Represented the United States at the World's Educational Conference in London.

1870   Died in Troy, New York.

SOURCES

Dictionary of American Biography, vol. 10, Dumas Malone, ed. New York: Charles Scribner's Sons, 1936.

Goodsell, Willystine, ed. *Pioneers of Women's Education in the U.S.: E. Willard, C. Beecher, M. Lyon*. New York: AMS Press, 1970.

Hoffman, Nancy. *Women's "True" Profession: Voices from the History of Teaching*. Old Westbury, N.Y.: Feminist Press, 1981.

Lutz, Alma. *Emma Willard: Daughter of Democracy*. Boston: Houghton Mifflin Co., 1929.

Lutz, Alma. *Emma Willard: Pioneer Educator of American Women*. Boston: Beacon Press, 1964.

Read, Phyllis, and Bernard L. Witlieb. *The Book of Women's Firsts*. New York: Random House, 1992.

Rudolph, Frederick. "Emma Willard," in *Notable American Women, 1607–1950: A Biographical Dictionary*, vol. 3, Edward T. James, Janet Wilson James, and Paul S. Boyer, eds. Cambridge, Mass.: Belknap Press of Harvard University Press, 1971.

OPRAH WINFREY
(1954–)

Oprah Winfrey's story is one of the most inspiring stories in modern America. Born in poverty in rural Mississippi, she became the most popular television talk show host in the country and one of the richest women in America. She also has become one of the most respected and most beloved of all Americans, a role model for countless numbers of people.

Referring to her love of books, Oprah has stated: "Reading books is the single greatest pleasure I have" (Lowe, 21).

Oprah Winfrey has always loved books, and reading has been a significant factor in her development as a person. Moreover, she has frequently shared her love of books with her millions of fans. She is given credit for popularizing many high quality books which languished on the shelves of libraries and bookstores until she mentioned them on television.

Oprah Winfrey was born in a tiny Mississippi town on January 29, 1954. She was the product of a one-night stand between her birth mother and father. Her father, Vernon Winfrey, left town shortly after that and did not know for some time that Oprah had been born, not until he received a birth announcement with a note asking for some clothes.

At various times during her childhood, Oprah lived with her grandmother, with her birth mother, and with her father and stepmother. Her childhood experiences were mixed. At times during her early years she led a normal, happy life, learning reading, writing, arithmetic, public speaking, and social skills, and she was admired by many for her talent and beauty. At other times her life was most unhappy. A low point occurred when she was raped by a cousin. For some time after that she engaged in casual sex.

When she was only seventeen Oprah was hired as a part-time news-caster for a radio station. Shortly thereafter she began television work where she achieved great fame. The *Oprah Winfrey Show* became the most popular such production on television, eclipsing even the phenomenally successful Phil Donahue program.

In addition to her success on television, Winfrey became an accomplished screen actress. A high point was her nomination for an Academy Award for her performance in *The Color Purple*. Moreover, she has been universally praised for her work in *Beloved*.

Winfrey formed her own production company, Harpo Productions, Oprah spelled backwards. The company has made a number of films and television specials, frequently based on critically acclaimed books.

Winfrey has received numerous awards not only for her work in the entertainment industry but also for her leadership in social causes, including women's rights and minority rights.

Oprah learned to read when she was a very small child. "I learned to read, at age three," she noted, "and soon discovered there was a whole world to conquer that went beyond our farm in Mississippi" (Adler, 268).

Oprah's grandmother, Hattie Mae, was a strict disciplinarian who insisted she learn reading, writing, and arithmetic.

Determined that she should get the best possible education, Hattie Mae tutored the little girl so that she could do arithmetic, read, and write by the time she was three. There was no television in Hattie Mae's home, and reading became a pleasure for Oprah that would always remain with her. (Mair, 8)

Even when only three, little Oprah was such a good reader and recited so well that she began doing readings at the local Baptist church, and she acted in church plays. Although some of the children were jealous and thought she was a little show off, ladies in the congregation loved her and correctly predicted she would go far. Later they were undoubtedly amazed at how very far Oprah would go in the world.

In one of her first recitations before the entire congregation, three-year-old Oprah told the story of Jesus' resurrection on Easter. "Jesus rose on Easter Day. Halelu, halelu, all the angels did proclaim!" She impressed the adults who both praised Oprah and her grandmother. (Mair, 8)

On one occasion Oprah was paid $500 for giving a speech to a church group. That was a huge amount of money for a youngster.

Unfortunately for Oprah, she was sometimes made fun of by other children because she was smart and did a lot of reading.

I was the smartest, but no one praised me for being smart. I was teased because I was always sitting in a corner, reading; people made fun of me for that. . . . My books were my only friends. (King, 44)

When Oprah lived with her father and stepmother, they insisted she get good grades in school and read good books. Oprah and her stepmother visited the public library regularly, and the girl was required to read at least five books every two weeks. She also had to write reports on each book she read. Oprah did not mind that at all because she loved reading so much.

The book reading broadened Oprah's vocabulary, general knowledge, and taught her much about her black heritage through the works of such authors as Margaret Walker and Maya Angelou. There was an "electric connection" between teenage Oprah and Angelou's autobiography *I Know Why the Caged Bird Sings*.

The book is Angelou's own story of being buffeted between parents, with a mother in Texas and a father in California. She tells the tale of a young girl who is raped and so traumatized by the experience that she loses the power to speak for many years, a story to which Oprah could relate. (Mair, 27)

In later years Oprah and Angelou became close friends.

Oprah entered all-black East Tennessee State University, and while there she distinguished herself with her dramatic readings and her acting in university plays. Years later one of her professors, Dr. Jamie Williams, saw Oprah in the movie *The Color Purple*. He remembered how fervently she delivered readings from Margaret Walker's *Jubilee* while in college. "The intensity of how she remembered her black heritage came blazing through then and in the film" (Mair, 90).

Even after becoming world famous, Oprah still found time for her books, going home after even the busiest days at the television studio and collapsing with a book. She found history, biography, the Bible, and women's books all stimulating.

Books about and by black American women of the past and present have been especially significant for Oprah Winfrey. Sojourner Truth, born a slave, escaped from her master and became a noted preacher, feminist, and abolitionist. Harriet Tubman, also born a slave, escaped to freedom and returned to the South a number of times to help other slaves escape.

Winfrey's favorite contemporary black women authors include Alice Walker, Toni Morrison, and, as noted above, Maya Angelou. She also, on one occasion, noted that Zora Neale Hurston's *Their Eyes Were Watching God*, published in the 1930s, was one of her favorite books.

Alice Walker's Pulitzer Prize winning book, *The Color Purple*, had such an impact on Winfrey that she bought many copies of it and gave them to numerous friends. She was especially taken with the character of Sofia, a very strong woman who was abused by her husband and by prison guards, but never lost her dignity. When she was offered the opportunity to play that role in the movie version of the book, she jumped at the chance. She gave an outstanding performance and was nominated for an Academy Award as best supporting actress.

The film received eleven Academy Award nominations, including the one for Winfrey. Unfortunately, neither the movie nor Oprah received an award at the Oscar ceremony. She later noted that she was stunned that the picture was ignored by the Academy.

For years Oprah Winfrey has shared her love of books with her millions of fans. Her on-air book club has had a phenomenal effect on sale of books. Once mentioned on her television show, a book's sales skyrocket. According to Donahue, "Oprah Winfrey . . . moves books not copy by copy but rather truckload by truckload" (Donahue, 1D).

Just a mention of a book on Oprah's show often sent its sales skyrocketing. Jacquelyn Mitchard, an author virtually unknown, had published her novel *The Deep End of the Ocean*, a beautiful literary work. It received great reviews, and had sold a respectable 100,000 copies. After Oprah discussed it on television, it sold a phenomenal 750,000 copies, reaching the top of the best seller lists and holding its own against major veteran authors Stephen King, Scott Turow, and Mary Higgins Clark.

Toni Morrison's *Song of Solomon* and Jane Hamilton's *The Book of Ruth* also received huge boosts in sales after being showcased by Oprah.

When she recommended Marianne Williamson's book, *A Return to Love*, in February 1992 it immediately sold 70,000 copies and ultimately went on to sell 750,000 in hardcover and 500,000 in paperback. Her endorsement of Robert James Waller's novel, *The Bridges of Madison County* . . . gave the novel stunning staying power on the best seller list where it stayed for 102 weeks! (Mair, 124)

Callan Pinckney's diet-health book *Callanetics* languished on the shelves of bookstores, selling fewer than 12,000 copies total. Not long after Oprah's recommendation on television, the book's sales topped 300,000. As noted by Deirdre Donahue, "Winfrey's on-air book club has emerged as an unprecedented force in thrusting serious fiction to the very top of the best seller charts" (Donahue, 1D).

One secret of Oprah's success at making books best sellers is that she is such a passionate reader herself. Reading all the time, her enthusiasm for particular books shows, and she recommends only those she has read and loved.

Clearly, reading has been most influential in Oprah Winfrey's development. As she stated:

Books showed me there were possibilities in life, that there were actually people like me living in a world I could not only aspire to but attain. Reading gave me hope. For me it was the open door. (Adler, 268)

IMPORTANT DATES IN OPRAH WINFREY'S LIFE

1954   Born in rural Mississippi.

1973   First employed as television news reporter and anchorperson, working at various stations for the next dozen years.

1985   Began the *Oprah Winfrey Show* in Chicago.

1985   Appeared in *The Color Purple* for which she was nominated for a Golden Globe award and an Academy Award.

1986   Received Woman of Achievement Award, National Organization for Women.

1987   Received Emmy Award for Best Daytime Talk Show Host. Received the same award for a number of years.

1989   Received Entertainer of the Year Award, National Association for the Advancement of Colored People.

1998   Appeared in *Beloved*. The film and her acting received excellent reviews.

SOURCES

Adler, Bill, ed. *The Uncommon Wisdom of Oprah Winfrey: A Portrait in Her Own Words*. Secaucus, N.J.: Birch Lane Press Book, 1997.

Bly, Nellie. *Oprah! Up Close and Down Home*. New York: Zebra Books, 1993.

Donahue, Deirdre. "Has Oprah Saved Books? Her TV Book Club Is Turning Viewers into Readers and Creating Best Sellers," *USA Today*, December 12, 1996.

King, Norman. *Everybody Loves Oprah! Her Remarkable Life Story: An Unauthorized Biography*. New York: William Morrow, 1987.

Lowe, Janet. *Oprah Winfrey Speaks: Insight from the World's Most Influential Voice*. New York: John Wiley & Sons: 1998.

Mair, George. *Oprah Winfrey! The Real Story*. Secaucus, N.J.: Carol Publishing Co., 1996.

Nicholson, Lois P. *Oprah Winfrey*. New York: Chelsea House, 1994.

Waldron, Robert. *Oprah*. New York: St. Martin's Press, 1987.

SELECTED BIBLIOGRAPHY

Conway, J. North. *American Literacy: Fifty Books That Define Our Culture and Our-selves*. New York: William Morrow and Co., Inc., 1993. Discussion of the influence on American society of works written by prominent scientists, politicians, writers, and others.

DeGregorio, William A. *The Complete Book of U. S. Presidents*. New York: Barricade Books, Inc., 1993. Includes brief statements on the reading interests of most presidents.

Devine, C. Maury, Claudia M. Dissel, and Kim D. Parrish, eds. *The Harvard Guide to Influential Books: 113 Distinguished Harvard Professors Discuss the Books That Have Helped to Shape Their Thinking*. New York: Harper & Row, Publishers, 1986. Each noted Harvard professor lists and annotates several books that influenced him/her.

Gilbar, Steven. *The Open Door: When Writers First Learned to Read*. Boston: D. R. Godine in association with the Center for the Book in the Library of Congress, 1989. Writers comment on their favorite childhood books.

Howell, R. Patton, ed. *Beyond Literacy: The Second Gutenberg Revolution*. San Francisco: Saybrook Publishing Co., Inc., 1989. Notable scientists, Nobel laureates, philosophers, and others discuss the importance of books and reading in modern society.

Nash, George H. *Books and the Founding Fathers: A Lecture to Commemorate the Year of the Reader*. Delivered on November 1, 1987. Washington, D.C.: Library of Congress, 1989. Includes comments on the book and reading interests of a number of early American leaders.

Sabine, Gordon, and Patricia Sabine. *Books That Made the Difference*. Hamden, Conn.: Library Professional Publications, 1983. Some celebrities and ordinary Americans note one or two books that influenced them.

Swartz, Ronald B. *For the Love of Books: 115 Celebrated Writers on the Books They Love Most.* New York: Grossett/Putnam, 1999. Contemporary writers note several books that made a strong impression on them.

Many reference works, such as those listed below, contain a brief note on the reading interests of subjects who found reading important in their lives. More detailed information on the topic can be found in the works listed in the sources sections at the end of each profile.

Contemporary Authors. Detroit: Gale Research Inc., vol. 1, 1962–.

Contemporary Black Biography: Profiles from the International Black Community. Detroit: Gale Research Inc., vol. 1, 1992–.

Current Biography. New York: H. W. Wilson Co., vol. 1, 1940–.

Porter, David L., ed. *Biographical Dictionary of American Sports: Basketball and Other Indoor Sports.* New York: Greenwood Press, 1989.

Magill, Frank N., ed. *Great Lives from History: American Series,* 5 vols. Pasadena, Calif.: Salem Press, 1987.

Magill, Frank N., ed. *Great Lives from History: American Women Series,* 5 vols. Pasadena, Calif.: Salem Press, 1995.

Telgen, Diane, and Jim Kamp, eds. *Notable Hispanic American Women.* Detroit: Gale Research Inc., 1993.

INDEX

About the Author

JOHN A. McCROSSAN is Professor Emeritus at the University of South Florida School of Library and Information Science. He previously worked as a reference librarian, library director, classroom teacher, and State Librarian of Vermont. He has taught at the University of Michigan and Kent State University, and his many articles have appeared in such journals as *RQ, Library Journal, American Libraries, Journal of Education for Library and Information Science,* and *Advances in Librarianship.* An authority on reference services, he has served as president of the Reference and Adult Services Division of the American Library Association and remains active in the field.